122 RULES
Mafiya

122 RULES

Mafiya

Book Three in the 122 Rules Series

DEEK RHEW

Tenacious Books Publishing

Published by Tenacious Books Publishing

Published by Tenacious Books Publishing in 2025
Tenacious@TenaciousBooksPublishing.com

This book is a work of fiction. Names, characters, places, and incidents are either the product of the author's imagination or are used fictitiously.

Library of Congress Cataloging-in-Publication Data
Rhew, Deek. First edition.
122 Rules - Mafiya / Deek Rhew
ISBN 978-1-7338974-9-5 (print)
ISBN B0FX13JZS1 (e-book)

Cover Image: © ShutterStock
Cover Design: Anita B. Carroll www.race-point.com

Printed in the United States of America

www.TenaciousBooksPublishing.com

I dedicate this book to my father, who taught me the importance of service, honor, and duty—both through his military career and his role as a dad. You may stand just over five feet tall, but you are the biggest man I've ever known.

Prologue

Jimmy "The Vault Slayer" Rice perched on the wobbly barstool, nursing his third PBR. The underground saloon had all the sex appeal of a wet camel in a string bikini. It reeked of stale beer, BO, and hopeless dejection. Still, he felt more at home here than in his own roach-infested studio apartment. He and the bar shared a mixed-drink relationship: one part lethargy and two parts mutual disdain, with a hefty splash of self-loathing.

The tables and chairs looked as though they'd been dredged from a dumpster sometime around the turn of the century. The pool table's mummified felt had yellowed and cracked like skin in the final stages of melanoma. The barfly patrons didn't look any better than the furniture.

Jimmy took a long pull from his sweating beer. When he set it down, he perfectly aligned the bottom of the bottle with the water ring on the counter.

In the dingy mirror over the bar, a big-bellied, broad-shouldered man—with arms as thick and stubby as fire hydrants, scuffed knuckles, alcohol pickled eyes—pushed through the door. A gun bulged beneath his thrift-store suit. Jimmy recognized Ivan Labanov, former heavyweight champ turned lieutenant in the Mafiya's Mogilevich brigade of the Gabisonia Enterprise.

The behemoth waded across the room. When he dropped onto the stool beside Jimmy, the exhausted vinyl seat cried out in pain. "Vodka," Ivan said, his Russian accent as thick and salty as fish chowder. He held up two crooked fingers. The barman dropped a dirty glass onto the counter, filled the double, and moved on.

Jimmy nodded at the man's drink. "Tough night?"

Ivan's dark eyes cut toward him. A grunt. Enough said.

"Man of few words," Jimmy replied. "I respect that." He took a sip of his PBR and set it down, aligning the bottle with the water ring on the counter once more. "Well, whatever your woes, your drink is on me tonight. Because I am celebrating." Ivan grunted again, which Jimmy interpreted as "Thanks."

Jimmy continued filling the conversational void. "By this time next week, I'll be out of my dumpy apartment and living in a condo in the Hills with a couple of sugars. My *colleagues* and I just scored a deal that will make us rich." He smirked, rubbing his thumb and forefinger together as though pinching a pair of hundred-dollar bills. "Filthy. Rich."

Ivan glanced at him, small pinpricks of interest lighting his lifeless eyes.

Jimmy pretended not to notice and looked around the rat trap bar. "I grew up just down the road. My old man used to drink here before he run off. Mom's in the clink for turning tricks. Haven't seen or heard from her in years. I've got nothing holding me back. I'm gonna take my share and beat feet for——"

A snippet of the news anchors' patter drew his attention. Jimmy's head snapped up, his focus zeroing in on the TV mounted over the bar.

On the smudged screen, a dozen cop cars blocked the street outside a brownstone. Guns drawn, lights flashing.

He stared. "That...that's my building."

As the closed caption reported *Shots fired*, Jimmy bolted to his feet.

A man brandishing an automatic weapon stumbled from the roof, plummeting six stories to the concrete below. A thick flurry of Benjamins corkscrewed lazily in his wake, littering the chaotic street like snow.

The news camera zoomed in on the fallen man—dark hair, scuffed leather jacket—as the money fluttered through the air.

"No! No! No!" Jimmy shouted at the TV.

The bar had gone quiet. All eyes on him.

He ignored them.

On the fuzzy screen, a black-clothed SWAT team stormed the apartment complex.

Jimmy held his breath.

The news anchors continued their patter, though Jimmy had no interest in what they had to say. His sole focus remained on the front door of the grungy apartment complex.

The SWAT team reemerged, marching three men in handcuffs before them.

The closed caption announced, *Suspects apprehended. The men are purported to be The Flying Dutchmen. An infamous gang of thieves alleged to have stolen millions in bank and treasury bonds earlier in the day.*

Jimmy dropped onto his stool as if an LAPD cruiser had parked on his shoulders. He stared off into space and downed the last of his PBR. When he set his bottle on the counter, he didn't bother aligning it with the water ring.

Ivan studied him in the dirty mirror. "You know?"

Jimmy's hand shook as he motioned to the barkeep for another beer. When it arrived, he emptied half the fresh bottle in a series of quick gulps. He didn't look at Ivan; he just stared at the dark brown liquid before him.

His phone rang. Jimmy reached into his coat, retrieved it, and read the screen. *Los Angeles Police Department.*

He stared at the name for a beat before glancing at Ivan.

Their eyes met. Complete understanding passed between them.

Jimmy tore the battery from the back of the phone, tossing both pieces onto the counter. He ran his fingers through his hair. "Yeah, I know those men," he said at last—exhaling a long, ragged breath. "I also know that I'm completely screwed. I'm broke *again*...and homeless *again*." He smacked the bar top. "Fuck my life!"

Jimmy reached into his pocket, took out a few crumpled bills, and dropped them onto the counter. He stood. "I need to go. Sorry, I promised to buy your drink, but I'm so poor I can't even afford to pay attention. I'll catch you next time, my friend." He turned, but Ivan gripped his arm, stopping him.

"No family. Your friends," Ivan waved a beefy hand at the TV, "gone too. Where you go?"

Jimmy shook his head. "I don't know. But if I don't find somewhere to lay low, I'll be 'gone' soon enough." He gestured at the phone. "The police have my number." He pointed at the TV. "There's evidence in that apartment implicating me in the robbery this morning, and a bunch of other hits we did. Most of it's small-time stuff, but still... I don't even want to think about how long I'd go away for if it all came out."

"Sit." Ivan commanded.

Jimmy's gaze flicked to the huge, bruised, and scabbed hand gripping his arm. Ivan only needed to squeeze, and Jimmy's bones would snap like kindling. He stared the big Russian in the eyes as he took his seat.

"What you do?"

Jimmy glanced about. The conversations around them had resumed. No one paid them any attention. "You mean for a living?"

"Dah." Ivan released Jimmy's arm and tilted his head toward the screen. "I've heard of this group. The Flying Dutchmen."

Jimmy eyed him suspiciously. "Who hasn't?"

"You part?"

"You a cop?" Jimmy retorted. He tensed as though preparing to outrun the Russian knee buster.

Ivan gave a sharp shake of his head. "Nyet. Nyet." He jerked his chin toward the screen. "You part of Dutchmen?"

Jimmy met the man's eyes and took a chance. "I was. Now I'm unemployed."

Ivan considered, leaning in until his vodka-ladened breath backhanded Jimmy across the face. "What your skill?"

Jimmy fought the urge to recoil from the halitosis assault. He dropped his voice. "I'm a picklock. The guys call me The Vault Slayer."

Ivan studied his face as though gauging his seriousness. He held up an anaconda-sized finger. The knuckles were bruised and splotched with blood, though none of it seemed to be his. With his other hand, he pulled out a phone and made a call, the low Russian syllables incomprehensible over the backdrop of slurred bar voices.

After a minute, he terminated the call, primly tucking the phone into his breast pocket. "We have opening. You need job and place to stay. You come with me. We keep you safe." Ivan stood and led the way to the door as though Jimmy had agreed.

The Russian mobster had phrased it like an offer, but they both knew it wasn't one. When the Reds requested your services, it wasn't healthy to say no.

What choice did he have?

Jimmy glanced once more at the TV, stood, and followed.

They stepped into the balmy night. Ivan led him through the shadows between streetlamps, stopping at a lonesome corner. They waited.

The moon was full; the intersection deserted except for scattered trash and a vagrant slumped in the gutter. A lone siren howled somewhere in the distance. Jimmy's gaze swept the twisted wire fence surrounding a vacant lot, alert for whoever Ivan had called.

He'd just begun to wonder if he should leave while he still could when the growl of a powerful engine split the night. A dark sedan, headlights off, screeched to a stop in front of them.

The front doors flew open, and two men got out. He didn't know the bald passenger, but he recognized the broad-shouldered driver—Mikhail, hired muscle with a rap sheet longer than the Magna Carta.

Shit moved fast. Jimmy's self-preservation instincts flared, urging him to run the instant Mikhail opened the back door. But it was too late. He'd already seen too much. These guys would never let him just walk away.

The car's weak dome light revealed spiderweb tattoos covering the bald man's scalp—then the universe went dark as someone yanked a fetid burlap sack over Jimmy's head. "Do not take off," Baldy ordered, his voice gravelly and thick with a Russian accent.

In any other situation, Jimmy would never have allowed himself to be blinded. But when someone from the Mafiya told you to leave your hood on, you left it on. He didn't believe they intended to kill him.

Not yet anyway.

Rough hands patted him down, pulled the cigarette case from his pocket, and clicked it open.

Jimmy's heart thumped hard against his breastbone.

If they found the false back and the police-issue micro cell, some difficult questions would inevitably follow. He could survive the interrogation. Probably. Maybe. But he was glad he'd chosen to leave his LAPD shield at home, or the thugs *would* have put his lights out.

Permanently.

He'd been undercover as Jimmy "The Vault Slayer" Rice for so long and had gotten so deep into his character—first as a member of The Flying Dutchmen and now infiltrating the growing Mafiya presence in his hometown—he sometimes forgot his real name, Frank Boreman, and his role as an undercover officer with the LAPD.

Jimmy recognized the faint *snick* of the case closing. It was stuffed back into his pocket. Someone shoved him into the back seat and slammed the door shut.

The car tilted hard to either side as the men got in. The engine revved. In a quiet protest of rubber on asphalt, the car accelerated. With a snap, the radio blared some indecipherable slasher metal music—Satan's Seizure or Cannibal Corpse—rattling the windows and vibrating Jimmy's bones.

The death rock sounded like poltergeists joyriding bulldozers through a nitroglycerin plant—furious, chaotic, unstoppable. As they drove, Jimmy tried to map their route—counting turns, guessing speed—but he lost track fast. The drive felt eternal, but at last, the car came to a hard stop.

The front doors opened. The car lurched as the passengers disembarked.

Someone yanked his door open. A cool breeze and the salt air of the Pacific swaddled him as a fist grabbed his collar and pulled him out. Gulls cried in the distance. He thought he could hear the gentle clanging of steel and fi-berglass boats bumping against rubber bumpers.

By his estimate, they hadn't traveled far enough to reach Long Beach. That meant the Port of Los Angeles. He tried not to picture the endless miles of body-hiding ocean within easy reach of his new Mafiya friends.

Hands shoved him across asphalt, onto a metal gang-way, and up a short ramp. Cold sea spray stung his face. Gentle swaying. Water lapping at what could be a hull. A boat.

He was pushed into a seat. The floor vibrated as the engine came to life.

Mikhail said, "*Idti.*" *Go.*

The motor growled, and the boat pulled away. A few minutes later, chains rattled, and something clanged off the deck. Despite his effort not to worry, Jimmy flinched.

Every nerve in his body screamed to fight. It took all of his will to keep from pulling off his hood. Such an act would almost certainly end with his death.

The telltale flick of an igniting lighter. The occasional cough. The rattle of loose equipment.

Hooded time, while riding in a Mafiya boat, proved to be as difficult to measure as counting the dark matter mol-ecules making up the universe. They may have traveled an hour, or perhaps three, when he sensed the sea swells change. The slap against the hull less frequent and more pronounced. The dips deeper.

He detected another underlying growl and what sounded like a small waterfall. It took him a moment to put the pieces together. Not a waterfall. The wake of another boat. By the sounds of it, something large.

Voices called out. Something—a rope maybe—slapped the deck.

Men shouted in Russian.

Someone hauled him to his feet and shoved him forward. His legs, butt, and arms had gone numb and didn't operate quite right. His feet tangled. He stumbled and fell. Cold shivers snaked up his arms as his palms splashed into the icy film covering the deck.

Strong hands grabbed him, yanking him back to his feet.

The hood was torn off his head. Before him, a rope ladder hung down the black steel hide of a much larger ship. Two men waited at the top, backlit by halogens. Waves splashed like geysers, misting him with frigid seawater.

Mikhail—feet spread in a wide, stable stance, a line lashed to the rail—grabbed the bottom rung of the ladder. "Idti! Idti!" he yelled at Jimmy and pointed.

Oh, hell no.

When he hesitated, the bald man shoved him hard.

He damn near fell overboard. Rather than plunge into the cold black ocean, he dropped onto the deck.

"Idti! Idti!" Mikhail screamed again.

"Yeah. Yeah," Jimmy said. "Got it." He found his feet. In a half squat, he gripped the ladder. The fishing boat not only went up and down with the swells but also varied its distance from the larger vessel by six or seven feet. One moment it butted against the ship, the next a canyon of raging ocean yawned between the two.

Jimmy took a deep breath, trying to time it just right. When the two ships came together, he scaled the first third of the ladder as fast as he dared. He barely cleared the rail when Baldy seized the ladder, pulling himself up the first few rungs. The smaller boat's motor revved, and the two vessels separated. The ladder swung wildly, smacking against hard, cold steel.

The fishing boat veered away and sailed off into the dark.

His death grip faltered, but he miraculously held on. He glanced up. A man, distant as someone perched atop Mt. Kilimanjaro, motioned for him to climb.

Jimmy didn't need to be told twice.

He scampered up the side of the ship, Baldy close behind. Rough hands grabbed his arms and pants, pulling him aboard. Baldy came over the rail, dropped to the deck, and jammed the hood back over Jimmy's head before pushing him forward. They crossed the wide bow and went through a door, then traversed a dank hallway. A squeak of hinges—another door being opened—and he was ushered inside.

The stuffy room smelled of old fish, burnt oil, and ancient dust. "You stay," the gravelly, accented voice of the stranger ordered. The door slammed shut.

Jimmy waited a few seconds before peeling off his hood. The unfiltered stench of fish and damp fabric hit him, swallowed by a darkness as black as a sealed coffin.

In front of him, a small flame flared to life with a quiet *zing*.

"Jesus!" Jimmy yelled, cocking back a fist.

The flame licked the tip of a cigarette. Its glow cut through the blackness, revealing a bird-thin, meth-pocked face before sputtering out.

"I don't think Jesus is coming to save you," the cigarette-owner said. "No salvation here."

Jimmy let out a long breath. He didn't entirely trust things wouldn't turn violent, but the voice lacked tension. Only resignation. Defeat. His body shook as the surge of adrenaline whooshed through his veins. "Who are you?"

"Name's Myles. You?"

"Jimmy." He dropped his fist, his nerves still electrified. "When you said Jesus wouldn't be coming, what did you mean?"

"I mean, everyone on this tub is doomed to Hell. There ain't no reason for your god to come 'cause ain't no one here gonna be making it to the pearly gates when they bite it. You dig?"

"Yeah, I think so. Where are we?"

Myles chuckled humorlessly. "You've gone where all sinners end up." The tip glowed bright as Myles took a drag. "Welcome to the *Vengeance*."

Chapter One

Sam Bradford skimmed the blue-green ocean, his surfboard slicing the surface like a spaceship gliding across the atmosphere of a newly discovered planet. A humid breeze tousled his shaggy hair as the mid-afternoon sun warmed his shoulders.

On the glossy nose of his board, a painted hula girl winked. *Nice ride, sailor.*

The sea churned with the raw energy of an early autumn storm—edgy and unpredictable, like a dish sharpened by a dash of cayenne and a flash of heat. As the wave lost power, Sam slipped into the water, his wetsuit protecting him from its September chill. He paddled past the breakers and then straddled his board, gazing toward the horizon—at everything and nothing.

Against a sky of faded denim, a brown pelican as large as a pterodactyl drifted on the breeze. Folding its wings, it plummeted, knifing into the crystalline ocean. Moments later, it bobbed up with a flailing fish in its long bill.

As the prehistoric-looking bird enjoyed its snack, Sam inhaled the briny air and closed his eyes. During the exhale, he released some of the residual tension that still clung to him like wet sand.

His life before the Cove had been ruled by clocks, codes, and an unbreachable internal fortress built to control the chaos of his world.

Something—his brother's death, serving in the Marines, his divorce, or the fallout with The Agency—had suffocated his natural chill, leaving him restless and raw. Cruising the highway of life, he'd taken a wrong exit and gotten lost on the back roads leading nowhere.

But out here, the cogs and gears of the clock held no dominion over him. The only knives were the frothy edges of the ocean waves. The only pain came from sore muscles. Out here, he was just Sam—the boardhead who worked at Max's shop, drank beer, and chased swells.

He scooped a palmful of ocean water. The little pool shimmered with a kaleidoscope of colors—his microcosm of calm. All around him, the sea teemed with unfathomable dangers, but in that tiny patch of peace, he could forget.

Forget the faces of those he'd killed.

Forget the oath he'd sworn.

And, most importantly, forget his final, career-shattering Agency mission.

That op had seemed textbook—like the thousands before it. It had been anything but.

He'd discovered—almost too late—that his mark, Monica Sable, wasn't an enemy of the state as he'd been told, but a witness brave enough to testify against a drug lord.

The Agency—the one he'd trusted, bled for, and sworn to serve—had sent him to silence her permanently, all to spring a mob boss from the clink.

Sam hadn't pulled the trigger. But he could never forget the betrayal. It was the shark circling in his pool of tranquility.

As part of the fallout, Monica had ended up in the crosshairs of the psychopathic assassin, Tyron Erebus. The deranged hitman had followed her to the Cove, where he'd nearly leveled half the town trying to kill her.

After Sam and some locals had put the madman in the ground, he'd asked his Agency handler, Josha, for an extended leave. The request had been immediately granted.

Three soul-searching months later, Sam still couldn't find a reason—any reason at all—that would explain why The Agency had tried to eliminate an innocent woman for a drug lord. No matter how hard he stretched his imagination, he kept coming up empty.

The Agency tides, it seemed, had turned—the darkening difference palpable, though not fathomable. Those sharks he sensed—razor-toothed and hungry for blood—circled just out of sight. And when they bit, he might not see them until it was too late.

He could have pressed Josha for answers, except it had been radio silence between them for the past three months. Besides, asking his handler questions might lead to uncomfortable conversations neither of them wanted to have.

Maybe it was better this way—he and The Agency pretending the other didn't exist. Perhaps this boardhead life didn't fit him exactly. But it was a hell of a lot better than the disaster he'd left behind.

With an exasperated sigh, he dumped the palm-sized pool back into the ocean.

Ahead, the brown pelican took to the air. As it soared away, the crashing waves beckoned. Sam just needed to let go and embrace his inner surf rat.

He drew in another deep breath of sea air. When he pushed it out, he released all thoughts of The Agency, his uncertain future, and Josha. Out here with the gulls, the dolphins—and yes, even the sharks—none of it mattered. Out here, nothing could disrupt the sanctity of his saltwater temple.

Peace out. Oooohmmmm.

His watch buzzed.

He ignored it and instead focused on fertilizing his root chakra in the garden mulch of transcendence.

To help grow into a better, more enlightened Sam, he'd taken a series of meditation classes taught by Max's girlfriend, Abby. Her techniques were supposed to nourish his aura—or something like that.

Inner peace. Inner peace.

The mantra circled in his mind like a vulture zeroing in on a deer carcass. As per Abby, nagging the universe with positive affirmations—what she called "verbal manifestations"—like a toddler begging for cookies would make the cosmos cough up enough Serenity Oreos to send him into a diabetic coma of joy.

The lessons learned under Abby the Om Whisperer's gentle tutelage brought world-altering calm to everyone else's chakra. Yet his chi rolled its eyes in exasperation, while his "spiritual voice" ridiculed the kumbaya theatrics with the dry sarcasm of a drunken pirate.

Still, he was evolving, damn it! He *could* find his higher self. Or whatever. So, channeling his inner monk, he chanted the phrase that was supposed to chill him out faster than a burrito in a North Pole freezer.

His wrist buzzed again, bursting his Zen bubble with a pinprick of irritation.

Probably Max wanting him to cover another shift. Or someone needed a surf lesson. Or his party-hard boss was throwing an impromptu beach kegger. As his temple of placidness collapsed under a tsunami of rancid kombucha, Sam clicked the message.

He stared in confusion.

Maybe his Zen had drifted with him from his state of flow, resulting in hallucinations... No, that wasn't right. Flow state and visualizations? Whatever. Maybe his new mantra should be *Pay attention during Abby's class* because his serenity tugboat had just hit the rocks.

He rubbed his eyes.

Still there.

Chief Palmer.

To describe his relationship with the chief as competitive and contentious would be like describing Montezuma's Revenge as passing gas. The chief—who still blamed Sam for Tyron Erebus' rainstorm of shit that had almost burned down the town three months ago—had made it clear he wanted Sam to make like a tree and leave. To be like an amoeba and split. To channel his inner Dorothy and hit the Yellow Brick Road. Though they hadn't argued in several weeks, perhaps the chief had found yet another inventive way of telling Sam to get out of Dodge.

He clicked the text. All traces of Abby's meditative tranquility vanished in a pulse-rattling second.

A body washed up on shore. Looks like murder. This seems like your wheelhouse. Want to take a look?

Sam read the message three times, convinced he'd misunderstood the string of characters—that perhaps by reexamining it, he could extract its true meaning. But as with the sender's name, he'd interpreted the message just fine the first time.

A murder.

Why did the chief think Sam could help? Sheriff Austin had probably already called it in to the state or county police. They could take the lead.

No one needed Sam's help to investigate anything.

Yet, the chief had reached out to him personally. The man hated him, so he must have had a hell of a good reason.

Sam rolled his shoulders, trying to ease the sudden strain in his muscles. No. That life lay in the past. Perhaps permanently. An investigation, even one outside of The Agency, would be a gateway drug leading straight back to the road he'd fought to escape and the world that no longer fit.

As he read the text again, his trigger finger itched—a sensation he hadn't felt in three months.

Why don't you just delete that message and forget you ever saw it? Chet's voice surprised him.

During the war, Chet—his gut instinct personified—had warned him of danger long before his physical senses had detected anything. Listening to his gut had often saved Sam's life, as well as the lives of the soldiers under his command.

Like the absent itch, it had been months since his conscience had spoken up. With Erebus' trail of terror concluded and Sam's long-term vacation begun, his instincts had little to ponder and even less to say.

For the first time in years, you've created a semblance of a life, Chet continued. *You've even found a few people who aren't completely repulsed by your presence. You should think long and hard before giving it all up.*

Sensing his inner conscience's underlying sarcasm, he braced himself for whatever wrath burned in Chet's heart. *Yeah, maybe.*

What maybe? You haven't killed anyone since Erebus, and by your own pathetic musings, it doesn't sound like you've missed it.

My musings aren't pathetic.

Really, Sparky? Because from where I sit, you sound like a whining, self-serving deadbeat who would rather throw away the country he swore an oath to protect instead of fighting for it. That's what you used to do, right? You used to believe in something so much you were willing to die for it.

That was before The Agency sold out, Sam snapped.

And that changes your personal convictions how? Besides, you don't know that. You don't know shit because you've been drinking beer and singing kumbaya with your pot-smoking homies. Maybe you should take this invitation from the chief as a sign from the universe that it's time to stop feeling sorry for yourself and get back into the game.

Chet might have a point. Maybe Sam had been so focused on not getting involved—so determined to keep the door closed on all those ugly, unanswered questions—that he'd just as soon quit as confront his old employer and deal with the ramifications of being proven right. *Fine, I'll help the chief. I don't know what I could offer, but I might owe him.*

Chet scoffed. *Yeah. No kidding.*

Sam, straddling his hula girl surfboard, bobbed up and down on the gentle Pacific currents. He scanned the ocean as if peace lay just over the horizon, while trying not to think about bodies. About death. About his gateway drug.

At last, he turned his board inland and caught the next ride to shore. He didn't know if he'd try to pull back the blanket of corruption shrouding The Agency or if he'd leave that problem for another day. For now, Sam had a murder to solve.

Chapter Two

Sam dropped his board off at home and showered. As he dressed, he glanced repeatedly at the floorboard where he'd hidden his Sig Sauer. Since his life in the Cove no longer required him to kill, he'd forced himself to stop carrying his piece. Yet even after all these months, leaving the Sig behind felt like leaving a kidney.

A few weeks into his self-imposed banishment from the real world, his resolve had crumbled. He'd strapped on the pancake holster and gone to work with the gun snugged at his lower back. The sensation of carrying the weapon had been as euphorically blissful as an alcoholic's first sip of bourbon after a decade of sobriety.

He'd forgotten about the Sig until an hour into his shift when Max called him out. "Hey! I thought you said you were done with your old life?"

Sam had paused from rearranging boards at the back of the store, confused. "I am."

"Oh, yeah?" Max nodded at his back. "That tells a different story."

When he'd bent over, his shirt must have pulled up, exposing the weapon.

"My friend," Max said, "you can't live in two worlds. You're either in this one, or"—he pointed at the Sig—"you're in that one. Decide."

Sam hadn't carried since, and as much as he wanted to justify bringing the gun with him, he couldn't see how investigating a dead man warranted breaking his streak.

Unarmed Sam pushed through the front door and walked the mile to the Alabaster Cove Medical Clinic.

From behind her desk, Savannah looked up and smiled when he entered. "Hey, Sam!" Her gaze traveled his body as though seeking riches she might plunder in the darkest hours of the night.

Her curled, blonde, blue-tipped hair framed a narrow face so caked with makeup, he bet she got annual stockholder thank you letters from the likes of Ulta and Maybelline. Tomato red lipstick, glittery fingernails, and some bronzing paste slathered onto her cheeks made it look as though she'd attempted to conceal her pretty features and striking blue eyes the way a hunter might conceal himself in a duck blind.

Sam had bumped into her on several occasions at Max's beach parties, sans the suburban war paint. He had trouble associating that attractive forty-something divorcee with this garish clown who showed up at the office each morning.

When did the circus come to town? Chet asked.

On the beach, she looks normal. The difference is...um...startling.

Well, you haven't done the horizontal tango in a while. And she's staring at you the way a starving T-Rex might eye a steako-saurus. Bet you could be playing doctor on an exam table in about five minutes if you dealt your cards right. It's such a sure thing, not even you could mess it up.

Having awakened from his three-month coma, his inner conscience seemed to be feeling feisty.

First, there's no such thing as a steakosaurus. Although... Sam held Savannah's too-direct gaze for a moment. *You're not wrong. Second, all that crap would rub off on me. I'd come out looking like a mime in heat.*

Sam crossed the small waiting room to her desk. "I'm guessing you know I'm here to see the chief."

This woman is practically ripping your clothes off with her eyes, Chet observed. *Given the pathetic state of affairs you call a love life, I recommend you take her up on her offer.*

That's twice you've called me pathetic since you roused from hibernation.

He shrugged. *I wasn't asleep; you're just so boring there wasn't anything to talk about.*

Savannah nodded. "He's been waiting for you." She dropped her voice. "Fair warning, he's not happy it took you so long to get here."

How dare I inconvenience His Majesty by not standing on the clinic lawn waiting to be summoned! Keeping his sarcasm in check to avoid exacerbating his fraught relationship with the chief, Sam said, "I'll try to be more prompt the next time a dead body washes up on shore."

The receptionist let out a little giggle. Leaning forward, she whispered, "The chief's not exactly known for his patience. He's——"

The door at the end of the hall buzzed and clicked. Chief Palmer, wearing black scrubs and two days' worth of five o'clock shadow, pulled it open. "Sam." He motioned with his head for Sam to follow.

Sam smiled and gave Savannah a little wink. "Thanks." He headed down the hallway.

Au revoir, Chet sang to the receptionist.

Chief Palmer punched a code into a wall-mounted keypad and led Sam inside.

The stench of rotten flesh and rancid shellfish hit Sam in the face as he walked through the door. Though frigid, the room felt stuffy from the acrid, too-familiar reek of death. On the table lay a sheet-covered body. From the far side of the narrow room, Polly Cahill gazed at him with vibrant green eyes.

She'd tied her long dark hair up into a bun. Her loose black scrubs whispered about the graciously curved figure concealed in the utilitarian garment.

The chief motioned to her and said, "I believe you are *acquainted* with Polly Cahill, our paramedic practitioner."

She nodded at Sam. "We met on the beach the night..." She paused. "Well, three months ago."

A small, faint scar on her forehead and another on her cheek commemorated the fateful evening Erebus had used explosives to turn the wooden dock into a fiery inferno of death. The blast had thrown her about ten feet before she'd been buried by debris. Did she remember he'd saved her life?

"Sure," he said. "You were one of the EMTs that came to help. I've also seen you patrolling the beach. You're a member of RU." The locals shortened the name of the Alabaster Cove Beach and Rescue Unit to the acronym

RU. He'd latched on to the local dialect more out of habit than any conscious effort to blend in.

"I'm actually team lead for RU," she said.

"I stand corrected."

She handed him a pair of latex gloves. "We thought you might assist in this case."

He took them from her but didn't slip them on. *We? I thought the chief had requested my presence.* "I don't understand why you think I can help."

"Ordinarily, I'd agree with you," Polly replied. "Having you here would be totally unnecessary and a burden."

Is that what I said?

"But," she continued, "this is unusual. The state police, as you've probably guessed, will be here to claim the body soon. We need all the help we can get to quickly determine the cause of death and where our John Doe might have died."

"So a male," Sam said. "And you don't have an ID."

"Not yet," Polly replied crisply.

The chief added, "The sheriff may have prematurely called in the staties. I believe this might be a matter for the Coast Guard. If we got the jurisdiction wrong, it'll be my ass, not his."

Something's not right, Chet said.

Yeah. His explanation sounds plausible, but my bullshit detector is screaming like I'd wandered into a congressman's confessional. Maybe I'm being set up?

Chet remained quiet for a moment. *I don't think so. But they aren't being straight with you. Don't bail…for now. Let's see where this goes.*

"You want my help because of what happened three months ago?" Sam asked.

The chief and Polly exchanged a knowing glance.

"I don't exactly know your background," she said carefully, "but word is you have ties to a federal organization of some kind."

This was a problem with remaining in the Cove. Too many people knew too much and fueled the flames burning through the gossip mill. If it had just been an urge to spend an extended leave in a beach town, he could have moved to one of a million places around the world where he would have remained anonymous. But something had compelled him to help undo the damage done by Erebus—the most sadistic psychopath Sam had ever encountered.

Three months later, he still couldn't figure out why it bothered him so damned much. During his career with The Agency, he'd hurt hundreds of people and felt no guilt, no remorse, no burning desire to offer recompense. Yet he'd remained in this intelligence nightmare, where the determined wagging tongues turned over every rock and shook every tree until they uncovered—or made up—the details of every man, woman, and child who set foot in town.

He gave Polly his best aw-shucks smile and a slight shake of the head. "Those are just rumors. You know the way people talk. I did some undercover work for the Marines. When something like what happened with Erebus goes down, training just kicks in. You know? The rumors have turned me into some kind of larger-than-life FBI or CIA agent. I assure you; I am neither."

For anyone who had directly asked him, he'd been able to avoid their questions with this practiced yarn. But Polly appraised him as though she could read straight from his brain. She smelled the half-truth as clearly as he could smell the corpse rotting on the exam table. More than just distrust and intelligence lingered in her eyes—instinct, intuition, and something else. Something darker.

Uh-oh, Chet said.

Yeah.

You're going to have to be a lot more convincing. I would suggest applying a healthy dollop of rule twenty-five.

Rule #25:
Saying nothing is sometimes best.

The lies most difficult to detect are the ones never spoken. Avoid saying anything when silence will suffice. The more details added to a story, the easier it is to detect dishonesty. Get in, say what needs to be said, then get out. Do not be lured into attempting to extricate yourself from a hole of your own making. You will only bury yourself.

—*122 Rules of Psychology*

Sam remained quiet, holding her gaze.

Polly crossed her arms, her focus never leaving his eyes. "Chief, would you mind excusing us for a moment?"

Palmer glanced between them, his expression troubled. "I'm going to go see how long until the state police arrive." He set his clipboard on the counter, dropped his gloves in the trash, and left the room.

As the door closed, Polly leaned back against a cabinet. "I don't know your history, and frankly, I don't care."

"Polly, I——"

She cut him off with a sharp look. "The rumors are, of course, just that. I get it. But you're something. Not FBI. Not CIA. Those sorts of spooks smell like plastic and have all the charm of cheap bread. You're more like what the porn or used car industries would send to DC as their head lobbyist, oozing with charisma and knowing just what to say to the weak-minded."

Until this moment, Chet said, *I never believed in love at first sight. But brother, I'm head over heels with this girl. This is the first time anyone has summarized you so succinctly and accurately. If you don't marry her, I will.*

Sam ignored him.

"I could have run a background on you," she continued, "but I didn't see a need. Marines, probably retired, and possibly some paramilitary or security forces."

What about *her* background? She wasn't a simple, small-town girl with sharpened intuition. She carried the weight of a heavy past. Her ponderous, somber aura practically had atmosphere and gravity. "I don't know what you think you know——"

Polly raised a gloved finger, cutting him off again. "Bradford. Let's get one thing straight. If we're going to have any chance of working together, the one thing I'd ask is that you not lie to me. I'd much rather have you say nothing at all than try to feed me your tired old BS. Is that clear?"

Hear, hear! Chet sang. *Rule number twenty-five, baby!*

Sam scoffed at his inner conscience. *What about it?*

She and I agree. You should turn silence into your religion.

Polly's gaze sharpened, as if she could hear their banter.

Sam shook his head. "I understand your position. But since we're being frank, let's get something else clear. I'm a *volunteer*. Your chief asked *me* to come in, take a look, and give my opinion. That's all. I haven't agreed to anything. In fact, as far as I know, there is no case to work."

Polly regarded him with her intelligent, knowing eyes.

Sam held her gaze.

She nodded at the dead man. "How about you look and then decide if there's anything worth pursuing?"

Sam waited a heartbeat before answering. "Fine. But I'm not making any promises." He pulled on the latex gloves she had given him.

"Understood." Polly pulled back the sheet.

The man's skin, bloated and pale, stretched over swollen cheeks like wet leather. The epidermal layer had begun to slough away, revealing greenish patches of decay. Sea creatures had spent a week dining on his soft tissue, leaving behind ragged pustules of partially digested flesh. His shrunken lips were peeled back from yellowed teeth, giving him a jack-o'-lantern rictus. Cloudy, sightless eyes stared as though terrified by the visions they'd glimpsed beyond the veil at the moment of his crossing. "Do we have anything to determine the ID?"

"No. No driver's license or wallet. I emailed the technicians his fingerprints. It's the weekend though, so I'm not expecting a response anytime soon."

"You don't have access to AFIS or NGI?" Sam asked, referring to law enforcement's Automated Fingerprint Identification System and the FBI's Next Generation Identification biometrics system.

She shook her head. "We don't have the resources for direct access, so we share a third-party contract with dozens of other small-town municipalities throughout the state."

Sam bent over, studying the cadaver's green-and-purple face. He'd glimpsed a bullet wound in the man's chest, but he averted his gaze, purposely ignoring it. In his experience, paying too much attention to the most obvious thing could prevent him from seeing details that might otherwise be missed. "It looks like he was beaten up shortly before he died." He leaned in closer, examining the wounds that couldn't be explained by the man's time in the water. "Huh."

"Huh, what?"

He frowned. "I'd say this man was beaten up at least twice. Once a few days before he died, and the second immediately preceding being tossed into the ocean."

Polly said nothing for a few seconds, then admitted, "That was my opinion as well."

"These injuries don't look like they came from a club or a bat, or anything as sharp as a crowbar."

Polly frowned. "What makes you say that?"

Sam pointed with a gloved finger. "Look at his nose. If he'd been struck with a blunt instrument, it probably would have killed him instantly. Shooting him would have been redundant."

Polly didn't reply.

"And here." He indicated some blotchy mottling. "It's hard to tell for sure because of the discoloration, but these bruises look like they could have come from knuckles." Sam made a fist and held them over the injury pattern. "In fact, I'd wager that our assailant was a lefty. Notice how the nose is more bruised on the left side. Here,"—he pointed at a purple patch on the man's forehead—"this was made with a right hand, but the rest of these were made with a left. It's no guarantee, of course. But it's just more likely."

Again, Polly didn't reply.

He held his gloved fist against the bruise again, noting the diminutive size. Sam pulled back the man's lips, exposing the discolored and worn teeth. His gaze slid down the man's neck, to the swollen throat and the saucer-sized purple patch along his esophagus. "This could be a punch, but the lack of a knuckle pattern makes me think it's a boot kick." Sam looked over the man's arms and clean fingertips. The vic's ragged nails hadn't come from a fight or trying to claw his way free of a box or crate; they looked as though he'd habitually chewed on them.

He, at last, focused on the bullet wound in his chest, studying it for a minute without comment. "Did you do an x-ray?"

"I called the tech in, but he's not here yet."

Sam gripped the man by the shoulder. He turned him over and froze, staring at the tattoo where an exit wound would have been—had there been one. He glanced at Polly, who nodded. "It's one of the reasons we thought you might be interested in this case."

The image of the hound snarled with a mouth full of needle-like teeth. *Teufel Hunden* was inked in gothic print over a tattered, waving American flag. Sam translated the familiar German words. "Devil Dog."

"Right. He was a former Marine."

Sam gave her a sharp shake of his head. "There are no *former* Marines. Once a Marine, *always* a Marine."

Polly didn't argue.

Sam had his own shoulder ink. His depicted an eagle, globe, and anchor. *USMC* in a crescent script underneath. *Semper Fi* printed above.

He gently laid the man back down. *What happened to you, brother?* To Polly, he asked, "Anything else of note on the body?"

"There's more bruising on the abdomen and some on his legs, but like with everything else, it's hard to differentiate that from the mottling."

"Personal effects?"

She pointed to the pile on the counter. "I've already gone through it, but you take a second look while I photograph the body." Pulling out her cell phone, she began snapping pictures. The integrated camera clicked again and again in the quiet room.

Sam examined the man's jeans, checked the pockets, and searched for hidden sleeves or items sewn into the fabric—but found nothing.

That. Chet pointed. *The smokes.*

A floral design was etched into the tarnished silver surface of the cigarette case. Sam pressed the small button on the side, and the lid popped open. The ocean had turned the cigarettes to mush. He held the case up to his nose, inhaling the sharp blend of tar and nicotine. Turning it around, he squinted at the faint lettering on the gray-and-white paper that used to be the cigarette sleeves.

He flipped the case itself over in his hand several times. *It's too heavy,* Sam told Chet. *Almost as if...*

From back in the lobby, the front doorbell tinkled faintly. Chief Palmer's and another man's voices drifted down the hall as they talked to Savannah.

Polly, squatting at the head of the table with her camera focused on the man's scalp, glanced at the door. "Shit. Staties are here already. I thought we'd have another hour. They're about to confiscate our evidence." She continued taking pictures.

On a hunch, Sam dumped the mush of cigarette pulp into his palm and pressed experimentally against the inside of the silver case. The bottom-left corner clicked.

This looks a lot like the one you had on that assignment in Monterey, Chet noted. *Wonder if it works the same way?*

Sam pressed three spots along the back of the cigarette holder. A narrow door popped open.

Got it.

While Polly remained focused on photographing the victim's injuries, he tilted the case up, dumping an ultra-flat mobile phone into his hand. He pocketed the cell, closed the hidden compartment, scraped the mess of cigarette pulp from his palm back into the case, and snapped the lid closed.

As he returned the holder to the evidence tray, the outside voices drew near.

Together, he and Polly rolled the body to the side so she could photograph the Marine tattoo.

Sam grabbed a glass from the counter, wiped it down with his shirt, and pressed the victim's left fingers to it. He repeated the process with the right hand and returned the glass to the counter.

Someone typed into the security keypad.

Polly covered the body with the sheet.

Sam dropped the glass into a plastic bag Polly held open for him. He slipped it into a pocket of his Bermuda shorts just as the door opened.

A state trooper—a thin man in his late twenties with a bushel of fire-red hair and matching long mustache—followed Chief Palmer into the room. The officer's badge identified him as Trooper Lane.

The chief paused as he looked between Polly and Sam. "Everything okay?"

"Sure," Polly said. "Is the ME here? I've done some preliminary—"

Palmer held up his hand. "No. Trooper Lane has come to secure the evidence until the ME arrives."

Polly frowned. "You're not here to take the body?"

The trooper shook his head. "No, ma'am. I'm here to ensure the crime scene isn't tampered with."

She gave him a withering glare. "Trooper Lane, this isn't a crime scene. This is our morgue. And until the ME comes to officially claim the body—"

"Polly," the chief interrupted, "the officer *is* officially claiming the body. The ME was tied up on another case and is running behind. You and Sam need to step away. It's out of our hands now. Trooper Lane is going to remain with our victim until the doc gets here."

She arched a brow at the police officer. "So, you're just going to sit in here with the corpse?"

His cheeks flamed as if they'd caught him with his hand in the proverbial cookie jar. "Yes, ma'am. Those were my orders."

"For how long?"

He looked uncertain, his face turning crimson until it matched the smattering of freckles splashed across the bridge of his nose. "I don't know, ma'am. Tomorrow. Maybe the day after."

"This is *highly* unusual." She glowered at him. "Are you trying to tell me there's only one ME?"

Trooper Lane cowered under her steely, interrogative gaze.

Polly had him in her crosshairs, her finger on the trigger.

"I... I'm not sure, ma'am." He swallowed. "I just know what I was told."

Chief Palmer came to the young man's rescue. "Unusual or not, we'll put the body in the cooler. Trooper, you can park yourself in a chair beside it. Orders are orders."

Trooper Lane let out a relieved breath and looked around. "Where is it? I don't see——"

The chief inclined his head at a steel door at the rear of the room. "The door will be bolted shut. The drawer will be locked."

"I'll need a key," Trooper Lane informed him.

Polly narrowed her eyes.

The officer cringed. "Please?"

The chief also looked annoyed but told him, "You have my assurance, it's very secure. We've never had a break-in. Not once."

The police officer took another breath and focused on the chief. "I know this is an odd request, but my orders come from up high."

Polly and the chief exchanged a look. Matching confusion and annoyance darkened their eyes.

The chief muttered something about bureaucracy. "I get that those are your orders. I'll allow you to stay here, but the keys are *mine*."

Trooper Lane did not look happy, but he didn't argue.

Polly huffed as she skirted the two men and stalked out the door.

Sam yanked off his gloves. After tossing them into the trash, he followed the gentle sway of Polly's hips as she led him down the hallway. The entire scene had left him unsettled. The chief and Polly had a point. He'd never heard of a police officer babysitting a body before in a secure facility. If the staties thought it was a case worth pursuing, they'd have sent the ME right away. Something about it smelled worse than the man's decaying flesh.

The lump of the glass in one pocket and the dead man's cell in the other beckoned with mystery. The weight of them far exceeded their mass. The old familiar pulse urged him to dive into the digital depths of the phone to see if he could unravel what had happened to their dead Marine.

But that tempting gateway drug led to his old life. He couldn't go there. Polly and the state police would have to solve this case without him.

Chapter Three

Polly muttered under her breath as she marched down the hallway.

Sam followed her through the waiting room. He'd almost made it to the front door when Savannah called after him. "Hey, Sam!"

He stalled. The drinking glass he'd hidden in his shorts pocket created a considerable bulge. He draped a hand over it, wishing he'd found something slimmer to capture the victim's fingerprints. Feigning an innocent, inquisitive expression, he turned to the receptionist. "Yes, Savannah?"

Her gaze flicked to his hand, her eyes growing extra wide with surprise. The stretched material of his front pocket stuck out well beyond his large palm. By attempting to hide it, he'd unintentionally made the bulge look less rounded and more pronounced. She dragged her focus back to his face. Her too-white teeth blazed from her clown makeup smirk. "I forgot to have you sign in," she said. "Need your number...for the records."

"Oh, sure." He stepped up to the desk, which thankfully hid his shorts.

She handed him a tablet. He filled in his name, address, and phone number. Her sharp gaze remained on his face while he worked, though in his peripheral vision he thought he saw her curious glance fall to his waist a couple of times, as if she might see through the counter.

When he handed her the tablet, her long nails clicked against the surface. "Thanks, sweetie."

Keeping his pocket away from her, Sam nodded and left.

Polly stood on the walkway, the bright sunshine and happy blue sky a searing contrast to the annoyed, disapproving expression on her face. She practically had a rain cloud storming over her head.

He held out his hands. "It's not my fault your clinic has a sign-in policy."

She huffed, turned, and strutted down the sidewalk.

Sam fell in step beside her.

"We went through all this trouble to bring you here," she said, her words short and clipped. "I've shown you the evidence. What are your observations?"

Sam bristled. He'd had about enough of her attitude. He'd stayed in the Cove looking for some quiet time to work through his issues with The Agency and to help rebuild what Erebus had destroyed. These two RU jokers had crushed the first serenity he'd found in years to play a ludicrous version of Guess My Motives. And ever since he'd joined their merry little party, Polly had been treating him as though he'd asked her for the favor and not the other way around.

The chief's explanation had been plausible but total crap, and they all knew it. Later, Polly had said they thought Sam would be interested because the victim had been a Marine. On the surface, the reasoning seemed credible, but it smelled off. As though she'd stretched the facts to fit their motives.

And after she'd read him the riot act about telling *her* the truth, they were playing some game and expecting him to believe them. It reminded him so much of an Agency assignment—though in this case, he was the mark instead of the instigator—it made him want to tell them both to take their case and shove it.

He'd spent his entire Agency career guessing and second-guessing everyone's motives as they lied, cheated, and hid. Polly needed to take her own advice and get on with the real reason they'd brought him in.

So, what do you think it is? Chet asked, breaking into Sam's introspection. *Why you?*

I'm not sure, but my gut says they both needed me.

That's not what you really think, Chet contradicted.

Oh, yeah, Freud? What do I really think?

You think she requested your help.

Polly, as though sensing she'd become the topic of a heated conversation, glanced at him but said nothing.

Sam considered Chet's conclusion. *Yes. You're right. I think Polly asked the chief to bring me in on the case. But I don't know why.*

The lady is waiting for you to say something brilliant, his inner conscience observed. *Give her your thoughts. As you get deeper into this, you should be able to root out the truth.*

Something about Polly's assured, quiet self-confidence resonated. As if she had considerable experience controlling those around her. He doubted it would be easy to manipulate her into revealing a truth she had no intention of revealing. It was an odd quality for a small-town paramedic practitioner.

The systematic, unemotional way they had fallen in lockstep as they catalogued the cadaver's injuries and his personal effects had felt oddly natural. As though they'd worked a hundred cases together. Perhaps her training would prove similar to what he'd received from the Marines and The Agency.

Or maybe a background check would turn up a previous career working in a big city, where overdoses and murder were a dime a dozen. She would have to be quick, but methodical—same as him.

Either way, he would look into it.

Sam took a breath, stamping down his doubts and questions about her motives, and began rattling off his clinical observations. "Whoever shot our victim was at least ten feet away. He's been in the water several days, but there still would have been powder burns if they'd been close."

He waited to see if she would add something. In his experience, small-town law and medical professionals almost universally felt a desire to prove their capabilities to their big-city counterparts by overstating the facts of a case. Polly, who remained quiet, didn't seem to have a need for self-aggrandizement.

"I didn't see any evidence our vic had been tied up," Sam continued. "They didn't weigh him down."

"They probably thought that dumping him in the ocean would be more than sufficient to hide the evidence."

He nodded. "Based on the tearing of the skin and lack of exit wound, the bullet was likely a hollow point. Even something as small as a nine-mil full metal jacket probably would have gone through and through. Might have been a little bigger, but not much. I really wish we could have gotten that x-ray. Even better, I'd like to have gotten the bullet itself."

Polly's angry gait slowed as she guided them into the park. She seemed to relax now that they'd transitioned to a safe topic.

"I noticed a puncture wound on his arm," Sam said. "It looked postmortem. You get a blood sample?"

"Good eye. Yes. Because our local lab is limited, they're only able to do a standard tox panel—alcohol, weed, a few narcotics. Even though I requested a rush, it'll still take a day or so. Everything in the Cove runs at hippie speed. We don't have the equipment for a deeper screening, so I sent another sample to our third-party provider."

"Won't the chief put a hold on it now that the case has been turned over to the state police?" Sam asked.

"He can't stop what he doesn't know about."

Sam didn't reply. The more they talked, the more Polly confirmed his suspicions that she, not Palmer, drove this investigation.

They drew near a blue-and-yellow street coffee cart built out of a converted VW Bus. The vehicle's roof had been removed and reattached with a series of collapsible arms to allow the occupant to stand. Beneath a complementary striped vinyl awning, a serving window and counter had replaced the upper half of the van's wall.

"Buy you coffee?" Polly asked.

"Is that a bribe from a city official?" He gave her his most flirtatious smile.

Dude, Chet said. *That's not going to work. She is so not into you, and she's too smart to reveal her secrets just because she finds you annoying.*

Maybe she wants to tell me. Maybe she only needs a little push.

Sometimes I wonder if you're paying attention at all. Why exactly did The Agency hire you? You're supposed to be able to read people. This chick has practically assigned a town crier to announce all the ways she finds you despicable. If your intention is to get burned by the fire of her wrath, then by all means, keep at it.

Polly stopped. She stared him in the eyes for several seconds, her expression a cornucopia of emotions. None of them pleasant. "Bradford, I have tried being patient and cordial, but evidently, subtlety is lost on you. So let me be blunt."

Here it comes, Chet said. *She's about to drop the hammer like it's hot.*

"My friends call me Sam."

"Bradford," Polly repeated. "I do not like you."

Chet burst out laughing.

Sam ignored him.

Polly continued, "I moved here to get away from the crazy and forget the rest of the world. I want peace and tranquility. You led a madman to my town."

"No. I—"

She barreled over the top of his objections. "People I knew, people I cared about, were hurt. Some of them were killed. I'm not interested in getting to know you. I'm not interested in dating you or being your friend. I'm sure you can find some local girls who are more than willing to overlook your incompetence and destructive propensity."

Polly leveled a glare at him so hot it could have melted the polar ice caps. "Now, put away your smile. I'm immune to your fake charms. I've been asked to get more information on this case, and that—unfortunately—involves the distasteful task of working with you. But I'll do it because I'm dedicated to my job and want to get justice for this murdered *Marine*." She let out an exaggerated, exasperated breath. "Any questions?"

Did my heart love till now? Chet sang. *This girl is perfect.*

Sam studied her too-direct gaze, the set of her jaw, the corded muscles clenched in her neck. Yes, the pain inflicted on her friends had pissed her off, but it didn't explain this over-the-top rebuttal. She had asked for him. Of that, Sam had no doubt. Perhaps she regretted her decision. But some other motive lurked just beneath the surface. He still saw no sign of the rationale behind that motive. Not yet anyway.

He could have called her out, but she wouldn't admit it. All he'd do was cause an argument and make her dig in that much harder. For now, he'd let her keep her secrets. He'd get to it. Eventually.

"No, ma'am," Sam replied, giving her his best unperturbed expression.

She snorted, her glare hardening. "Since this is likely going to be your only compensation for your contributions to this case, I ask you again. Would you or would you not like a cup of coffee?"

"Sure. I take it black."

Though they'd been well out of earshot, the proprietor, a grizzled man in his late fifties, had been watching them. No doubt cataloging the exchange and filling in their words with his own imagination.

Polly stepped up to the cart and scanned the menu. "Two cold brews. No cream or sugar."

Reggae drifted from a speaker on the bus. The proprietor hummed and swayed with the beat as he filled their cups. Sam and Polly took their coffees and wandered down the path.

"You've given me your clinical analysis," Polly said a few minutes later as they strolled through the park. "But I figured out all of that already."

"I thought that was why you brought me in?"

"No. The *chief* brought you in because he wanted you to go beyond the physical details. What does your experience tell you about what happened, and does it help you identify our vic?"

Deny. Deny. Deny.

Sam knew the chief cared, but maybe not as much as Polly had insinuated.

Still, a Marine had been murdered. He'd play along for now if it'd help her figure out what happened. "I believe our Marine was working undercover. My gut says he's a detective, though I wouldn't rule out DEA or something else. The people he was trying to infiltrate either had a Russian in charge, or this was a Russian op. Something happened that drew their suspicion. He blew his cover, though he could've just crossed the wrong person who'd wanted to prove how tough she was. Really, there are a thousand possibilities. I think he was hoping she'd only use him as a human punching bag as punishment for perceived wrongs, but things went further than he'd expected. He got shot, either by her or someone else, and thrown overboard."

Polly froze mid-sip. She lowered her cup and stared at him. "How could you have possibly gotten all that from the physical evidence?"

Sam stopped and faced her. "Let's start with what's obvious. He was shot and beaten up at least twice."

She arched a brow.

"This indicates gang or organized crime," Sam said. "Not a mugging gone wrong or a crime of opportunity. He's a Marine, trained to fight back, but he had no defensive wounds. That means—unless he was drugged—he let her beat him up. Probably hoping she'd get the anger out of her system, and he could remain in her employ. The size of the bruises means it was an average-sized woman or a small man. I'm thinking the former."

Polly appeared thoughtful but didn't reply.

"Next, let's consider that he washed up on shore here in the Cove. My guess is our sheriff claims the vic was murdered in LA and dropped off a pier."

Polly said, "Yeah, that's my understanding of his conclusion."

"The problem is the Pacific Current runs from Alaska down to the equator, with a hard push east. According to Max, who spends a lot of time studying such things, that eastern drive has been exacerbated by the storm out at sea. The wind has been pushing hard. Besides the extraordinary kick-ass surfing conditions, you may have noticed the extra debris that's been washing up on shore."

She didn't reply, but she also didn't argue the point.

Sam continued, "If our John Doe was dumped in LA or some other city, he wouldn't have made it this far south. While it's possible someone could have dumped him within a few miles of here, I find it unlikely an undercover cop would be working out in the middle of nowhere between the Cove and LA. And no criminal would have driven so far to dispose of a body in the ocean. There's just no reason to."

"Meaning he had to be out at sea when it happened."

"Right. While this is pure conjecture, factoring in the storm and the number of days he'd spent in the water, I estimate our man was over twelve miles offshore. Most likely in international waters." Sam played into the story they'd spun by saying, "You and the chief will have to work out the jurisdictional angle he was so worried about. That's not my area of expertise."

If his comment sparked an emotion in her, she didn't show it. "Your reasoning is as sound as can be expected at this point. Except, how could you know this is tied to the Russians?"

"I didn't say it was tied to the Russians. I said whoever was running the show was *probably* Russian."

"Okay, why was this person *probably* Russian?"

"The cigarettes," Sam replied as though his simple statement proved everything.

Polly furrowed her brow. "There weren't any of the cigarettes left. It was just pulp."

"Yeah, but there was a slip of faded wrapper with OMOPKAH on the label. It was faint but still legible. That's the Russian brand, Belomorkanal. I had an instructor in college who smoked the same kind. Aside from the name, they have a very distinct odor."

She didn't look convinced. "This is a serious stretch. Maybe he just liked that brand."

Sam chuckled. "No. No American likes that brand. It's a very harsh flavor. It's what they call an 'acquired taste.' Besides, those cigarettes aren't exactly available at your local mom-and-pop. My prof had some relatives back in the motherland who mailed him some occasionally, but generally, those smokes have to be smuggled into the country. Your typical Russki, criminal or not, wouldn't have so many lying around they'd be willing to share. Since our Marine had a case full, someone he knew had plenty."

Polly processed this information as she began walking again. "Like I said, it's a stretch."

Sam matched her pace. "Of course it is. But you asked me to give you my opinion based on the evidence."

"I suppose," she admitted. "What about the undercover part? Why do you think he's a cop and not a criminal?"

"Because he's a Marine."

"You're letting your own bias cloud your judgment."

"No, I'm letting math guide my hypothetical. Of course, someone in the military could go to the dark side. It happens. But statistically speaking, that's not as likely as someone post-active-duty entering law enforcement."

"Okay, maybe."

"Also, our guy's teeth were unusually worn, and he chewed his nails. He was under *a lot* of stress for a very long time."

"Yeah," she said, "I noticed that too but didn't think much of it. Lots of people are stressed."

"True. But add in that his teeth were only lightly stained. He hasn't been smoking those cancer sticks for very long. They're tar heavy and make a mess of the smoker's mouth."

"So, he was lighting up to fit in," Polly surmised.

"Right."

She seemed to mull this over. "I don't know. That doesn't necessarily add up to undercover."

"Well, there was also the cell phone."

Polly stopped and turned to him. "What cell phone?"

"The one that was custom designed to be undetectable and hidden in the false back of the cigarette holder. Didn't it strike you as odd that our soldier had a silver case?"

"Wait. What? You're saying there's a cell phone in that case?" Polly glanced back the way they'd come, as if considering returning to the clinic. She faced Sam, irritation twisting her expression like a hurricane. "Why didn't you say something? We could have used that."

"Weren't we supposed to turn over all the evidence to the police?"

"I don't care about *their* investigation," she snapped. "I care about *my* case."

Her lone determination struck Sam again. *I care about my case.* Not the chief's, not "ours." Hers.

Why is she pushing so hard? Chet asked.

The shit with Erebus started with a body washing up on shore. Maybe she's just jumpy?

Maybe. Doesn't smell right though.

No, it doesn't, he admitted.

"So, you aren't going to turn me in for holding on to this?" Sam slipped the phone from his pocket and held it up.

Her expression transitioned to incredulity. "I suppose I could let it go. This time." She took the phone from him.

He considered holding onto it. It seemed unlikely, but if she ghosted him, he'd never see what was on it. Never know what happened to the Marine. But Polly seemed more than just wrapped up in the case. She was invested. It had pulled her in.

As the lead for RU, she'd surely found dead people before. While Sam felt confident she would have done everything necessary to solve those cases as well, he didn't understand what was so special about this one.

And despite her supposed abhorrence of him, she wanted him involved. In fact, she'd insisted he be part of it.

Like her, he felt the pull and thrill of the hunt. The mystery of who had put the man on the slab needed solving, but the biggest mystery of all was Cahill herself.

Chapter Four

"Hold this," Polly said, shoving her coffee at him. Sam took her cup. He thought she'd wait until they were somewhere less public to work on the victim's phone, but she fussed with it right there in the middle of the park. It didn't exactly look conspicuous, but still, it would have been better to conceal the evidence he'd stolen from a crime scene.

"It's dead," Polly said, after a few minutes.

Sam held out his hand. "I was going to dry it out. It still might work, depending on how much water got inside. If we stick it in a bowl of rice, it could draw out the moisture, though the salt may have damaged the—"

She leveled an exasperated look so hard it felt like a punch. The air around her seemed to crackle with her enraged energy. "Don't worry about it." She slipped the phone into her pocket and took her coffee back. "I have better ways that don't involve *food*." She'd made it sound as though he'd suggested a shaman lay healing hands on the phone's silicon components. Pivoting on her heels, she marched away.

Sam fell in step next to her as she stormed through the park like a typhoon. Only an occasional slurp, as she sipped her coffee, broke the verbal lull.

A storm of emotions seemed to swirl like a dust devil inside her. The more they walked, the more she transitioned from pondering, to brooding, to frustration, and—at last—to anger.

Sam would have paid big money to read her thoughts.

What's she so mad about? Chet asked.

You tell me, Captain Sensitive.

His inner conscience shrugged. *No idea, but spending time with her is like playing with matches in a dynamite factory.*

Sam had about run out of patience. Despite her denials, Polly had asked him to come in to help solve the murder under false pretenses. He could have let her anger roll off as she blasted away at him, but he didn't need to.

He said to Chet, *If she comes after me with whatever shit's going on in her head, I'm done.* He thought it over for a second. *In fact, I think I'm done anyway.*

What about justice for our murdered Marine? Chet asked.

I can't do anything about that if I'm only serving as Polly's punching bag. He side-eyed her. *And she looks like she's ready to start swinging.*

Maybe she's thinking about how you let Erebus blow up half the town and kill all her friends.

Which she knew before asking me to help! If she wanted to keep me away, if my very presence pisses her off, then why the hell call me in?

We keep coming back to that same question, Chet said.

And we keep not coming up with any new answers. Sam glanced at Polly and took another sip of his coffee. *Rage or no rage, this chick is an untrustworthy gateway drug. Following her will only lead me back to my old life. Except, The Agency of yore may not be the one I'd be returning to. It's better to focus on peace and quiet so I can figure out what comes next. I don't have to solve a murder, and I don't have to put up with her drama. She's not Josha, and this isn't a matter of national security.*

"How confident are you in your hypotheticals?" Polly asked, interrupting his conversation with Chet. Her voice sounded calm, professional. He had no idea what had spawned the hurricane, nor what had quelled it. It only appeared that the internal storm seemed to have simmered down.

Still wary that her seemingly somber winds may turn into a funnel cloud of fury once more, Sam thought over her question. He'd only been brainstorming earlier without intending to quantify his theories until he had more facts. "Maybe sixty percent. There are still a lot of unknowns. You need to get into his phone and run his prints. Here." Sam slid the bagged cup from his shorts pocket and handed it to her. "Until *you* get more information, I think you've gone about as far as you can." Time to make his intentions clear.

Something—heat, a challenge, a warning—flashed in her green eyes. She'd caught the subtle shift in his pronoun use. "You're not bailing on me, are you, Bradford?"

"I've consulted on the case." He added, "As you asked."

Instead of continuing to beat the ruse that his participation had come at the request of the chief, she said, "This is far from over. I could still use your help." Polly pointed back at the clinic. "*He* could use your help."

A surprising pang of guilt stabbed at him. Of all the military ops he'd fought in, he'd never left a Marine behind. Not once. Polly would have surmised this and was turning the screws on his dedication to his fellow soldiers that went so deep it was instinctual.

He swallowed the feeling. Emotions, especially guilt, were the levers and pulleys *he* used to control others. He would *not* allow someone else to do the same to him. "Ms. Cahill, I'm not qualified to see this through. I'm just a guy who's watched too many detective movies. This is a matter for the police to——"

Polly halted mid-stride. Turning, she leveled her gaze at him. "What did I tell you about lying to me?"

You want to talk about lying? How about knocking off the games and try being straight with me for once? Though he wanted to lob accusations at her like hand grenades, she'd only deny any wrongdoing. He'd redirect the conversation to confirmable, solid ground. That was how he'd come out on top. He put some sizzle and a hint of righteous exasperation into his words. "And what did I tell you about me being a *volunteer*?"

Anger darkened her tone. "You and I both know you're way more than some guy who's watched too many detective movies, and I don't believe for a minute that you're willing to let the death of a fellow *Marine* go unresolved."

That guilt poked him again. *Son of a bitch.* "I didn't say I was. The police——"

"Are incompetent and not motivated to find out what really happened. We both know how this will play out. Marine or not, they'll take the sheriff's ridiculous conclusions and run with them. Hell, they haven't even bothered to send the ME. Just parked some rookie cop to babysit the body so they can claim they maintained the chain of evidence. So, unless our John Doe turns out to be a celebrity, or rich, or a serial killer, or——as you suspect but haven't proven——a cop, they'll assume he's a criminal that crossed the wrong perp and got himself killed. They'll assign a first-year detective to it for a few days. When that guy doesn't make any progress, they'll drop it into the cold-case folder, where it will stay until it's archived. No justice will be served. No arrests made."

Damn it. He couldn't deny her conclusions.

What are you going to do? Chet asked.

I can't let a Marine's killer go unpunished. But fuck her for trying to manipulate me.

It feels like she's reading from our playbook, Chet observed. *She seems to understand the lessons from The Agency better than you do...not that it takes a lot.* He paused. *Lord. Could you imagine the force she'd be if she were a trained operative? She's wielding Rule Ninety-seven like a sword and doesn't even know it.*

Rule #97:
Everyone has an emotion that can be leveraged.

No matter how devoid of emotion an individual appears, everyone possesses a weakness that can be exploited. Narcissists—who do not experience empathy, joy, happiness, or sadness in conventional ways—are particularly susceptible to negative emotions such as anger, jealousy, and self-righteousness. Any disruption to their perceived reality, or to their position at the top of it, can quickly provoke rage. Conversely, empaths—especially those who have been manipulated or abused by narcissists—tend to be more attuned to manipulation. Use caution when employing traditional psychological tactics such as gaslighting, fear, or guilt. Individuals who have used these methods, or have been victims of them, are often faster to detect and resist manipulation.

—*122 Rules of Psychology*

Polly would be unstoppable, Sam admitted. *The Agency could use someone with her raw talent and skill. Actually, maybe not. She and The Agency of old could have reigned terror on criminals across the country. This new Agency wouldn't want anything to do with her. She's too likely to see through their bullshit and would refuse to take on cases like Monica's.*

You don't know that. Not for sure.

No. Not for sure.

Maybe, after you wrap this up, we could focus on that next.

Sam didn't reply.

"You want to play all coy with your background?" Polly said. "Fine. I don't care. What I care about,"—she put a hand to her chest—"is figuring out who murdered a cop and dropped him into the ocean hoping the sharks would devour the evidence so justice was never served." She fixed him with a steely, accusatory gaze. "Isn't the Marine's motto something about never leaving a man behind? Are you telling me you're quitting on a fellow jarhead?"

Sam bristled as she echoed his earlier thoughts. He saw her manipulation as clearly as an oncoming train, but he couldn't seem to step out of the way. The worst part was, he agreed with her. If she'd been wrong, it would have been easy to dismiss her accusations. But her words struck home like an arrow through the heart. *You little trickster.* He held her gaze. "You're really pulling out all the stops."

Polly arched a brow. "You didn't answer the question."

This chick is a predator, and right now, you're the prey, Chet observed. *She's boxed you in.*

Sam's mind returned to the little pool of water in his palm and the sensation of sharks lurking in the depths. Had he just glimpsed a glint of teeth and coal-black eyes? It seemed improbable, yet also probable. *So she has. I guess I'll go along...for now.*

But two could play this game. He might have lost this battle, but the war waged. She'd accused him of playing coy, but she hadn't exactly offered details of her past either. A thorough background check would reveal enough of her secrets that he could gain the advantage. "Alright, Stevie Jobs. Once you've gotten the information off the phone, call me. We'll figure out what comes next."

Chapter Five

Exhaustion gnawed at Sam's bones like a mangy hound. After ordering a background check on Polly through a deep-dive investigator he'd met on one of his assignments, Sam had stayed up until the early hours of the morning scouring the internet for intel on his new partner. Though the AIs, search engines, and even the dark web had returned thousands of hits, none of them had proven relevant.

There should have at least been a genealogy about her online. But according to the web, "Polly Cahill" of Alabaster Cove didn't exist. She hadn't revealed where she'd grown up or her parents' names. He might get her to shed some light on her history through casual conversation, though, so far, she'd remained tight-lipped about everything except the case.

Sam had searched using her phone number, combined with the town's name and anything else he could think of, but had found nothing substantial. Switching gears, he'd searched for a series of similar names, including Pauline, Patricia, and Priscilla. Nothing. He'd even tried less common root names like Apollina and Petronella.

She may have learned her habit of referring to people by their last names while working for the government, military, or even the police. This tidbit might prove useful if he had more to go on, except those agency systems would be locked tight. Even if he knew which to target, he'd never gain access on his own.

Likewise, if he could have hacked into the clinic's computers, he could have gotten her pertinents, but without an Agency assist, he was shit out of luck. He needed specific information to find anything useful, but without finding anything useful, he couldn't get the specific information he needed.

He'd paid extra for the rush on the background check, but the job could still take anywhere from three days to three weeks. If he asked Josha, he'd receive the results within hours. But given his shaky relationship with his employer, and the fact that the request had nothing to do with Agency business, he refrained.

Sam would have to learn patience if he planned to live in a non-Agency world.

Perhaps he'd become too reliant on Josha and team. If they parted company for good, he'd need to learn to dig up dirt without the crutch of their super-computers. Of course, if he no longer worked for The Agency, he may not have a need to look into anyone's background.

Having lived in the Cove for three months, he'd had more than enough time to dig into hers and everyone else's past but had chosen not to since finding dirt on people didn't fit with his new tranquil lifestyle. Sam had, of course, heard rumors about her, but everything reeked of speculation. Until now he'd had no need to pursue the truth about the elusive paramedic practitioner. He might have to reconsider letting people keep their private information private—it paid to know about those hurtling through his solar system.

As if on cue, Sam's phone buzzed and Polly's name blazed across the screen. He read the message: *You asked for more information. I have it. On your way over, get me a large quad, non-fat, triple pump, extra whip, double cup, extra hot mocha with a sprinkle of salt from Sand, Surf, and Brew.*

Below that, she'd included her address.

Chop-chop, Chet said. *Best get on it.*

Who does she think I am, DoorDash?

You're her assistant, Chet said with a slight grin. *Now be a good little gopher and run along to get your new CO her coffee.*

His inner conscience's exuberance only ground sand into Sam's raw nerves. *We're going to have a serious conversation about our roles.*

I don't think it'll be a very fruitful discussion until your girl gets her caffeine.

Sam rubbed his tired eyes as he considered his next move. Like Josha, and the military before him, Polly had assumed her priorities superseded his. He would help her reevaluate her understanding of the pecking order. They were equal partners or nothing at all. But in this instance, he would do as she'd asked since the coffee might help quell her orneriness. Plus, a shot of caffeine might take the edge off his own exhaustion, giving him the patience needed for their upcoming discussion.

Sam's phone vibrated again. Another message from Polly. He clicked it: *If Doogie's running the show, tell him I said to say hi to his mom and not to forget the salt this time.*

Chet chuckled and said, *You can always tell how high maintenance someone is by their coffee order.*

Sam reread the set of instructions, no less intricate than a rocket engine maintenance manual. *If that's a stick by which to measure people, then Ms. Cahill is slightly more complicated—and maybe as temperamental as—a nuclear power station.*

Amen, brotha.

He read her message a third time. In a flash of insight, he retrieved his computer and accessed the San Diego County Recorder's website.

Aren't you supposed to be fetching your boss her coffee? Chet asked.

Lesson number one: Sam Bradford is no one's errand boy. Polly can wait.

He entered the address she'd just provided. According to the deed, the house was owned by Security International, Inc. Finally, something specific to go on. But what had, at first, felt like a lead turned out to be another dead end. The digital universe rebuked his requests for more information on what smelled like a shell corporation or a trust.

Exasperated, yet unsurprised, he closed his laptop. He could tap back into the gossip vines. Maybe slivers of intel lingered deep within the cornucopia of rumors.

His phone buzzed again. *Where are you?*

Only through a Herculean effort did he resist the urge to reply with snark and sarcasm, though the battle had been razor-close. He typed out a response. Cordial, yet it still relayed the underlying message that her urgent orders were not his top priority. *Caught up on something. On my way soon.*

While he wanted to make sure she got the point, he also didn't want to unnecessarily provoke the bear. Time to get moving. His faux CO awaited her morning pick-me-up.

Sam pulled on his jeans and an old sweatshirt so threadbare the fabric felt as if it might come apart at the slightest provocation. Before slipping on his shoes, he paused, looking around the humble house he'd called home since moving to the Cove. This simple structure was more than adequate to fit his new lifestyle, which he'd lose if he went back to The Agency. Polly was as much a gateway drug as his Sig Sauer. If he followed her down this path, he risked sacrificing the serenity he'd established.

And yet, he couldn't deny the thrill pumping through his heart. The mystery and pace of it called to him. Luring him the way the bells and flashing lights of a casino would tempt a gambling addict to place his mortgage payment on red.

These last months living in the Cove had been therapeutic, but the analytical side of his mind had grown hungry. The itch to solve a problem, to track down a villain and remove him from the gene pool, prickled. And he longed to scratch it. Though solving the riddle of a dead man didn't fit exactly, it was close.

Add to that the enigma of Polly Cahill herself. Who was she really, and what were her true motivations? He sensed these incongruent pieces tied together. That he'd only glimpsed a fraction of a picture so large, it would suck him in like a black hole.

Sam approached the proverbial crossroads. One way led to potential peace and tranquility. To carefree sanity. The other path to danger, a life that changed from day to day, and an uncertain future.

He opened the floorboard where he'd hidden the backpack containing his Sig Sauer. After unlocking it and slipping the computer inside, he retrieved the Agency-issued cell phone. He stared at the gun lying in the pack's maw and once more waged an internal debate as ferocious as marauding tribesmen fighting over an ancient slice of holy land.

This case wasn't really a *case*, per se, but more of an investigation. And the dead man wouldn't pull a gun or a knife, requiring Sam to protect himself. Itch or no itch, if he had any hope of remaining in the Cove and keeping the peace he'd discovered, he would have to resist.

For now.

He was already tempting fate just by working with Polly. He could only put off the final decision—all in or all out?—a little longer. Soon, he would have to commit and live with his choice.

Sam resecured the pack and left his gun behind. Again.

Inside Sand, Surf, and Brew, a Beach Boys classic provided harmony to the comforting aromatic melody of ground coffee and cinnamon rolls. Nets draped from the open beam ceiling. Surfboards stood at attention, anchored to the rough-hewn walls like soldiers. Patrons lounged like wasted alley cats on a couch in the front window while others lingered in clusters, chatting in the rustic pine chairs scattered throughout the open space. The glassy concrete floor shined, its swirling patterns of blue and green reminiscent of a Disney cartoon's version of the ocean.

Sam stepped up to the surfboard countertop. The kid behind the bar looked to be about twenty, with a knit hat and a curly mop of sandy-blond hair that hung down over his eyes like a sheepdog's. Sam ordered a large black coffee for himself and referred to his phone as he rattled off Polly's recipe.

The kid smiled. "Got it. One Cahill Heart Attack comin' up."

Since the pimple-faced barista didn't wear a name tag, Sam asked, "You wouldn't happen to be Doogie, would you?"

His smile grew. "Yeah. How'd ya guess?"

"Ms. Cahill told me to tell you to say hi to your mom and for you not to forget the salt."

Doogie laughed—the sound relaxed and ringing of a carefree, unjaded lifestyle only enjoyed by the very young and the very innocent. "Got it." He entered the order into the cash register. "That'll be fifteen seventy-five."

Did I miss you asking for a ribeye with those coffees? Chet asked.

Right? Sam dropped a twenty on the bar top and told Doogie to keep the change.

Behind the counter, the barista pumped, banged, steamed, and poured; machines hissed; and a blender whirred.

Damn, Sam said to Chet. *No wonder it cost so much.*

At last, the young man handed him the drinks.

No steak.

"And I didn't forget the salt," Doogie said, dropping Sam a wink.

Sam made his way to Polly's, the hot drinks almost scalding his hands despite the protective cup sleeves. By the time he arrived, the cool morning air had taken the edge off the heat. He set his coffee on the porch so he could knock. From deep within the house, a small-dog yip echoed with all the ferocity of a baby koala.

As Sam picked up his cup, Polly yanked open the door. Clad in an old sweatshirt and a pair of faded jeans, she held out her hand. "Coffee."

Sam obliged.

She snatched it and pointed at his boots. "No shoes." She spun and marched back into the house, her stock-inged feet silent on the hardwood floor. Her long, dark hair—hogtied in a ponytail—bobbed along behind her.

The owner of the bark scampered around the corner. The fluffy dog probably weighed all of seven pounds and looked like a terrier mix of some kind. It danced and pranced inside the entryway.

Sam bent and scratched its neck.

The canine gyrated with such excited exuberance, it might have been hopped up on its own "quad."

"Saundy!" Polly called. "Come!"

Saundy, who had rolled over onto her back so Sam could scratch her belly, bounded up like a grasshopper.

Nails scratching on the hardwood, she sprinted toward her mistress' voice.

Sam raised his emotional blast shield as he prepared to go to battle. Time to lay down the law with his new partner and level the playing field.

Chapter Six

Polly had peppered the chicken-yellow sheetrock with photographs, maps, and other bits of evidence centered around the dead man's face. What the police called an Investigative Wall or Murder Board. Coffee in hand, she stood, focused on the mural of intel. While Sam wanted to dive in and learn what she had unearthed, that wasn't what had captivated his attention.

A luxurious cloth-covered wooden bench, piled with thick blankets, filled the alcove of a bay window. On either side, and extending to the corners of the room, ran floor-to-ceiling panes of glass, interlaced with white, crossing muntin frames.

Beyond the windows, past a rise of dunes covered in sea oaks, the ocean crashed against the shore. Open, hinged sashes at the top of the glass wall allowed the whispered chorus of collapsing breakers to fill the space with an ancient lullaby, as enchanting and serene as a hymn lilted by a primordial choir.

"Wow," Sam said, gaping at the spectacular view.

Polly glanced at him. Her eyes cut to the breathtaking panorama, then back to Sam. "Yeah," she said. "The house itself needed a lot of work when I bought it, but it was worth it for that view."

You mean when Security International bought this house, he thought absently.

Sam spent almost every day at the beach, but this magical canvas captivated him as though laying eyes on surf and shore for the first time. The wavy panes of glass seemed to amplify the rays piercing the never-ending patchwork of caramel-colored clouds. Sunbeams shimmered in a bouquet of colors, reflecting off the water and dazzling the room in prisms of oceanic hues—as though the house hadn't been built on dry land but had been constructed within the placid fathoms of the sea.

He tore his gaze from the vibrant tableau and focused on Polly's Investigative Wall. In one section, she had pinned pictures of a ship—an old freighter by the looks of it—including varying views of the deck, bridge, bow, and stern. In another, maps and charts. In a third, surveillance images of figures who clearly hadn't known they were being photographed.

At first glance, the intel appeared chaotic. But the more he studied it, the more he sensed a method to her madness. The information flowed like an intricate flower, starting with the man in the middle. It spiraled outward in streams of logic, from cohesive thought to cohesive thought. In its own way, it rivaled the ocean view, its beauty one of reason and deduction instead of natural phenomenon.

A million cop shows and movies depicted Investigative Walls. Hers was too organized, too meticulous to be an imitation of televised fiction. This reeked of strate-gized habituality.

With this new revelation, Sam ruled out a history in the military or government. While she may have been em-ployed by something as elite as the FBI, he felt confident that her background check would reveal a history in police work. Perhaps even a detective.

Sam made his way across the old, meticulously restored hardwood floor. Orbiting the neutron star of intel like a third-ring planet, he asked, "What is all of this?"

Her gaze remained on the mural. "This was on Frank's phone."

"Who's Frank?"

"Our Marine." She removed a page of text from the wall, replacing it with another.

"I take it you managed to turn on the phone." As soon as the words left his mouth, he internally cringed. His mind was still fuzzy from a lack of sleep.

She cut her sharp green eyes at him for a second. "Yep. No food required." Sarcastic condescension tinged her voice.

He waited for her to say more, but she remained fo-cused on her work. "Care to fill me in?" he prompted.

Polly took an extended sip of her coffee before letting out a long breath. "Yes. I suppose I should take a break anyway. I've been at this all night." She set her cup on the coffee table, made from a polished slice of tree trunk, and stretched her arms over her head, reaching for the ceiling. She rolled her head and arched her back. Instead of beginning her debrief, she flowed through a series of elaborate stretches, her joints popping like a bag of Orville Redenbacher.

Though her weapon of choice was a blade of irritation instead of a dagger, Polly had proven as adept at slicing through his patience as a trained assassin. She seemed to think Sam waited at her beck and call. That she could do whatever she pleased, and he would bide his time in patient adoration.

Sam had been about to launch into his practiced lecture about their roles and respect and equality when she turned toward him and he got his first good look at her face. Dark crescents hung under her puffy eyes. When she'd said she'd been working all night, she meant *all* night. Back in the military, he and his soldiers sometimes had remained awake for days at a time, only catching the occasional cat-nap. Around the twenty-hour mark, people got a look about them, like they'd hit the bottom of their reserves, and each subsequent ladle dipped into the energy well came up dry.

She wasn't in the right place to have what would undoubtedly be a confrontational conversation. He would wait.

When she finished a routine so complex it would make an Olympic gymnast sweat, Polly picked up a random pile of papers. Dropping onto the blue-denim, overstuffed couch, she folded her legs underneath herself as if transitioning from paramedic detective to swami.

Sam took a stool across from PI Cahill and set his brew on the coffee table next to hers.

"Meet Frank Boreman." She handed him a picture of a handsome police officer in the traditional uniform—starched navy shirt, matching cap, black tie—and a stoic expression. He looked competent and ready to take on the world.

His shield identified him as a member of the Los Angeles Police Department.

She read off his badge number, precinct, rank, and other particulars. "He's in the middle of a divorce. Family lives in Minnesota. As you predicted, he was working undercover. He'd spent a year gathering evidence on a gang known as The Flying Dutchmen, who specialized in high-end bonds, bank and jewelry robberies, and even dabbled in art theft. The bust had been epic, splashed across the news, and resulted in dozens of arrests, collapsing entire criminal chains from bank executives to black market art dealers."

A slew of questions flooded Sam's mind. First and foremost: how had she come by her intel? He'd spent hours researching her and turned up bubkes. Unless "Frank" kept a dossier on his phone, she must have discovered the dead man's identity through his fingerprints, which would require an in with law enforcement or the feds.

Instead of giving voice to his misgivings, he let her tell the tale in her own way at her own pace. Pretending as though her revelations were as routine as researching Sand, Surf, and Brew's coffee menu, he asked, "Didn't that bust just happen a week ago?"

Polly pulled a page from a random pile of notes and set it on the table in front of him. "There's not a lot more here than what was in the news. What the pencil-neck reporters didn't know was that Boreman leveraged the opportunity. He stayed undercover to infiltrate the Russian Mafiya."

Sam skimmed the document and let out a whistle for both Frank's audacity and Polly's extensive intel. "Those are very different beasts. How did he go from one to the other?"

"It was a matter of opportunity. The Mafiya's not just growing in the LA area, it's thriving. The police there were caught with their pants around their ankles and have been desperate to catch up. When the Dutchmen went down, Boreman 'just happened' to be next to an enforcer named Ivan Labanov in the new, up-and-coming Mogilevich brigade of the Gabisonia Enterprise. It was, of course, a complete setup so Boreman could get inside. Unfortunately, he disappeared the next day. Even his cell went dark."

With this revelation, Sam reconsidered the condition of the body versus time in the water. It didn't change his estimate. "But he wasn't in the ocean for a week. If he blew his cover, it wasn't right away." He pointed to the pictures on the wall. "Based on these, I'm guessing Frank spent the missing days on a ship."

"It seems so. There are a few missing pieces. The Mogilevich brigade specializes in debt collection. As far as anyone knows, they only work within the city limits. No ships involved."

"It fits with what we talked about yesterday. And guessing you don't yet know this connection to the boat."

"No, this is a different brigade. The captain's a woman named Levka Belikov. Levka means 'lion.'"

"That's not ominous."

She took a sip of her coffee and continued her story. "According to the status reports on Boreman's phone, the ship is the *Vengeance*." Polly looked at him expectantly, as if the name had some significance.

"I feel like you think this should mean something to me."

Polly stood, coffee in hand. She pointed to a document tacked to the top left of the Investigative Wall. "May twenty-sixth, nineteen-eighty-three. *Return of the Jedi* is in the theaters, Ronald Reagan is president, and the US–Soviet Cold War is hot. According to various unnamed sources, the top-secret plans for Reagan's so-called 'Star Wars' program—a ground and space–based missile system that supposedly would protect the US from a nuclear attack—are stolen by a KGB operative by the name of Nikolai Gorshkov."

Sam waited. How the hell could a Cold War crime from the previous century be connected to Frank Boreman's murder?

"According to unofficial reports, and a few leaked documents, Gorshkov slipped out of the US with a tape drive containing the schematics he'd downloaded from a server in the Pentagon. He chartered a boat that took him into the North Atlantic." She tapped a blurry image of a fishing boat. "At this point, the records get a little murky. He transferred to a trawler. From there, the trail gets cold until he transfers again to a ship in the Skagerrak. That ship is..." She held her hand up to Sam, indicating for him to finish the sentence.

"I'm guessing it's the *Vengeance*."

She pointed at him. "Wrong! It's *Novorossiysk*, which was captained by Vladimir N. Chernavin."

All the Russian names and words rolled fluidly off her tongue. If he had to guess, Polly spoke at least English and Russian. "Okay. How could I have known that?"

"I didn't expect you to, but I'll get back to why that's important in a minute. This is the point in the story where things get interesting."

"Oh, I can't wait."

She traced a line on a map of the world. "From the Skagerrak, the *Novorossiysk* sails into the Baltic Sea. It's headed to the Port of St. Petersburg, where Gorshkov will be escorted to Moscow. Except the *Novorossiysk* doesn't make it. On June third, nineteen-eighty-three, a fire detonates the munitions stored in the hold." She picked up a felt marker and made an X in the middle of the sea. "The ship is nearly ripped in half and sinks somewhere in the middle of the Baltic. All aboard are lost. The *Novorossiysk* is never found."

He saw where this might be headed. "At least according to official reports, that's the story."

"Right. However, in a few *unofficial* reports, it's purported that the US was so desperate to stop the stolen plans from falling into the hands of the Russians, they sent a black-ops submarine code-named *USS Pathfinder* to torpedo the *Novorossiysk*. Following the sinking, the Kremlin denied stealing the plans and even denied the existence of the *Novorossiysk*. The Navy, of course, claims there is no *USS Pathfinder* in their fleet. And, doing their part, the US denied destroying the ship."

"Had either side officially reported the incident, it could have led to World War III," Sam surmised, though he still didn't know how any of this related to their present situation. "What does this have to do with Frank Boreman?"

"According to the Soviet maritime archives," she said, "the *Novorossiysk* could not have been the ship Gorshkov took into the Baltic, because that ship had already been at the bottom of the sea for twenty-five years."

And the hits just kept on coming. "What? You're kidding."

"I'm not. The *Novorossiysk* was a battleship that had exploded and sunk near the Black Sea port of Sevastopol in the nineteen-fifties." She made another X on the map.

Sam did some rough mental math. "Those two points must be—what?—four-thousand miles apart?"

"About forty-five hundred." She tossed the felt-tip pen onto the coffee table.

"But if the *Novorossiysk* had already been sunk, then what ship went down in eighty-three?"

"According to a recently declassified CIA report, Russian propaganda claimed to have lost one ship. But that was a fake report meant to mislead. In reality, it was actually an old icebreaker known as the *Vengeance*."

"I'm still not seeing how that's connected to the ship in Frank's messages."

Polly gave him a dimpled grin as if about to pull a rabbit from her sleeve. "The captain, Vladimir N. Chernavin, who supposedly died in eighty-three, was rumored to have served at a high-level post in the Russian Mafiya until he passed in the early two-thousands. Chernavin had one daughter, Levka Chernavin. Levka wanted to earn her own street creds, so instead of leveraging her father's name, she took her mother's maiden name. Belikov."

The incongruent pieces Polly had been laying out fell into place, creating a dramatic scene worthy of a major motion picture. "Levka's father, who had ties to the Mafiya and KGB, purportedly piloted a ship that had been sunk twenty-five years earlier and reported going down again in the middle of the Baltic. A brigade leader in the Russian Mafiya captains the resurrected *Vengeance*."

"This is all circumstantial and based on unsubstantiated rumors, but that's the gist of it. I've printed the details, which are included in the copies of everything I've made for you."

Sam scratched his head, his mind whirring with thoughts of ghost ships, dead captains brought back to life, a ship risen from a watery grave, and a murdered undercover detective. He skimmed through the printouts of Frank's reports. Some of the text was garbled, and the remaining bits had little information. "Are these all of Frank's reports?"

"Yes. There's not a lot. I think there were more, but because of the damage to the phone, most of what he'd typed up was lost. I pieced together some of it but couldn't salvage most of the text."

Despite the loss of Frank's reports, Polly had gathered a significant amount of intel on the Russian Mafiya and, specifically, on the brigades. Time for the million-dollar question. Her answer would probably reveal more about her than the reports on Frank, the *Vengeance*, and the Mafiya combined. Sam asked casually, "How'd you figure all this out?"

Polly continued to focus on the Investigative Wall as she returned to the couch. She picked up a stack of papers, studying them as though needing a reference to answer his question. "Huh? Oh. Our third-party tech came through with the AFIS fingerprint identity faster than I'd expected. A few internet searches gave me his background and the history of the Cold War. All the rest is off Frank's phone." She said this with false air of nonchalance, but a slight note of something sharp—anxiety, perhaps—betrayed her casual delivery.

No, Chet said. *No way, did she get all of this off a "few internet searches." She's hiding something. A lot of somethings.*

Yeah, no kidding, Sam replied.

Let's put aside the Cold War reports for a moment—which or-dinary citizens wouldn't have access to in a million years no matter how much the CIA declassified. Polly has been emphatic that their outside company wouldn't be working on weekends. But say that's true—even though it feels about as genuine as a politician's smile. Undercover police operations, especially ongoing ones, would never be available online. Your girl isn't just snowing you; she's conjured a full-on blizzard.

Yeah, but if I call bullshit, it's going to lead to an argument.

Maybe try using a little charm for once instead of always being so tactless.

Hey! I can be charming and tactful when I want.

Chet scoffed.

Sam said, "This is good work."

She glanced at him, arching a brow. "But?"

"Well." He selected his words carefully. "I'm not in law enforcement, but I wouldn't think they'd post information about ongoing investigations on the internet."

Polly shrugged as she crossed her feet at the ankle.

Whatever came next would be a lie. The lips strive to deceive, but the body will always speak the truth.

"Not everything is off the web," she said. "I have a friend in law enforcement who owed me a favor."

All kinds of alarm bells clanged in Sam's head.

Though Polly had just confirmed his suspicions that she'd at one time been a cop, the fabricated half of her story smelled as pungent as a fish market outhouse. This small-town paramedic conveniently had an undisclosed contact willing to provide her inside information on one of the most closely guarded secrets in the LAPD. Not even for a sibling in blue would a detective who valued their career—not to mention the safety of their fellow officers—be willing to break such a sacred protocol. She'd either used some sort of leverage, had underplayed her law enforcement contact, or her information came from somewhere else she would never be willing to disclose.

And when she'd mentioned the new bratva, she'd tried to make it sound as everyday as reporting basketball stats on a fantasy league. But crime organizations didn't exactly share their org charts. She had criminal knowledge she had no business knowing.

He had no doubts that the intel she'd provided was accurate. But Polly's explanations of how she'd come by it had more holes than all the Florida golf courses combined.

She laid another page on the table, obviously trying to divert the conversation. "This is the only picture we have of Diego Gabisonia."

He studied the blurry outline of a man in a suit. *Supposedly you found all this secret information online, yet this is all you have on its leader?* "Of the Gabisonia ilk you mentioned earlier?"

"One and the same. He's the vor of the Gabisonia Enterprise. He and his lieutenants are the fastest growing bratva on the West Coast, maybe even the world. At the rate he's expanding, he could own every drug, weapon, and human trafficking operation in LA within a year."

While the mystery around Polly grew by the second, he put that aside. It was relevant and he would unearth the truth, but right now, it was a distraction to the case. Sam took a sip of his coffee as he studied the image. The face of the enemy. It was people like Diego that The Agency used to send him to hunt down and remove from society.

His trigger finger itched.

Polly said, "We know about the Dmitry Mogilevich brigade. I suspect Mogilevich sold or gave Frank to Captain Levka. I think either she or someone on the *Vengeance* killed Frank and dropped him into the ocean."

She fixed Sam with a hard look. "And you and I are going to prove it."

Chapter Seven

Sam focused on Polly's determined green eyes. The set of her jaw. She was used to facing the impossible and coming out on top. "You think you can prove a brigade—which we know almost nothing about—killed Frank Boreman?"

"Don't be ridiculous. It's much too big a job for one person. You and I will prove it *together*."

"We're talking about the Russian Mafiya. I would think that the vor and all his knee-busting, kidney-stealing, body-dumping lackeys might be more interested in staying off everyone's radars. I don't know your background, Ms. Cahill, but you should know that's not a two-person job."

She arched a brow. "You're saying you're not up to the task?"

"I'm saying the National Guard isn't up to the task. There's a reason the police have a team dedicated to infiltrating these guys. And, let me remind you, the one officer who got inside floated up to your beach with a bullet in his chest."

"I—" she began, but her phone buzzed. She pulled it out and read the screen. "I need to call the office and give the chief an update."

Polly started to head to her room but paused as she went inside. She caught Sam's eye. "You think about your fellow Marine and what justice you believe he deserves."

She keeps throwing down that same ace over and over, Sam observed.

It means she probably doesn't have any other cards to play, Chet replied.

I admit, it's a good card, but eventually, it'll lose its effectiveness.

Maybe it's time you stop farting around with the internet and commercial background checks and get the lowdown on your new girlfriend.

Sam hesitated. *You think Josha's in the mood to do a favor for his most disgruntled and insubordinate employee?*

Chet chuckled. *Come on. You and I both know that's why you brought your Agency phone. You thought it might come to this.*

I didn't know it would get this deep.

And yet, on some level, you did.

As much as he didn't like it, Sam couldn't argue. Somehow, he'd known the shit might get hairy and he'd need to call in a favor from his handler.

Monitoring Polly's door, Sam pulled out his Agency-issued phone. He entered the password and pressed his thumb to the screen, completing the device's security protocols. On the home page, he clicked a few buttons to access a hidden menu.

Agency phones came standard with an application allowing operatives to find out anything on anyone at any time. Enter a few parameters and hit a button. After being blessed by the operative's handler, the request went to the underground super-servers. The system's AI fulfilled the request from whatever computer systems held the data.

No firewalls, no security software, no protocols blocked The Agency's machines. Nothing was off limits.

Nothing.

But first, it needed to get past Josha.

Sam entered Polly's pertinents—her name, address, and phone number—then paused before hitting *Send*.

You click that button, Chet said, *and you'll be getting a call before you can put it in your pocket. You ready for that?*

I don't know if I have any choice. Too many questions needed answers. He had to know who he was working with and what her true motivations might be. *Besides, weren't you the one just a minute ago telling me to stop farting around and get to the bottom of this?*

And I stand by what I said, Chet replied. *I just want to be sure you're ready for the ramifications. You know how they feel about off-the-books investigations.*

Everything we do is an off-the-books investigation.

Touché, Chet said. *But you know what I mean. Off The Agency's books. It's not the call I dread as much as the guys in black camo who will come and take you away in the middle of the night. Not that I'm worried about your dumb ass, but if they get you, they get me too. And I'm too beautiful and charming for prison life. My butt would be more popular than Space Mountain. Every thug, murderer, and kidnapper in the joint would want to ride my glorious cheeks.*

Dude, that's wrong on so many levels.

Chet shrugged. *You wouldn't understand the tormented life of the aesthetically resplendent.*

Sam hit the button.

Three seconds later, his phone buzzed. The caller's identification read *Blocked* of course.

Told ya, Chet said.

Sam had been hoping his handler would just rubber stamp the request. He hadn't been expecting it, just hoping. Sighing, he kept his voice low as he answered. "Hello, Josha."

"Hi, Sam. What can I do for you?" As usual, his handler made no effort at small talk.

The two of them hadn't talked in three months. Since The Agency knew everything about everyone every second, Josha already knew why Sam had requested the information on Polly. The call was a formality. But a decade ago, Sam had signed on the bottom line, agreeing to play the game. Time to dance. "I need some information," Sam whispered.

Josha paused. "On who?"

Exasperation tweaked Sam's nerves like a Taser. *You know very well who.* Keeping his voice low and calm, he said, "Polly Cahill. She's a local paramedic." He thought for a second. "No, she's a paramedic practitioner."

Over the line came the muted but familiar rap-tapping of a keyboard. Josha was an infamous multitasker. He might have been pulling up Polly's information, or he could have been putting together the assassination plan for some whacked-out terrorist that had stumbled onto American soil.

Or he could have been putting a hit out on Sam.

The clack and clatter halted. A note of guardedness colored Josha's voice. "I'm reviewing your request. Are you certain about the name? Polly Cahill?"

Sam's heart gave a hard thump. In all the time they'd worked together, he had never heard that tone of—concern? unease?—before. "Yeah. Polly Cahill. I don't know her middle name. Figured you would. I tried to do some preliminary research last night but couldn't find anything."

"I don't doubt it." Josha's voice had been so quiet, Sam hadn't been sure his handler had actually said anything, or whether Sam had heard him correctly. *I don't doubt it.* What could he have meant by that?

A deafening silence blared down the line.

Finally, Josha said, "I don't recall giving you a case."

"This is for a private investigation."

"I see. That's not in your job description. Plus, you're supposed to be on vacation, remember? A concept which seems very difficult for you to embrace."

"Yes," Sam hissed a little too loudly. He dropped his voice and gave Josha a brief rundown of the situation. The keyboard on the other end of the line rattled away like a machine gun as he talked. "But there's something very off. It doesn't sit right."

"I see," Josha said again, but he made no further comment.

Anger flared white hot in Sam's gut. If Josha had something on his mind, he should just get on with it instead of muttering and leaving uncomfortable gaps in the conversation. "Is there something you're not telling me?" Sam asked.

"No." The hesitation had left Josha's voice. He sounded more like his old self.

Sam would have loved to study his handler's face. Trying to get a bead on the man would have been a million times easier if he could have read the deception in his eyes. Of course, he'd never seen Josha. Not a single time. He didn't even know what his handler looked like.

"One of the reasons we brought you on was because of your instincts," Josha said. "If you think something is off, then I trust you."

But now Sam wondered—and not for the first time—if he could trust Josha. They'd been on rocky ground since the Monica case. Sam had hoped they'd find some sure footing once he'd finished his vacation, but now, things seemed even more uncertain.

He waited for his boss to continue. It would do no good to poke him. His handler would start talking when he was ready.

"Alright," Josha said. "I'll let you run with this."

Sam let out a pent-up breath.

"But I have a few conditions."

Sam checked the hallway, but Polly must still have been talking to the chief. "Okay, shoot."

"First," Josha said, "do not get involved with anyone regarding the Frank Boreman case. You are only acting as a consultant for Ms. Cahill."

Sam didn't understand the condition. Though Polly had delusions of taking down the Russian Mafiya, their odds of success lay somewhere in the neighborhood of zero to nonexistent. Given that, instead of asking for clarification, he said, "And second?"

"Second, you are to report any findings to me. Keep me looped in on everything that's happening."

"Will do. Anything else?"

Josha paused once more, and again, a dagger of worry stabbed Sam's heart.

"Last, be careful."

Be careful? Sam had faced mob bosses, drug lords, deranged assassins, politicians, pimps, and thieves——sometimes only armed with his wits and Josha's well-wishes. Never, in any of those cases, had his handler told him to exercise caution. He sensed some significance in the warning, but he couldn't fathom what Josha wanted to convey.

His handler's muttered phrase came back to him. *I don't doubt it.*

The more he thought about it, the more he believed he'd heard correctly. But Sam didn't know what to make of the odd statement. Why would Polly not be anywhere on the internet?

Something didn't add up.

His handler continued, "You went way too far with Erebus. Took too many unnecessary risks. I had to answer some very uncomfortable questions to some highly pissed off individuals who wanted you thrown in a dark cell in a deep pit. But I stuck my neck out and calmed them down."

"Thank you, Josha."

"I'm not after your appreciation. I want you to know that what you did got attention up and down the chain. It's important for you to understand the stakes of going off the rails again. I'm giving you some latitude because, from what I see here, there might be something of interest. Be careful how you use this latitude. It could become the rope that hangs you. Don't disappoint me."

"I won't," Sam said, but the line was already dead.

His phone buzzed again with an email notification. Josha had sent the requested intel. The Agency was fast, but usually, it took a few hours for the type of deep dive he'd requested. Yet one more oddity in a series of oddities.

Polly's bedroom door opened.

Sam quickly dropped the phone into his pocket.

She'd swapped the ratty sweatshirt and jeans for work scrubs. "I've got to go into the office. The chief wants me to handle the press and work with the State Police." She handed him a thick manila envelope. "This is everything I have on Boreman. Study it, and we'll meet up tomorrow. I'll text you when I'm available."

Sam didn't need a written notice to recognize an invitation to leave. Polly's terrier danced around his feet as he headed to the door.

Polly picked Saundy up, petting her head. She opened the door, and blazing sunshine cut into the shadowed hallway.

Sam put his boots on and stepped across the threshold. He paused on the stoop. "You can trust me, you know."

Polly's emerald-green eyes locked in on his. "I don't trust anyone. Things are simpler that way." She set the dog on the floor, told her to be good, and followed him outside, locking the house behind her.

Without another word, Polly marched down her walk-way and turned toward the clinic. Sam followed at first but then went in the opposite direction toward his own house. He finally had some intel on his elusive partner. Time to unlock her secrets.

Chapter Eight

Sam pushed through the front door of his modest, single-room home. He hadn't bothered to fasten the cheap lock, which could have been picked by an adept three-year-old. The air conditioner, a block of rust parked on a disintegrated pallet behind the house, looked like it hadn't sparked since Nixon wore diapers.

Sam didn't mind. In fact, he enjoyed the warm humidity blowing through the windows he never closed. Graceful ocean breezes waltzed through the house to the gentle tempo of the sea's rumbling waves.

Overhead, the vaulted exposed-beam ceiling joined like rib bones to the rough plank walls. His lumpy mattress lay on the hardwood floor in the corner, opposite a threadbare couch with tired springs. His hula girl surfboard waited in the corner. Should the mood strike him, he could be out the door and taming the Pacific in less than three minutes.

The humble space contained nothing unnecessary. Basic. Essential. It fit him like his old sweatshirt. Comfortable and worn. A bit past its best-by date, but with many years of life still left in it.

Like him.

At night, serenaded by the crickets and the ocean, he envisioned a life free of his job as a federal assassin. He had plenty of money. If he bought the joint, it would save the owner the trouble of knocking it down and building something nice.

Without The Agency and anything resembling responsibility, he could live out his days in peace. No more death. No more obligations.

Except he knew better.

Young, pre-divorced, pre-military, pre-Agency Sam of twenty-some years ago may have been happy living that dream. But his soul had too many miles on it. Having seen too much death and injustice, he'd developed an appetite for righting wrongs so strong it felt like a compulsion.

Residing in a small town, giving surf lessons, and working in Max's shop wouldn't rid the world of evil. That was *existing*, not *living*. It lacked purpose and didn't contribute to the betterment of society.

He'd sacrificed everything to the causes of freedom and liberty until he barely recognized himself. Yet, it never felt like enough. As though he still had a debt to pay. Though to whom he owed—the universe maybe—and for what, he couldn't say.

Sam tossed the envelope Polly had given him onto the rickety dining table. The thick bundle of papers slapped the worn Formica like a backhand to the face. He started the music app on his phone, streaming it to the speakers placed strategically throughout the room. The house filled with warm, melancholy guitar riffs and the dusty, soulful voice of Beth Hart as she sang about being caught out in the rain.

Sam knelt, opened the floorboard, and rolled the combination on the strap anchoring his backpack to a metal loop drilled into the concrete foundation. When the clasp clicked, he removed the chain and lifted the bag out of its hiding spot, revealing a small metal box beneath.

He almost ignored it but instead reached in and pulled it out. The hinges gave a soft squeak as he opened the lid, releasing a scent dusty and dry, like ancient memories long forgotten. A bottle of sand from Afghanistan where he'd done his first tour. Dog-eared photos of the men he'd served with—some of whom never made it home. Sam picked up his old dog tags, winding the chain through his fingers, thinking about oaths and honor, blood and sacrifice.

Promises to never leave a brother behind.

We'll find who did this to you, Frank.

He shook his head. Dropping the tags back into the box, he returned it to the hole in the floor, unsure where his foolish sentiments had come from.

Sam entered the code into the lock embedded into the backpack's stiff composite shell—a unique layered sandwich of Kevlar, anti-RFID mesh, and nylon. Maybe he should order a sleeved blanket made from the same fabric. It should be warm and fuzzy, like the kind hawked on TV. Only his version would also be bulletproof, knife-proof, and impervious to explosives.

The perfect gift for the dictators, warmongers, and Agency operatives in your life!

Sam pulled back the double metal zipper, retrieving his computer and Sig Sauer. After setting both on the table and plugging the computer in, he plopped down in a dining chair and opened the laptop. He threaded his way through the security layers to retrieve Josha's email and began to read.

Polly had been born and raised in New York City. Her father, Rexford Ray Cahill—of Germanic descent—was an Army master sergeant. After retiring from the military, he'd become a PSO—Protective Service Officer—for the Speaker of the House. Both he and Speaker Hillman were killed in the Geneva bombing. Their bodies were never recovered.

Her brother, Liam Allen Cahill—also born in New York City—had been a corporal serving in Syria. Two days after his father died, Liam's convoy ran over an IED, killing him and sending several of his fellow soldiers to the hospital. News of his father's passing hadn't even reached him yet.

Mother and daughter had taken the sudden destruction of their family differently.

Her mom, Camila Lace Cahill—maiden name Dioli, of Italian descent—devastated by loss, joined a political activist group fighting for the global ban on assault weapons.

Polly, a junior in high school when she'd suddenly become an only child, went the opposite direction. As Sam had suspected, she'd become a cop. She graduated early and entered the police academy a week after turning eighteen.

Sam ran a search on Camila Lace Cahill but found nothing of substance. He paused over the keyboard and then tried again, this time using her birth name. This second search resulted in a thousand hits and read like the "who's who" of political activists.

Sam scrolled the long series of articles. He clicked an image. A dark-haired woman with sharp cheekbones, a hooked nose, and the same intense green eyes as Polly stared back at him. He started one of the many videos, listening as Camila passionately spoke about the dangers automatic weapons posed to our civilization. She had a natural presence. An "It Factor" so many in Hollywood sought, but so few possessed.

Though he understood her position and why she'd taken such a hard stance, he disagreed with her solution. A sickness had infected society like a cancer. And like any sickness, it needed to be eradicated. The removal of weapons, automatic or otherwise, wouldn't heal the illness afflicting humankind. The misuse of guns was only a symptom. Anything from planes to trucks to toxins could be substituted for bullets. The cure lay in the reformation of those who spread their diseased values like a plague.

And if they couldn't be reformed...well, that was why The Agency hired people like Sam.

Were Polly's views on fixing what ailed society similar to his? It didn't seem out of the realm of possibilities, considering she'd elected to go into law enforcement instead of activism as her method of curing the world of its sins. If she and Sam aligned on removing scumbags instead of weapons, could Polly and her mother debate the merits of their differing opinions, or was the chasm between their philosophies too wide to cross?

Camila's arguments were compelling and well thought out. Unlike many who had taken up the anti-gun cause, she struck him as the sort of person who could hold an intellectual conversation without resorting to name calling and media-invented clichés. That increased the chances mother and daughter had remained close.

Sam paused the video of Camila speaking at NYU. He studied her eyes, the set of her jaw, the determination and conviction in her face. He'd seen this same intensity in Polly's expressions. She had the same "It Factor" as her mother. The same drive. The two women probably shared stubborn streaks that wouldn't be deterred by a runaway bulldozer, least of all politicians and their self-serving motivations.

Sam turned back to Polly's history. In her youth, she'd mastered martial arts, which she incorporated into law enforcement. She had a colorful record with the Boston PD. Sprinkled among the commendations, her voluminous work history included reprimands for excessive violence and disciplinary citations for failing to follow orders, and she was twice suspended for incidences of applying deadly force with her service weapon. In both cases, Internal Affairs had determined she'd been justified, though they had still issued black marks on her record.

Eight years ago, her law enforcement career ended abruptly.

He scrolled through the supporting documentation, discovering a few pages of redacted notes from a court proceeding. Why hadn't they included the entire case? Government incompetence being what it was, maybe someone had misfiled or accidentally deleted them. A special app on his computer revealed the limited text—a direct examination by a prosecutor named Tattersall.

Tattersall: Is it your sworn testimony that you had no warrant when you attacked the victims?

Cahill: Victims? They weren't victims. These men were cartel drug dealers.

Tattersall: Alleged cartel drug dealers, and you didn't answer the question, Detective. Did you or did you not have a warrant when you attacked the victims?

Cahill: We were following a suspected distributor. We chased him into the abandoned mall. There was no time to get a warrant, nor did I need one. Our actions were justified.

Tattersall: Justified? Interesting choice of words. So, according to you, you were justified in murdering seven men?

Cahill: I did what I had to do to save my officers.

Tattersall: But you didn't save any of them, did you, Detective?

Cahill: No.

Tattersall: In fact, there were no witnesses to your crimes.

Cahill: That's not a question, Counselor.

Tattersall: No, Detective. I'm just trying to understand your motives during the sequence of events. Can you walk us through what happened?

Cahill: We followed the suspect into the building. As we breached the perimeter, Officers Talbot and Jervis each took a round.

Tattersall: Meaning they were killed?

Cahill: I didn't know it at the time, but yes.

Tattersall: Did you attempt to aid in any way Officers Talbot and Jervis?

Cahill: I couldn't. Officers Baldwin, Mains, and I got into an extended exchange of gunfire with the drug dealers. Talbot and Jervis were in the open. Had I attempted to assist them, I would have been killed too.

Tattersall: I see. So, it was their lives or yours?

Cahill: No. I wanted to save them but couldn't. Had I tried, we all would have been killed.

Tattersall: With two of your officers down, why didn't you retreat and call for backup?

Cahill: I did call for backup, but retreating wasn't an option. We were pinned down. They had automatic weapons. We couldn't escape.

Tattersall: But at some point, you did escape. Isn't that correct?

Cahill: No. There was a hallway off the back of the room. I got out and circled around to flank the perps. Along the way, I had to clear several rooms, during which I ran out of ammunition.

Tattersall: How could you possibly continue without ammunition?

Cahill: I used Krav Maga to subdue several suspects, then used their weapons to disable the drug dealers attacking my officers.

Tattersall: Wow, you're a regular Jackie Chan. [Laughter in the courtroom] Subdue and disable? Interesting choice of words. You are attempting to imply that you follow protocol to arrest and detain. But in this situation, you are covering your crimes by incorrectly applying those standard police terminologies. The truth is you killed them.

Cahill: I did what I needed to do to save my officers.

Tattersall: Except the officers in your charge were already dead, correct?

Cahill: Yes. While I'd been trying to get back, both Mains and Baldwin were shot.

Tattersall: With everyone dead, the bulk of whom fell at your hand, no one's alive to refute your version of events.

Cahill: There is no version of my events. They happened exactly as I described. We were ambushed.

Tattersall: And you had no other motivation for the deaths of the victims besides protecting the public?

Cahill: They weren't victims; they were cartel members who sold drugs to anyone with a little cash, including children. It wasn't murder. It was a justifiable homicide. And no—I had no other motivation than to end a very dangerous situation.

Tattersall: You were working solely for the Boston PD at the time?

Cahill: Yes. Same as now. Same as every day I wear the shield.

The derogatory interrogation continued for a few more paragraphs before abruptly ending. Sam searched the rest of the documents but found nothing else.

Though Tattersall was the prosecutor, he presented his case more like a persecutor. He implied Polly had other reasons for killing those cartel members, but unless he had solid evidence, it was nothing more than a fishing expedition. He must have been hoping Polly would implicate herself. No chance of that.

Sam didn't need to be in attendance to sense the bloodlust or hear the way a narcissist could twist the narrative to fit his preconceived conclusions. That wasn't justice. That wasn't the truth. That was a politician with an agenda ramming a dagger into the back of a blue blood who would have sacrificed her life to save him or any other Bostonian.

Her captain followed and testified, as much as the prosecutor would allow, in support of Polly's actions. Ultimately, Detective Cahill had been found innocent of both murder and manslaughter charges, but the bureaucrats had stripped her of her gun and shield anyway. They labeled her dismissal as "Termination for Cause." He tried to find the supporting documents, but only found *Records sealed. Unavailable at this time.*

Sam frowned, unsure what to make of the concealed information. The Agency knew everything about everyone. Nothing was "unavailable" to them. Nothing. This made no sense.

How could The Agency, which had unrestricted access to all systems on the planet, not have Polly's complete file? The oddity left him feeling unsettled. With nothing more to be done at the moment, he let it go for now and continued reading.

Second careers didn't come easily to either ex-military or ex-law enforcement. Many ended up in some half-assed security job monitoring warehouses or babysitting rich juvenile delinquents. Polly had gone a different direction and enrolled in paramedic training.

Despite having no obvious source of income, her banking records showed regular monthly deposits that had begun when she entered school and continued until she graduated. Sam dug through the statements until he found a check stub. The payer's line——*Security International, Inc.* The same company on the deed to her house. Nothing in the file indicated if SI was a shell corporation, a trust fund, or something else.

He could request an Agency follow-up on her income, to find out about SI and to see if her termination records could be unsealed, but he had already gotten a call from Josha today. Best not to press his luck. Besides, if The Agency thought any of that was relevant, they would have included information.

Right?

A faint warning bell rang in the back of his mind. He felt snowballed. Shown a misleading, partially true version of her history. Like wandering through the false fronts of a movie set. It looked real enough, but the eyes could be deceived. Fooled into filling in details that weren't there.

After Polly received her paramedic practitioner certificate, she had applied for, and received, the job in the Cove, where she had been employed ever since.

According to the records, Polly spent very little of her income and had no personal assets and no run-ins with the law. She also had no regular monthly expenditures. Security International either made the mortgage and insurance payments for her or owned her house outright. Sam guessed it also paid her cell service and utilities and covered any vehicles she owned.

Polly Cahill had a nearly nonexistent digital footprint. Perhaps having her name smeared across the headlines had driven her underground. As a police detective, she would have known the tricks to hiding in plain sight.

The explanation, while plausible, didn't quite sit right in Sam's head.

He cycled through the attached photos. Polly as a baby with her parents, first grade, middle school, police academy, graduation from EMT training.

He thought for a moment and returned to her employment history, unsure what niggled at the back of his mind.

What's wrong? Chet asked.

I don't know. Other than the missing termination documents, there's nothing in her history that stands out.

Yet, the nothing kinda screams, doesn't it?

Exactly, Sam replied.

He reread her police service record. *Look here. Even as a rookie, she was busting people left and right. Racking up commendations, medals, and promotions, mixed in with regular disciplinary reports. But then later in her career, when she's even more experienced, things seem to slow down. Some of the events are over a year apart.*

Almost as if someone spread them out, Chet said.

Yes.

That doesn't make any sense. Chet remained quiet for a moment. *Unless this was modified to make it look like she was at the Boston PD longer than she was.*

Pulling that off would require the help of some big guns with political clout.

Sam scrolled through the list of her accomplishments again. Two years before the cartel bust went horribly wrong, Polly had received a Police Commission Unit Citation. An award she'd earned by running in and pulling a fellow officer from harm during a drug bust shootout. She'd taken a single round in the left buttock as she dragged the unconscious, bleeding man to safety.

Sam entered the officer's name, Zach Ghinhart, into the browser. The top hit returned a phone number and address. While it had taken the vast resources of The Agency to unearth Polly from a digital black hole, most people—including cops—could be found with a simple internet search.

Civil servants who patrolled the dregs of society were more likely to be victims of targeted violence by anti-government groups, anti-law enforcement extremists, and criminal organizations attempting to intimidate the police and keep them from doing their jobs. But politicians found it more beneficial to their careers to punish cops for publicly perceived wrongdoings instead of giving them the support they needed and deserved. Even worse, there was no policy to protect these sentinels of justice, who put their lives on the line for subsistence wages.

Whatever Polly had done to keep herself and her data private should be extended to everyone who carried a badge. But in his experience, law breakers had more rights and were treated better than law enforcers.

Shaking off the mental vision of himself railing against the political gestapo, he pulled out his cell phone. This wasn't the time or place for soapbox preaching. Taking a long breath, he closed his eyes.

Zach was trained. Served years busting narcissistic criminals who could lie to a priest without breaking a sweat. Sam had to be cautious, or the officer might detect the deception and could even try to contact Polly.

Rule #73:
Blend some elements of truth into your background story. It increases believability.

Stories are, by definition, fiction. Trying to formulate a past on the fly, while also making it sound believable, is difficult unless great thought and planning has gone into the structure and background. Blending elements of truth, no matter how trivial the details, into the tale lend it credence to the ear and can get it past the most honed of bullshit detectors.

—122 Rules of Psychology

Sam created a story, blending in as many elements of fact with his alternative history as he could. Though the conversation should be short, he worked in details about Polly's family, her days in school, her assignment on the force, and so on. He didn't want to be unprepared if the man turned out to be a Chatty Cathy and was feeling nostalgic.

Satisfied he had the basics covered, Sam relaxed his body and mind, slipping on the new character like a warm winter coat. He became this alter ego. Sam Bradford still existed, but in a different reality. His old self had become a simple observer.

He opened his eyes again as a different man. After entering a faux number and name into *Caller Mask*, an identification cover app on his phone, he dialed.

It rang several times before a male voice answered. "Hello." The man sounded hesitant, probably because Caller Id would have identified the connection originating from the sheriff's department.

"Zach Ghinhart, please," Sam said, in his most professional tone.

"Speaking."

"Mr. Ghinhart, my name is Buford Austin. I'm the sheriff for Alabaster Cove in California."

Our good sheriff would not be amused by this, Chet said, his own voice sounding quite amused.

"Oh." Zach seemed concerned and confused, probably wondering what connection he could have to a podunk agency in a town he'd most likely never heard of. "Hello, Sheriff. What can I do for you?"

Doing his best to funnel the lawman's tone and attitude, Sam said, "Polly Cahill, who used to work for the Boston PD, put you down as a reference."

Relief echoed in Zach's tone when he replied. "Cahill? I haven't talked to her in years. She put *me* as a reference?"

Had she kept in touch with anyone at her old precinct? Apparently not with the man she'd saved. "Yes, sir. I don't want to take too much of your time. I just have a couple of questions."

"Okay. I'm not sure what I have to offer, but go for it."

"Don't know if you know this, but Ms. Cahill has been a paramedic in our town going on about five years."

"I didn't, but neither does it surprise me. I always wondered what happened to her after..." He cleared his throat, "her *retirement* from the precinct. I tried looking her up once but couldn't find her."

Josha's words from earlier about her being invisible on the web echoed in Sam's mind. *I don't doubt it.* That niggling had become an itch. Someone with the Boston PD should have had the resources and information to contact her, yet Zach had been unable to find her. As capable as Polly was to drop from the public eye, she shouldn't have been able to hide from law enforcement. How had she pulled that off?

Zach continued, "I'm glad she turned that drive of hers into something else good."

"Indeed. Her service has been exemplary." Sam paused. "Her drive is why I'm calling. Evidently, being a paramedic isn't keeping her busy enough, as she's also applying for a deputy position. As part of my screening process, I have applicants include any notable commendations. It took a bit of arm-twisting, but Polly listed she'd received a Police Commission Unit Citation, among others, and that you were involved in the episode that led to her earning it. Though I asked for details, she deferred. Said the recognition was nothing more than her doing her job."

Zach laughed. "Of course."

"Sir?"

"Oh, I don't mean she didn't earn it. Hell, if it had been up to me, I'd have given her the key to the city. I just mean she's not into pomp and circumstance."

"So it seems. Can you tell me what happened?"

Zach took a long breath. "We got a tip that some local gangbangers had turned an old garage into their headquarters for packaging and distributing. Polly led the raid. I was a rookie, and it was my first big bust. To say I was anxious and excited would be an understatement. I saw someone come out the door, and I thought they had a gun." He sighed. "Wow, this was so long ago."

"Just tell me what you remember," Sam said in his best "Sheriff Austin" voice. *Just the facts, sir. Just the facts.*

"We were flanking the building and..."

"You fired," Sam guessed.

"Yes. To this day I wish I could take that back. Anyway, that tipped our hand. I was trying to get clear when I took a round and went down. Polly, who was either the bravest or stupidest person I've ever met, ran in and got me. Bullets were flying everywhere. She took one in the ass, of all places. I don't know why she wasn't hit more. We eventually got the guys. No casualties on our side. And Polly got the medal for saving me. I'm pretty sure she just tossed it in a drawer and forgot about it."

"On her application, she listed this happened nine years ago."

Zach fell quiet for a moment. "No. That can't be right. I left the precinct...let's see, ten years ago. Polly had been gone six by then. The bust happened twelve months or so before she left, so that puts her award at seventeen, eighteen years ago. Give or take."

"Ah, okay. She must have accidentally dropped a one from the application."

"Some women don't like to admit how old they are," Zach offered.

Sam pretended to chuckle. "Right you are, Zach." He paused for a second as he worked through how to ask his next question. "What can you tell me about the detective's dismissal?"

A guarded, defensive tone—as hard as a stone wall—replaced the casual one. "I think that's a question best left to Cahill."

Tread carefully. He gave it fifty-fifty odds Zach would clam up no matter how he phrased it. "I have talked it over with her and read the formal report. The details are sealed, as I'm sure you're aware." He gave it a heartbeat before continuing. Just us brothers, chewing the fat and calling the bureaucracy on its shit. "It seems, though don't know for sure, that she was hung out to dry. I know you weren't her superior, and you weren't involved in the incident. But you knew her at the time and something like that doesn't go unobserved by the force. So just tell me what you know."

It was Zach's turn to pause. He remained quiet for a full minute.

"I need to know whose got my flank if the crap hits the fan," Sam said.

At last, the ex-police officer said, "I don't have any first-hand knowledge of the accounts leading up to Cahill's early retirement."

"No. I imagine you don't. But people talk."

He would either defer again, or, if Sam had done his job and gained the man's trust in the last few minutes, he would spill. It could go either way.

"Sheriff, I honestly don't know what happened. There were accusations and rumors, but none of them gelled with the hero I knew. My opinion—and I'm not alone in this—is that she was a scapegoat. For what, I don't know, but someone had it out for her."

"Nothing hinky on her end that ever got your spidey senses tingling?"

"No. No way. Cahill was as honest and dedicated as they come. If you ask me, the shit-for-brains mayor was bending to some loudmouths with a bullhorn." He went on for a few minutes about policing by popular opinion and letting the media dictate policy.

There was nothing to be gained by letting this continue. Even if there were video recordings of Polly on the grassy knoll and stealing the Lindbergh baby, Zach would still defend her. It was more than just her saving him. He respected the former detective. That wouldn't have been the case had she been dirty. Time to wrap things up. "I appreciate your time."

"Sure thing, Sheriff." He paused. "I don't care what happened with that last case. It was utter bullshit. For the record, you will *never* find a better, braver, more dedicated officer than Polly Cahill. I promise, you won't regret hiring her."

"You're not the first person to say that," Sam said, as if he'd followed up with a dozen references. "Thank you, and have a good day."

Before Sam could hang up, Zach said, "Hey, Sheriff?"

"Yes, Zach?"

"After I left the force, I married and became a stay-at-home dad. Our little girl is three now. She wouldn't be here if it weren't for Cahill." His voice broke. Zach cleared his throat before continuing. "Anyway, we—my wife and I—named our daughter Polly in her honor. Would you mind telling her?"

"I will. Thank you for sharing."

They said goodbye once more and ended the call.

According to Zach, the rank and file hadn't smelled anything corrupt about the detective. Other than her being railroaded—most likely because she'd pissed someone off she shouldn't have—she'd been clean.

Also, Polly risking her life to save a fellow officer didn't surprise him. What should have—though also didn't—was that the timing of events as recalled by Zach didn't line up with the documents supplied by The Agency. It was possible the ex-police officer had misremembered; however, it seemed unlikely. He seemed pretty confident about the date, and besides, people didn't forget a near-death experience. Yet, Sam couldn't imagine his old employer had gotten the facts wrong. They knew everything about everyone.

Except for Polly's termination, Chet observed.

True.

Her background isn't entirely fake.

No, Sam agreed. *It's not.*

Like you being Sheriff Austin, it's a good mix of truth and fiction. The sort of story The Agency would create.

But that makes no sense. Why would The Agency falsify her background?

Maybe they didn't.

It seemed so obvious his employer had mucked with her history, Sam couldn't imagine why his inner conscience thought otherwise. *What do you mean?*

I mean, we don't work for the only federal entity. Others are quite adept at lying and manipulation. Plenty of three-letter orgs could have altered her work history.

Though Chet had a good point, it still didn't feel right. *"Who" isn't the only thing that needs answering. Two more questions are "what" and "why." As in, what was Polly doing for those eight years that are unaccounted for, and why cover it up?*

Those are the right questions, Chet agreed. *It's going to take some digging to get the right answers.*

Sam went through the files several more times before closing them, disquieted. There was more, a lot more, to Polly Cahill that he needed to know. Since it had been The Agency that had supplied his intel, he obviously couldn't ask for more. Without them though, he didn't know how to go about getting those answers.

Letting his subconscious work the issue, he pushed aside the hundreds of marauding thoughts now circling his mind. A few hours remained before his shift at the surf shop, so he picked up the manila envelope Polly had given him.

He might not solve the mystery of Polly Cahill right now, but he damn well could help bring justice to Frank Boreman. He opened the envelope containing the sordid details of the detective's last week on this earth, the Mafiya, and Captain Levka, a.k.a. the Lion, and began to read.

Chapter Nine

A couple of hours later, Sam pushed through the entrance underneath the miniature surfboard sign. *The Board Wake, Epic Fayle Designs* flowed in fancy script across its smooth surface.

As the door's little silver bell rang merrily, the comforting scents of hot wax and the sawdust floor greeted him. The three TVs hung from the ceiling around the room played scenes from *Point Break* and *Endless Summer*—two of Max's all-time favorite flicks. A triple set of modest shelves, containing everything from earplugs to bodysuits, stood in the center of the store. Posters of Max—and his impossibly perfect physique—riding waves or standing next to bikini beauty queens adorned the walls.

A wooden cabinet filled with custom, colorful boards perched on their tails took up the entire back of the store. Sam had handcrafted a few of these under Max's watchful eye and detailed tutelage.

"Sam!" Max called. The sun-kissed, effervescent shop owner, sporting a bright-blue tank top and a waterfall of dreads cascading around his shoulders, came around the counter. He clasped Sam's hand in his firm grip and pulled him into a quick one-armed hug.

No matter how long they'd been working together or how long it had been since they'd last seen one another, Max greeted everyone as though they'd been apart for months. He unabashedly embraced his personal motto: Life's short. Love.

A lot of people might underestimate the shop owner, passing him off as a simple boardhead. But Max, like Shakespeare, was an observer of people. He understood them and had the instinctive ability to see past their facades. He took everyone at face value. Instead of judging them for who they used to be, he accepted them for who they were now. He possessed keen intuition and trusted his gut, which was how a high school dropout had become such a successful business owner.

When undercover, Sam usually avoided people like Max and his girlfriend, Abby. Trying to pass off a fake backstory to either would be like trying to give a bank teller Monopoly money. Fortunately, Sam had come to the Cove as himself. And despite reserving the sordid details of his life, he'd sensed that Max had intuited a lot more than Sam would have liked.

"How's it hanging, bro?" Max asked, as though Sam had just gotten back from an overseas assignment instead of a day off from work.

"Had the best ride yesterday. You were so right about the storm."

Max kissed his fingertips, exploding them outward as though he'd just eaten the most delicious Italian meal of his life. "What'd I tell you? Perfecto!" He slipped into what Sam referred to as "Professor Mode" and gave a short, though technical, meteorological report on the effects of wind and barometric pressure on wave formation.

As the Professor wrapped up his brief lecture, Sam moved around behind the counter, stowing the backpack containing his notes from Polly in a drawer. "Where do you need me today, boss?"

Max headed to the back workshop entrance. "I've got a custom I need to finish this afternoon, so if you could mind things up here, that'd be great."

"Sure. Of course."

"Don't forget, we've got the party tonight."

"Right. Closing early."

For Max, the call of the sea superseded all, including regular business hours. When the ocean beckoned, he dropped everything to heed her voice. Even in the middle of the day, he'd park a *Gone Surfing* sign out front and lock the door.

"Tonight's gonna be off the charts," he promised. "We've been feeling the effects from the storm for the last few days, but the tastiest waves to grace our shores in over a year will be here this evening."

"Better than yesterday?"

"They'll be so orgasmic, your lady will need to take birth control or in nine months she'll be poppin' a pair of Poseidon's twins."

Sam laughed. "Good thing I don't have a lady then."

"You, my friend, are throwing away the natural gifts bestowed upon you by Aphrodite and Eros." He shook his head as though Sam's dating status were the saddest thing he'd ever heard. "Ain't nothing in the world as satisfying as having the gal of your dreams in your arms and in your bed."

"You're just saying that because you landed the best of the best. I've always suspected that Abby's Aphrodite or Eros in the flesh."

Max fist-bumped him. "Right about that, brotha. And I'm just smart enough to know it. But just 'cause Abs isn't on the market doesn't mean there's no one out there for you. Plenty of fish and all. Anyway, the usual crew's coming. You in?"

Perhaps a Max rumination might provide new insights into Polly that The Agency's background check had not. He just needed to nudge the conversation in the right direction. "I think so. Might have something going on. Depends on her schedule."

Max's face relaxed into a smile. "You got yourself a date. It's about time you courted one of our fine señoritas. Lots have had their eye on you, but you seemed to be in another world."

Sam let out a laugh. "Not exactly."

Max arched a bushy brow, the question obvious.

"Polly and I——"

His serene smile turned into a Cheshire grin. "You and Cahill? Rumor has it she's still pretty pissed at you for what happened with that lunatic a few months ago." Max absently rubbed the scar on his palm. During Erebus' reign of terror, he had broken into the woodshop and nailed Max to the floor with a pneumatic gun. If not for Max's refusal to give up—and a bit of luck—Erebus would have finished the job. "But, as they say, it's a fine line between love and hate. That friction will make things spicier than a habanero burrito. Word of advice: wear Kevlar-lined protection."

Sam laughed. "No. No. Nothing like that. The chief asked me to help her investigate the body that washed up on shore yesterday."

Max didn't look like he quite believed him, probably because the rumor mill also reported—accurately—how little Chief Palmer cared for Sam breathing on the same continent. His disbelief transitioned to confusion. "Not to underestimate her abilities or anything, but Polly's a para-medic. Isn't this a job for the sheriff?"

"You mean Sheriff Austin? The one who spends more time sampling the goods from the evidence locker than he does keeping the streets of our little town safe. *That* sheriff?"

He snorted. "Okay, maybe not *our* sheriff. But a compe-tent one. Or maybe the police, or the FBI, or someone."

"Polly's taken a special interest in this guy's death and doesn't want it to fall through the cracks. Besides, the victim's a Marine."

Max's gaze flicked to Sam's arm and the *Semper Fidel-is* tattoo. Understanding registered on his face. "And you don't want him to fall through the cracks either."

"Something like that." Sam hesitated, as though try-ing to find the right words to express his determination. He would find the scumbag and make them pay for what they'd done to a sibling in arms. "Polly wants to see justice done. I respect her for that. But there's something else driv-ing her." He would have liked to have added a bit about her brother and father being killed and about her being a detective, but since he wasn't supposed to know any of that, he refrained. "It's like she's taking it personally."

Max leaned against the counter, crossing his arms. "You know I don't worry about anyone's history. It only matters who they are now. But I might be able to offer you a bit of insight."

Sam waited. He'd planted the seeds. Time to see what sprouted.

The boardhead, his expression thoughtful, continued, "I know Polly came here about five or six years ago and has been pretty quiet about her past. Even the gossiping biddies haven't been able to pry any details out of her. And trust me, they've tried. But most of what you hear is probably made up."

Not exactly astonished by this revelation, or lack thereof, Sam said, "I don't take the bulk of what people say seriously. Especially about Polly. The more I get to know her, the less stock I put in the vines."

"And that's the right thing to do. I can't tell you anything about where she comes from because I don't know. But I can tell you Polly is a scales of justice kinda girl." He held his hands up in front of him, one higher than the other. "If the scale is way out of balance like this, she's going to try and make things even." He brought his hands together so they were level. "She wants to right the wrongs in the world."

Sam nodded. "It sounds like you admire her."

"I do," he admitted. "She sees the bigger picture and something deep in her core drives her. For example, most are satisfied with a paramedic cert, but Polly's got the extra schooling to be a practitioner, which allows her to do more doctoring stuff. I can't tell you what she can do, but I've never seen her turn folks away like our other EMTs. She volunteered to run the RU team. She wasn't drafted like so many, but *volunteered* to *run* it, and she puts in more hours than the chief. I feel like I work hard, but all I ever aspired to do was this." He waved a hand at the shop. "But she and my girl Abby, they've got a grit deep in their bones that I don't see anywhere else."

Saying Abby had drive was the understatement of the century. She owned half the successful businesses in town, lent money to entrepreneurs like Max, and spent her vast fortunes helping fix up the park, town hall, and anything else the city needed. Abby had the glowing, easy heart and humble demeanor of a pauper, but the checking account of a Wall Street tycoon.

Though professionally the two women couldn't be more different, at their cores, their similarities were undeniable.

"And," Max said, "I know you were in the military back in the day, but we never got into what you did after that. I always figured you'd tell me if you wanted, and if you didn't..." He shrugged. "Well, that's your business. But I saw what you did to take down that Erebus asshole and get justice for people like my sister."

Max's sister, April, had been Erebus' first Alabaster Cove murder victim. They had been close, and the loss had torn a hole in his heart. After almost becoming a victim himself, Max had helped Sam track and put down the psychopath.

He swallowed as if a lump of emotion had caught in his throat. "I don't know what set that guy off—if it was a mistake you made, like so many in this town believe, or you were just doing a job that no one else wanted to do. But I do know just how far you'd have gone and what you'd have sacrificed to stop him. Polly has that same fire. It reminds me of the way the ocean calls to us, you and me. I see it in the way you ride a wave. You and the ocean are one. It's one of the things we were *born* to do. Same as Polly. She's doing what she was born to do."

He paused, but Sam made no reply. His friend still had more to say, and Sam didn't want to interrupt his flow.

"The chief may have been the one to ask you to help with this investigation or whatever, but make no mistake, it came from Polly. And it's that indefinable quality the two of you share, as well as your backgrounds—maybe your demons too—that prompted *her* to ask for you. Not him. I'm not telling you anything you probably don't already know. But she's special, Sam." He sighed. "Enough ruminations, or speculations, or whatever. I've got a board to grind." Max glanced at the big silver watch on his wrist. "If we gotta close so you can go body hunting or whatever, let me know."

"I'm fine to do my shift."

"If you're sure."

"I'm sure," Sam said.

Max made his way to the back of the store. He started to push through the door, but stopped. "You should consider coming out tonight. If I know you, you already did your homework, read up a bunch on this guy and stuff."

Sam nodded.

"Yeah, well ain't nothing like the song of the ocean to help you put the pieces together." His grin made a grand reappearance. "Invite that girl of yours. Polly's great on a board and could probably use the time to think too."

"She's not—" Sam started, but Max had disappeared into the back. A few minutes later, the low whir of a sander drifted through the air.

Had it been most anyone else, Sam might have dismissed the man's musings as romanticized, perhaps even aggrandized. But everything he said aligned with what Sam had read, observed, and intuited. Polly had a fiery streak of relentless pragmatism that she expressed with contentiousness—which, even though it sometimes chafed Sam's nether bits—was part of what made her an effective leader.

He still wanted to find out why The Agency had provided an altered version of her background. He would keep digging until he found the truth of what she'd really been doing during those eight-odd years. Not because he wanted to get the dirt on her, but because he felt deep in his bones that it mattered. This time away was significant to him, to the murder investigation, and to what lay ahead.

Sam had questioned the Boston PD officer Polly had saved, and he trusted her. The chief trusted her to run RU. Max and Abby, two of the most intuitive people he'd ever met, trusted her.

Despite the mystery of the missing years, a hesitant flame of faith bloomed for the paramedic detective. Trust was a foreign concept to him, yet he trusted Polly

Cahill with a kinship he hadn't felt since he'd been in the trenches with his fellow soldiers.

Unease trembled Sam's heart. Having faith in someone was a vulnerability. It was easier to assume that everyone had an agenda. An ulterior motive.

Could Polly be what she claimed to be? It appeared so, but he was worried he was blinded somehow. Yet, if he was, so was everyone else. As Sam helped customers and worked the shop, he reexamined everything he knew—and everything he didn't—about his new partner.

Chapter Ten

Reflecting off the Pacific, the sky glowed nuclear. Orange, yellow, and pink flamed as if the gods had lit a hearth of cosmic embers on the edge of the universe. Glistening sparkles shimmered off the ocean as though infused with Christmas lights. The smoldering heat of the day, tempered by the infant evening breezes, had morphed into a comfortable dusk-time simmer.

Sam leaned back against a log, watching the bonfire dance, a cold beer in his hand. A playlist of music drifted from a battered speaker, as if the soul of Jimmy Buffett had joined the festivities.

Sam had almost returned to his house to review the Boreman documents one more time, but something urged him to join Max and the gang. Unexpected conversations came alive at these parties. Loose tongues—intoxicated by salty water, tasty waves, and cheap booze—lost their inhibitions, sometimes resulting in an unexpected nugget of information.

You're just hoping that Polly shows up in something a bit more revealing than her scrubs, Chet said. *Not that her scrubs aren't hot.*

Dude, first of all, as you've pointed out several times, Polly isn't into me.

It doesn't mean you don't want to see her in her RU outfit and...

Sam cut his inner conscience off before he could really get going. *Seriously, bro. We're on this case together. That's it.*

Chet scoffed, but didn't continue badgering him.

Bikini-clad women in festive cover-ups, eliciting images of Hawaiian luaus and Havana fiestas, swayed lithely to the music, their tipsy counterparts sporting jungle-themed shirts and board shorts. Other partygoers huddled in small groups, laughing and nursing their beers.

As Jimmy Buffett finished his saga detailing his search for a lost shaker of salt, a female singer with smoky vocals and a brooding timbre began a slow ballad about a funny valentine. The accompanist traveled the chords on the guitar's neck the way a man might make love to his new bride on their wedding night.

Three months ago, Max's sister, April, had been slain by Tyron Erebus' wicked blade. Her devastated wife, Kyme, had asked Abby to sell the couple's house and put everything else into storage. She hadn't returned to town since.

"Hold up! Hold up!" Max called out.

The crowd grew silent, all eyes on him.

"This was April's favorite song. Kyme played it every show." He raised his beer. "To April and Kyme." His voice cracked. He cleared his throat. "May your love ride the waves for eternity."

Everyone echoed the sentiment. "To April and Kyme!"

The dancing and relaxed conversations resumed.

Max had finished the custom order faster than expected, so he closed the shop an hour early. He and Sam had grabbed their boards and spent a couple of hours on the water. As always, Max had been spot-on with his surfing forecast. The waves, as thick and decadent as melted chocolate, made each ride smooth and effortless. Sam forgot about death, The Agency, his questions about Polly, and the Mafiya. The two friends devoured their fill of the luscious ocean, only returning to shore when the bonfire beckoned.

Though he'd been cutting waves with reckless abandon, his unconscious mind must have been sorting through the details of the Frank Boreman case, digesting the information he'd spent the afternoon reviewing.

New questions lingered. According to Frank's background, he had spent years on the gang task force. No matter how desperate the LAPD, why would they allow him to infiltrate the Russian Mafiya with no training and no support? They never should have sent him in alone. Never. It was like someone had chosen him to be the sacrificial lamb.

But to what end? Could it be they jumped the gun and allowed one of their best to walk into the Lion's den? Or had there been something more nefarious going on? If so, what?

Before his shift, Sam had hesitantly requested a background from The Agency on Frank. Josha hadn't called, but six hours later, the report hadn't shown up either.

Agency dives usually took less than two hours. It could be red tape because of Sam's vague employment status.

But Josha served as the intel gatekeeper, meaning he must have put a hold on the inquiry. Except, he'd also given his blessing to provide the assist to Polly.

The dissonance set Sam's nerves on edge.

He broke out of his reverie as a familiar blonde with blue-tipped hair stood in the waves. She picked up her board and sauntered to shore like a cat in heat. With the sun behind her, he couldn't make out her face, though he recognized the curves of her figure and her lynx-like sashay. She jammed the tail of her board into the sand, then stripped off her wetsuit—revealing a striking one-piece bathing suit the exact color of her blue eyes. She grabbed a bottle from the cooler and plopped down next to him. "Hey, Sam," she said and took a sip.

He nodded. "Hey, Savannah."

Without the clown makeup she wore to the clinic, she exuded a natural grace and beauty. A primal sensuality that the dollops of blush and mascara hid rather than enhanced. Sam couldn't figure out what she felt so insecure about that prompted her to resort to such extremes.

She tilted her head back, the curls of her hair spilling over the log and exposing her thin throat. In the dancing firelight, her cleft of cleavage plunged as deep as the Grand Canyon. She gazed up at the purple and pink tufts of clouds floating through the sky. "It's a perfect night out, don't you think?"

Sam took a very long pull on his beer and forced himself to follow her gaze. He studied the darkening sky. "It is."

"I grew up here, you know," she said. "Third generation."

He did know. In fact, he had memorized most everything he'd heard about everyone. Not that he had any reason to. It had become an unconscious habit. An occupational hazard. Also, out of habit, he didn't admit to having any knowledge of what he'd memorized. What people lied about offered a window into their psyche and the image of themselves they wanted to project versus the truth that lay as plain as the nose on their face.

"I didn't," he lied.

She rolled her head to the side and arched a manicured brow. "You didn't? Everyone knows everything about everyone here."

Sam gave a little shrug. "I'm not a fan of gossip."

She gave him an inquisitive look. "For someone who's the subject of so many rumors himself, that's a very laissez-faire attitude."

"I can't control what people say, but I can control how I respond and what I listen to. I choose not to get involved."

"Hmm." She turned back to the sky. "I got married here." She chuffed. "Got *divorced* here."

Batter up! Chet said. *This girl is lobbing a meatball over home plate that not even you could miss. Well, you could, but ninety-eight percent of the population——including those in comas and even the dead——couldn't.*

She's looking for a lot more than a one-time fling. Besides, Sam studied her face, *there's a trace of crazy behind those blues.*

Since when has any of that mattered? You've used and abused across the nation.

Those were all in the line of duty.

You're on assignment.

Sam shook his head at his inner conscience. *No, I'm not. I'm helping Polly with her assignment.*

I'm just saying, this girl has been undressing you with her eyes since the moment you met. Maybe you should return the favor. Like I said back in the clinic, it's been a while since you've done the horizontal salsa.

Bro...

Maybe you should just step aside. Chet rolled his shoulders and cracked his neck. *Let the professional take care of business.*

Sam ignored Chet's lascivious urgings and focused on the woman sitting next to him. Over the months, his friend Triniti had filled him in on the sordid details of Savannah's divorce. He had seen her ex——a portly man named Mark with so little presence, it was amazing cameras could capture images of him——around town. Even with Savannah's heavy-handed use of a blush-wielding trowel, she'd been an eight while her ex was a three at best. Mark had married *way* out of his league and had blown it big time.

Sam already knew the answer but wanted to keep her talking. "Kids?"

She shook her head. "No. Parenthood fit my mom and dad, but I'm too much of a free spirit."

"So now you work at the clinic by day and party all night?"

Savannah gave him a coquettish smile, a little color blooming in her cheeks. "Something like that. What about you?"

"What about me?"

"Saving the town one day, working in the surf shop the next, helping Polly solve a murder the following."

He shrugged. "I get bored easily."

Her surprised laugh sounded free and lighthearted. On the surface, she looked like a walking, talking mid-life crisis. But beneath the makeup and party girl attitude, she might be a genuine person. "Well, next time you're bored, let me know, and I'll take you out on the boat."

He, of course, already knew she'd gotten everything she'd wanted—including the boat—in the divorce. "You have a boat?"

Her cheeks flushed. Her expression turned to stone.

Uh oh. He'd hit a hot button.

"Yes," she said, her voice hardening. "Mark's lawyer was a drunken buffoon. Mine was a piranha. I got most everything, and Mark got next to nothing, as he deserved." A flash of something a little too wild—maybe that hint of crazy he'd suspected lingering just beneath the surface—lit her eyes for a moment. He'd seen people go too far, step over lines they otherwise would stop at, when they got too spun up.

During the divorce, Savannah had discovered something about herself that had left her disturbed to the core. Perhaps she'd learned what she'd be willing to do when backed into a corner. She'd looked past the reflection in the mirror and caught a glimpse of the savage darkness slumbering in each of us. Her darkness, it seemed, had awakened—even if for just a little while. It had left her raw and skirting a razor-thin edge that still threatened to swallow her if she stepped too close to it again.

This otherwise fun-loving and vibrant woman had struggled more than she'd let on. She'd survived, come out the victor even, but the experience had left cracks in the clay pot containing the madness.

Sam could almost feel the emotional tornado ripping through the trailer park of her sanity. She had a little more to say before she was ready to move on, but if he didn't change the subject soon, this would be all they'd talk about for the rest of the party.

"It's interesting," she said, that fervent heat lightning crackling in her blue eyes. "When we were together, I hated the boat. Mark was a stuffy drag who only wanted to fish. I could have done cartwheels naked around him, and he'd have told me to not make so much noise because I might scare away the carp or whatever. I know I'm not twenty-five." She waved a hand over her smooth, shapely legs. "But really. He turned this down for trout? I swear, the man should go hang out with Owen and Norman...not that I have anything against gay men," she quickly amended. "I love the fellas. I just don't want to be married to one."

Time to cool her down. "He had no idea what he had." Sam raised his beer and gave her his most understanding and disarming smile. The one that said he'd been there and done that. "May the short-sighted prude forever roam the lands horny and unsatisfied."

She laughed humorlessly, but her thermostat seemed to drop a couple of degrees. "I'll drink to that."

They clinked bottles and each took a sip.

"So, if you don't fish," he said, "what do you do out on the boat? Water ski or something?"

"Well, it depends."

"On what?"

"Who I'm with and my mood. Sometimes, as they said in *Top Gun*, I'm feeling the need for speed. So, I'll open it up and see how fast I can go. Sometimes I'll take some friends out and just let it idle and drive wherever. It's a pretty big ocean, so there's not much chance of running into anything." She paused. The ruddiness in her face from the earlier subject of Mark had faded. An excited pink with a touch of embarrassment now bloomed in her cheeks. "Sometimes, I go out to sunbathe."

"By yourself?"

That coquettish smile returned, transitioning to a sly grin. "Or with someone close. It's very relaxing, sitting out on the deck while the boat gently rocks. When you get too hot, you can skinny dip to cool back down."

Despite his best effort to stay impartial, Sam's throat had gotten a little dry. He took a sip of beer to wet it. Chet had a point. It had been a while since Sam had been romantically involved, and Savannah's sensuality radiated like a sex missile.

But now that he'd glimpsed the insanity, he knew that landmines lingered just beneath the surface of her mental and emotional landscape. If he frolicked in her field of wildflowers, it would be fun at first, but in the end, he might find himself handcuffed to the bedpost while the house burned down around them. He forced himself to focus. "That so?"

"That's so," she confirmed. A brief look of disgust crossed her face. "Though, I went out a couple of days ago, intending to work on my tan, but I had to come back in pretty quick."

"Why's that?"

"I go out far enough so I can't be spied on from the land—Peeping Toms and all—but there was this big, rusted heap offshore."

Sam's heart gave a hard thump, a tremor of energy traveling his nerves. All thoughts of illicit dalliances vaporized in a flash. "Like a barge or a cargo ship?"

She shook her head. "No. Seen plenty of those in my time. They're usually just passing through. This thing was anchored. It looked like an old freighter or something." She shivered.

Savannah had Sam's undivided attention, but he pretended to only be mildly curious. "I was surfing this afternoon and didn't see anything."

"You wouldn't go out far enough on a board. This thing was ten or so miles offshore."

Though most of the Pacific was too deep, there were random charted and uncharted seamounts and knolls off the California shoreline high enough for a ship to anchor. A captain just needed a good enough map or the right equipment to find them. And thirteen miles off the shore would put the ship in international waters, beyond the US jurisdiction, though the Coast Guard could still board it if they thought the crew was up to something hinky.

The pictures Polly had given him cycled through his mind. Savannah had referred to the ship as a big, rusted heap. That description could apply to the *Vengeance*. Also, the location fit where they may have dumped

Frank. Especially given the recent storm out at sea, the currents could have carried him inland from there. Except, if they'd murdered the undercover detective, why would they be hanging around, waiting to get caught?

Whatever their motives, it would be worth the time to do a sortie and check it out firsthand.

Chet laughed. *You really think Polly's gonna go for that?*

Maybe. She's not exactly predictable. But that's a problem for later. Right now, I need to see what else Savannah knows. We're not sure it's the Vengeance.

And yet, we both are.

Okay. Fine. I still need to do my due diligence.

Chet waved a hand at him. *Go ahead and do your thing, Matlock. But try not to screw it up.*

"Don't suppose you noticed the name on the hull?" Sam asked.

Savannah shook her head. "Is that important?"

"Not at all. Just curious."

She continued with her story, "I could have gone further north or south and been far enough away they wouldn't have been able to spy on me. And my boat can *move*, so they wouldn't have been able to follow me. But something about it felt...off. I don't know. I trust my gut to keep me safe. So, I came back to the marina." She took a pull off her beer. "I might try again tomorrow."

He wanted to ask her more, but first, he had to do a little social maintenance. She'd laid out an invitation. If he didn't address it, he might get nothing else out of her. "If you're nervous about the ship, I might be available tomorrow afternoon. And even if you aren't nervous, if you're looking for some company, I'd love to go."

She considered. "I'll call you if I decide to go out." She shivered again and wrapped her arms around her knees. "I don't know. It was pretty creepy. Maybe I'll just stick to surfing for the next few days." She glanced at him. "You seem to handle yourself pretty good on a board. Might even be able to keep up with me."

He gave her a mischievous, flirty grin. "Are you asking me on a date?"

Savannah cocked her head, an answering grin slinking across her thin lips. "I'm pretty sure *you* asked *me* out just a minute ago under the guise of keeping this damsel in distress safe from the big, bad boat." She pointed at him. "For the record, that was a pretty obvious tactic."

Sam laughed. "I suppose it was, but I think it worked." He dropped her a little wink.

"Touché."

"To first dates," Sam said, holding out his beer while mentally working through a list of excuses to cancel that wouldn't send her into a spiral. He didn't want to hurt her, but also, he didn't think it wise to step through that door. Not even once.

"To first dates," she agreed.

They clinked bottles again.

He let a little quiet slip past as they gazed out at the rolling Pacific. Then he said, "Hey, Savannah. Out of curiosity, what did the boat look like?"

She shrugged. "I don't know. I kept my distance."

"You said it was rusted and gave you a bad feeling."

She considered. "Yeah. Black and old. It didn't look like it was very well maintained. Even from a distance, I could see that."

"Any idea how big it was?"

"Not really. From far away, big things can appear small, and small things big. You know what I mean?"

Sam nodded. "But you said it wasn't a cargo ship?"

She scrunched her lips and looked up as she thought. "No. Not that big. But not a fishing boat either, like you see around here. Something in between."

"Rusty. So metal?"

She nodded. "Why all this interest in some old boat? Aren't you more interested in something a little younger and faster?"

You're losing her, Chet said. *Best put on the charm.*

He grazed her cheek with the tip of his finger. "You know I am..." Sam paused as though he had something to say but didn't know if he should.

She narrowed her eyes, and he could see the gossip salivating over whatever morsel Sam hesitated to offer. Lowering her voice, she said, "I can hear you thinking. What is it?"

He chuckled. "How can you read people so well?"

"It's just one of my skills that, if you're lucky, you'll get to see more of. Now spill."

Sam let out a long sigh as if she'd twisted his arm just hard enough to get him to tell her his secrets. He lowered his voice to a conspiratorial whisper. "When I was in the military, the guys used to talk about...pirates."

"Pirates!" she said a little too loudly. "Here?"

Several people glanced their way.

He kept his voice low. "Ssshhh. We don't want people becoming hysterical. Not everyone can keep their cool under pressure."

She took an absent drink, her excited eyes never leaving his face. "I'm totally cool under pressure."

I'll bet.

"I've heard about pirates on the news." She was practically drooling. "They rob cruise ships and hold people for ransom and stuff."

"Right. Me too. So, I'm sure I'm just being overly cautious. That's not what's out there. I'm positive."

"But you want to be sure that we—the town, I mean—are safe." She crossed her tan legs.

"Exactly."

She glanced around as if Blackbeard and his band of scallywags might descend upon their party, rob the men, and carry off the women to do unthinkable things to them. A notion that didn't look entirely unwelcome to her. "You don't think there are any here, in town, do you?"

Sam forced a laugh. "I highly doubt it." He paused again.

"What?" She leaned forward and put a hand on his knee. "What do you need?"

"I should check it out. Just to be safe. But I don't have a boat."

"I'll take you."

He took her hand. "You're incredibly brave. But I have dealt with unlikeable types before. I don't know if you know this, but in the Marines, I did some tours overseas. Seen some...stuff."

She looked like she was about to object. Sam didn't give her the chance. Gently rubbing her fingers, he looked into her eyes with his best concerned expression. "This town, and the good people in it, have been through enough. I couldn't live with myself if something happened to you."

Savannah held his too-direct gaze, and Sam could almost hear the tropical rainstorm moistening her down under. "You brave, wonderful man." She gripped his hand. "Of course. It's called the *Finders Keepers*. Row E, slip number three-oh-one. The key is under the seat. I had the GPS on, so you can just follow my last route."

"Which marina?" The Cove had two, Clearwater and South Harbor.

"Clearwater. Once you're done, come back and see me. If the coast is clear, we'll go out for a few hours. If not... we'll find something *else* to do."

Sam leaned over and kissed her on the cheek. Her warm, smooth skin tasted like salt. "Thank you. I'll let you know what I find. Hopefully, they've moved on, and all of this fuss will be for nothing."

"Pirates," she whispered. Her wide eyes found his again. "Be careful."

"I will. And Savannah?" He held her gaze.

"Hmm?"

"We need to keep this just between us."

She blinked as though he'd asked her to recite the Pythagorean theorem. Then nodded as realization dawned. "Of course, Sam."

He stood. "Thank you."

"See you tomorrow."

Sam smiled. "Wouldn't miss it for the world."

Dropping the false charm, he went back to Max's shop. After storing his board in the back, he grabbed his bag from under the counter and headed to town. He needed to find Polly. If he couldn't convince her to come with him, he might have to check out Savannah's mystery ship alone. Though, taking on the *Vengeance* by himself hadn't worked out so well for Frank Boreman. Hopefully, he'd do better.

Chapter Eleven

S am jogged to Polly's house. The windows were dark. He checked his watch. Nine-thirty. She must have gone to bed early or gone out. She'd want to hear what he had to say, so he knocked.

Inside, Saundy's nails scratched against the hardwood as she scampered to the door, barking her ferocious little dog yips. When Polly didn't answer, Sam rang the bell and knocked again. She said she'd stayed up the whole night working on Frank Boreman's phone and doing research. She could have passed out, exhausted.

No. That wasn't right. Other than the dog, the house felt empty. The hairs on his neck stood on end as goose-flesh pricked his body. There was no physical evidence to justify his feelings, but he nevertheless sensed a dark, foreboding presence lurking in the otherwise calm night.

As if something evil had arrived in town.

He could return home for his Sig. But if Polly was in trouble, he needed to act.

Sam dropped his backpack in a dark corner of the porch. He didn't want the bag to hinder his ability to move or give an assailant an easy way to grab him.

He sure wouldn't win any brownie points if it turned out Polly was just a heavy sleeper. Risking her wrath, he raised his foot, preparing to bust through the door.

Before he smashed his way inside, a thought struck him. Sam pulled out his phone. *Shit.* Three missed calls, all from Polly.

That sense of foreboding deepened into a premonition. He tapped out a message.

Where are you?

He waited for what felt like an hour, his heart knocking against his ribs. To his relief, the phone vibrated.

Come to the clinic. Now. Sam almost texted back, asking if she'd been hurt, but it would be faster to find out in person. Pocketing his phone, he sprinted down the road.

As he rounded the corner of Ron's Quick Pawn—*Cash in a Dash!*—he halted, stymied by the gruesome scene. *Shit. Shit. Shit.*

Police lights bathed the street in flashing neon. Two local squad cars sat parked helter-skelter in front of the clinic, as if the drivers had raced as fast as they could, skidded to a stop, and jumped out.

As an operative for The Agency, he had both visited and caused dozens of scenes just like this one. Years of experience had taught him one universal truth: Burglaries, trespassing, and similar misdemeanors didn't warrant such a show of force.

Someone had been killed.

Sam ran.

It could be anyone. Lots of people worked at the clinic. But maybe his earlier relief was premature. Yes, *someone* had responded from Polly's phone, but the texter could have been the chief, the sheriff, or one of the half dozen deputies.

He raced to the familiar yellow crime scene tape, ducking under it as though he had every right to do so. The fresh-faced deputy tasked with keeping people at bay had watched Sam approach. The young officer furrowed his brow in confusion at the sudden perimeter and protocol breach.

Sam ignored him as he absorbed everything, looking for the source of what had caused half the sheriff's department to come running. He had taken several steps toward the clinic before the deputy had the wherewithal to get in front of him. The officer held up a hand. "Sorry, sir. No one is allowed in." He pointed to the sidewalk where a small crowd gawked. "You'll have to stay back."

Heated irritation goosed by the premonition that something had happened to his partner made Sam want to lash out. But this man had done nothing other than his job. Besides, going on the offensive with a police officer wouldn't gain his cooperation. It would land him in cuffs.

Sam stopped, pretending as though he hadn't noticed the deputy. Even in the pulsing red and blue lights, Sam detected the man's white pallor and haunted eyes. This poor kid—who looked as though he could have attended his senior prom last week—may have been the one who found the victim or victims.

The deputy had just stared Death in the face. Ill-equipped to deal with true violence—savagery for the sake of savagery—the atrocities committed by man in the name of a god, a war, a political agenda, or to satisfy some twisted carnal craving, tainted the spirit and robbed an innocence most people never knew they possessed until hate devoured it.

Every event for the rest of his life would be infected by this moment. No matter where he went or what he did, a black-cloaked specter would linger in the back of this young man's mind, haunting his nightmares and darkening his dreams. The shadow creature would fester like a disease until the deputy either learned to live with it or tried to cage the beast with mind-altering substances—which would only temporarily mute the terrors playing out on the big screen behind his eyes. In reality, he'd be inviting a whole new monster to rip apart his life, one that would eat him from the inside out until nothing remained but a husk.

Though he sympathized, Sam couldn't wait around to follow the stringent protocols designed to preserve the crime scene. He needed to persuade the man to let him through. His partner may have been killed.

"Son," Sam said with authority. He glanced at the baby-faced lawman's badge. "Deputy Haines, Polly Cahill asked me here to assist." He held up his phone as if he'd just received the call. "I'm Sam Bradford."

Recognition lit the young man's eyes. "Polly didn't tell me she'd asked anyone to come."

Sam let out a small, relieved breath. She hadn't been a victim. But if not Polly, then who? The chief? This had to tie back to Frank Boreman. The man had washed up on shore, and now someone was killed at the same clinic housing his body. There was no such thing as a coincidence when it came to murder.

Sam could out-authority this newbie cop with a gallon of bluster and an imposing presence. He could make the poor, stunned deputy fold like a house of cards in a windstorm. "I need—" he began.

Another man's voice called out. "Let him through, Haines."

Sam and the deputy looked over at the clinic.

Sheriff Austin stood outside the entrance. He shook his head. "He's going to be nothing but a pain in the ass until you do. And I can guarantee he will eventually get his way. Might as well save us all the trouble."

Without waiting for affirmation from the deputy, Sam marched past the young lawman and joined the sheriff on the sidewalk. "What happened?"

"We responded to a silent alarm about an hour ago. Third one this week. The first two were false alarms. We think there's some faulty wiring or something. Palmer had ordered the security company to come take a look, but getting service in this town sometimes takes a while."

"So, when you got this one, you didn't think it was anything and took your time getting here only to find out someone had broken in and something had happened. Someone got killed." Sam tried hard to keep the accusatory tone out of his voice, but the sheriff picked up on it.

The big man narrowed his eyes, anger flashing in their inky depths. "It's a weeknight in the off-season. We run a skeleton crew. Deputy Haines was chasing down a domestic and came here right after."

"What did he find?"

Sheriff Austin scratched his forehead, lifting the brim of his hat as he did so. He ran his palm down his face.

Whatever waited behind the clinic's door had rattled the sheriff, who'd spent a couple of decades working for the LAPD gangs division. He'd seen it all. "Seems you already have an idea," he said at last.

"Let's just say, I've been to the afterparty of some ugly stuff."

The sheriff nodded toward the clinic. "Well, then, it's best you go see for yourself. But look quick. The staties are sending in their boys. Once they get here, they'll claim the scene and none of us will have access. We're just supposed to be securing things and biding our time."

Sam turned toward the door, but the sheriff caught his arm. "This is an active crime scene. I don't have to lecture you on the proper procedure to keep from contaminating it?"

Sam shook his head.

"I didn't think so." He took a deep breath. Almost as if to himself, he commented, "I moved here to get away from all of this shit. And until three months ago, everything was fine."

Sam searched for accusation in the sheriff's expression, but only resignation lingered in the man's tired eyes. He let go of Sam's arm.

As Sam approached the clinic, the sheriff said to one of his deputies, "Call in to HQ. Have them set up a roadblock. No one gets in or out of town without an inspection. We aren't letting this bastard get away."

The usual crime scene kit sat near the entrance. Sam covered his shoes with a pair of booties made from the indiscernible sticky material that seemed to have originated on Polyester Planet and snapped on latex gloves. Even though he'd let his hair get shaggy, it hadn't grown so long it warranted a net. He glanced back at the sheriff. Would he be coming inside too? But the lawman had lit a cigarette and seemed to be focused on something in the heavens.

Sam pushed through the door. The tang of copper and fecal matter assaulted him as he stepped inside.

The body of a man, maybe in his sixties, lay on the floor. He wore blood-soaked coveralls. A patch on his chest, which probably gave his name, had been soaked black—the letters indiscernible. The man's head lay at an impossible angle, the neck elongated. His shoulder appeared dislocated. His throat cut. Someone had stuffed a rag so far into his mouth, his jaw had distended like a snake's.

A pool of crimson about the diameter of a super-sized pizza spread out underneath him. The lights reflecting off the shiny blood indicated it hadn't congealed yet.

"That's Phil," a woman's voice said from the hallway.

Sam tore his gaze from the morose tableau.

Polly watched him. "He was the janitor." Her soft voice, not much louder than a whisper, carried the ponderous weight of sadness in the otherwise silent lobby.

"He was inside? The sheriff said they came because of a silent alarm."

She nodded. "It's a proximity system, nothing fancy. It just monitors the doors and windows. Phil always set the alarm when he was working. Even in a town this small, it made him feel better knowing the police would come arrest any drunks trying to break into our medicine cabinet." She turned and headed down the hallway. "Come on. Best see the rest."

Careful not to disturb any evidence, Sam followed Polly to the same room they'd been in earlier that day. She stopped outside the door and pointed at the floor. Bloody, smeared footprints led from the room to the rear of the building. "Careful of those. The forensic team will shit a litter of hedgehogs if we compromise the scene. There's nowhere in the room you can go, but you can look."

Avoiding the inkblot trail of red, Sam poked his head inside the doorway. Though a clear epicenter to the violence had been laid out like a White House Thanksgiving dinner, Sam averted his gaze. Gather the facts first, or risk missing something vital.

Rule #33:
Never follow the path that has been designated for you to follow.

If a scene has been staged, purposefully choose to not follow the trail. Examine everything else first. Get a feel for and assess the situation. Gather the supporting data and minutiae before turning your attention to the big picture. Otherwise, you take the chance of getting caught up and missing obvious clues. The perpetrator's intention is to mislead you. Change the rules. Take away their power by not playing their game.

—*122 Rules of Psychology*

The room looked as though a troop of poltergeists had ransacked it. The drawers had been pulled free of their tracks and tossed to the floor. The cabinet doors were torn from their hinges, the contents emptied and smashed. At the rear of the room, the steel door's handle had been blasted by what looked like a thousand bullets, as though machine-gun-wielding partiers had held an impromptu rave in the confined space. What remained of the lock hung in shredded metal fragments, the rest of it pulverized and scattered across the floor.

More bullet holes, which may have been ricochets, had turned sheetrock to powder—exposing the wooden studs beneath, which were pocked and chipped like fractured rib bones. Beyond the destroyed door, someone had pried open a drawer, using a crowbar or something similar. The steel tray lay empty, save the sheet once used to cover the body of Undercover Police Detective Frank Boreman.

He at last focused on the man—or what remained of him—in the chair. Zip ties secured Trooper Lane's hands and ankles. His bloodied, pulpified face matched the flaming red of his hair. Singed flesh showed beneath his ripped shirt. The burn marks looked as though they could have been made by an overclocked Taser. Nails missing from the end of broken fingers. Smashed hands and knees, probably the result of a pipe or hammer, completed the tale of the unimaginable pain this man had suffered during the final minutes of his life.

Rage over the senseless brutality pumped through Sam's veins. Even if they'd intended to end this young life, only a few years out of the academy, no reason in the universe existed for torturing him. None.

Seething, he turned to Polly. His anger reflected in her eyes, the hard line of her lips, the corded muscles of her shoulders and neck. "Have you worked out what you think happened?" he asked.

She tilted her head at the door. "The perps broke into the back, triggering the alarm. Based on the scratches, the lock may have been picked. They surprised the janitor and Trooper Lane."

He glanced at the empty morgue drawer. "They wanted the body."

She nodded. "Seems so. The chief forgot to give the trooper the key though."

"Which they didn't believe."

"That's what it looks like. They tore the room up and tortured the victims. When that didn't work, they used force to gain access."

Most people, when faced with this kind of brutality, would be horrified to the point of shock. Deputy Haines and, to a lesser extent, Sheriff Austin both had the haunted expressions of men who wouldn't be getting a good night's sleep for a very long time.

While Polly appeared disgusted and angered by the scene and the carnage surrounding her, she kept her descriptions of the scene short and clipped. The murderers were "perps." Trooper Lane and Janitor Phil, "victims." By keeping her emotions in check and her words professional, she helped prevent bias from sneaking into her report. Though years had passed since her Boston PD days, she clearly remembered the lessons and training she'd learned on the force.

After taking a deep breath to rein in his own anger, Sam asked, "I'm assuming that the sheriff has his men out looking?"

"Yes. But it's more a formality. Unless the perps fuck up and someone spots them, I'm guessing they're long gone. Even toting a body, they could be out of town in just a few minutes." She refrained from saying that the deputies hadn't been properly trained and had little to no experience with these kinds of crimes, though Sam could read between the lines.

If the local law found them, it'd be just dumb luck. And if they did happen upon the bastards responsible, they'd more likely than not end up like Trooper Lane.

Sheriff Austin appeared in the doorway. "Staties are here. Need you out." Without waiting for a reply, he turned and led the way out of the clinic. Polly and Sam followed. A pair of state cruisers sat next to the deputies' cars. The new arrivals expanded the crime scene and set up an extended perimeter.

A woman in a sharp brimmed hat and a uniform similar to the one Trooper Lane had worn stopped them.

"Excuse me." She looked pointedly at Sam and Polly. "Who are you?"

"They're with me," Sheriff Austin said.

She cut her eyes to the sheriff before returning her hawk-like focus to Sam and Polly. "I need to get statements from both of you. Also, I'm trying to maintain the chain of evidence. Having more people here makes it difficult to—"

"Janet," the sheriff said, cutting her off mid-lecture. Behind his back, he waved them to go. "My people understand the protocols. I assure you, the crime scene has not been compromised."

They turned and threaded through the crowd bathed in blue and red pulsing lights, leaving Sheriff Austin and his men to deal with the state police. The bodies were stacking up. If they didn't find those responsible and stop them, it could become the Erebus case all over again.

Chapter Twelve

Polly fell quiet, seemingly deep in thought. She held her shoulders tight and back straight while her boot-steps clicked against the pavement as though marching to war. Sam gave her time to process as they made their way to her house. Finally, she seemed to come out of her reverie, her jaw tight.

"Do we have any evidence of who killed Trooper Lane and Phil?" Sam asked.

She gave a sharp shake of her head. "Not yet. There are some random cameras on the street. We're hoping one of them recorded something. And, of course, the police are questioning everyone. Maybe they'll find a witness. So far, they've got nothing." She looked both angry and dejected.

"I have to admit, I didn't see this coming—not by a long shot."

"You and everyone else," she bit back.

"I'm sorry about Phil." In his capacity as an operative, he'd had to fake empathy and sympathy. It came with the job. But in this case, he meant it. No one should have died the way those men had.

She cut her sharp gaze in his direction as if looking for false platitudes. After a few seconds of studying his face, she huffed a breath. "It was shitty enough that Phil and the trooper were killed, but the way they were tortured... There's no excuse for that."

"None," Sam confirmed.

Polly turned up her driveway, the hint of salt air lingering on the cool night breeze. The quarter moon a mere sliver in the night sky.

Sam followed. "I came to your house earlier because I have some new information. That's when I saw I'd gotten three calls from you."

"I was trying to let you know..." Her words trailed off.

They stopped on her front stoop. Polly's door stood unlatched and partially open.

"It wasn't like this earlier," Sam whispered.

Understanding lit her eyes.

He reached to the small of his back for his gun, except he hadn't stopped by his house and picked it up. He silently cursed and vowed to *never* again go *anywhere* unarmed.

"Are you carrying?" she whispered.

He gave a quick shake of his head.

Pulling a Beretta from her purse, Polly flicked off the safety and held it at the ready. "Wait here." As she slid through the entrance, the darkness swallowed her compact form.

Sam closed his eyes for several seconds, allowing his pupils to dilate to their maximum size while he listened to every creak and cricket. The ominous silence draped his soul like a funeral cloak. He expected to hear Polly's terrier, Saundy, but the house remained as quiet as a tomb. A pang of dread for the little dog tightened his chest, but he didn't have time to dwell on her fate right now.

Mentally, he reviewed a map of the house. Living room, kitchen, bedroom, bathroom, dining room. In the foyer, stood a hip-height table adorned with knickknacks, including a few decorative figurines.

Anything? he asked Chet.

Clear, his inner conscience answered.

Going in low, Sam entered the shadowed hallway. Two steps. The table. He reached forward and gripped the glass Buddha statue he'd seen in his memory. It felt as heavy and solid as a river stone. Unfortunately, the figurine didn't make up for not having his Sig. Sam had always felt underdressed without his gun.

Now, he felt naked.

Stepping lightly to prevent the floor from squeaking beneath his shoes, he paused outside the kitchen. The quarter-moon's pale light drizzled through the window, misting the room beyond in a soft lunar glow. Unless drenched in darkness, the simplicity of the space didn't permit anyone as large as an adult to hide.

It's clear, Chet said quietly.

Despite his inner conscience's assurance, Sam went in low, keeping his back to the cabinets. As Chet predicted, no one lingered in the comfortable space. Likewise, no one waited in the adjoining dining room.

The living room proved as dark as a comet hurtling through the deepest recesses of space. Polly must have drawn the curtains before leaving.

Sam lingered in the entryway. He held his breath, listening for telltale sounds—breathing, shuffling from foot to foot, the soft murmur of the old hardwood. Anything to indicate someone lingered in the blackness. He inhaled through his nose, attempting to detect the aroma of body odor, cologne, or perfume.

Anything? he asked Chet again.

I can't get a bead on it, Chet said, sounding frustrated. He paused for a heartbeat. *If anyone's still in the house, this is where they'll be. Assume the perp's in there.*

Sam glanced at his mental map. Wall table to his right. Couch in the middle. Coffee table in front of it. Chair to the side. Armoire in the corner. The Investigative Wall along the far side.

He listened harder.

Nothing.

Skirting the corner, he ducked down next to the far side of the table, keeping his back to the wall, and stopped.

Move! Chet shouted. *Now!*

Sam pushed off. Too late. He froze as someone jammed the barrel of a gun against the vertebrae of his neck, a cold spike of fear shot down his spine.

In a nanosecond, a million images raced through his mind, his training snapping into place. The angle of the weapon based on the pressure. The position of the shooter's arm in relation to their body. Probable height and location of the wielder. A schematic as intricate as a salsa dance formed in his mind.

Drop. Swoop. Disarm. Gut punch. Head blow. His electrified body amped, ready to execute.

"Freeze, asshole," someone hissed from the darkness.

The familiar voice was so out of alignment with what he'd expected, only shock stopped him from pivoting and slamming her into the wall. "Polly?" he whispered.

"Sam?" She sounded as surprised as he felt. "I told you to stay outside."

Though they'd established identifications, she hadn't yet removed her Beretta.

He waited for the pressure of the cold steel to relent from the base of his skull, a flicker of frustration tightening his gut. *After everything, she still doesn't trust me?* Tension and anticipation sparked every nerve. Every muscle. He kept his focus riveted on the ex-police detective while also trying to monitor the living room. Someone could be there, and they could have a gun aimed at him and Polly right now.

Who exactly is the real enemy?

"Yeah, I don't listen very well," Sam said, aware that every breath, every word could help a potential attacker triangulate their position. He kept his voice calm, but his body rigid. If she didn't remove her gun in the next couple of seconds, he'd execute his disarmament plan and just have to hope no one else had them in his crosshairs. "My mother used to say I was incorrigible."

She snorted. "Your mom was a smart lady." Polly still didn't lower her weapon.

Dude, Chet said, *there's someone else here.*

Damn it! We don't have time for whatever game Polly is playing.
"You planning to shoot me?" he asked.

"I—"

From somewhere near the Investigative Wall, a muzzle flashed. The echoing cannon fire rattled the windows in their frames.

The wall beside Sam's head exploded.

Even as sheetrock peppered his face, Sam knocked Polly's gun aside and tackled her. She grunted as he shoved her to the floor and dropped on top of her, covering her body with his.

"Sam! Damn it! Get off!"

Another blast rocked the night. Sam's arm yanked back as though struck by a hammer. A bullet had found its mark.

Ignoring the wound, he kept his focus on the spot where he'd seen the flash. Sam rolled off Polly, eliciting another unhappy grunt from her. He pulled back his injured arm and hurled the statue still clenched in his fingers. As he released the Buddha, Sam launched himself off the floor.

In the dark, a man grunted in pain.

Another flash, the bang muted in Sam's ringing ears. A bullet whizzed by his temple like a wasp.

He aimed his bulk for the gunman's center mass. Miscalculated. His shoulder ricocheted off the man's hip and he plowed into Polly's coffee table, smashing it flat.

Even as the furniture collapsed beneath him, he spun, sweeping his feet into what he hoped would be the man's knees. In the pitch black of the room, he caught the intruder in the shin.

With that point of reference, Sam sprang, grabbing for the guy's arm. Found it. Drove the weapon up. Another blast roared, the sound a deafening hammer in his already ringing ears. The light fixture overhead shattered, raining down shards of glass that stung his skin like a swarm of angry bees.

Sam rammed his fist into the man's solar plexus.

The intruder cursed and brought the gun down like a club. The hard steel bit into Sam's shoulder.

Pain exploded from the point of impact. Sam's arm vibrated. The nerves buzzed and zapped as they shorted out.

With his good hand, Sam grabbed the man's wrist and twisted.

The intruder let out a high-pitched yelp of pain. The schoolgirl-like cry might have been comical had the owner not been trying to kill him.

The man struck, his fist colliding with the top of Sam's head.

Sam twisted, trying to put his body weight into the move.

A granite-hard fist smashed into his nose, flinging him back. Though stunned, the sudden momentum gave him the leverage he needed, and he yanked the gun out of the man's hand. As he fell, he brought the weapon around and pulled the trigger. In the muzzle flash, he caught a blurred glimpse of the intruder, who had already started to run.

Sam crashed once more onto the busted-up coffee table, the broken edges jabbing his ribs and butt. When his gun hand hit the wall, the weapon flew from his grasp and skittered across the hardwood.

Though the gunshot's echo rang as loud as every church bell in Rome, Sam detected the heavy clomp of retreating footsteps. He tried to get up, to chase after the man, but the wooden table had struck a nerve in his back, causing his diaphragm to spasm, making breathing impossible.

Damn, not again, he thought, a surge of frustration burning through his chest as the killer slipped away.

He rolled onto his side, pushing up with his wobbly arms while attempting to inhale.

He'd almost regained his feet, intent on giving chase, when the barrel of a gun rammed into his forehead. "Freeze," Polly's voice came out in an icy hiss. "Move and I'll blow your fucking brains out."

Son of a bitch. Again? A wave of anger crashed through him—after taking a bullet for her this was the thanks he got?

Sam tried to speak but couldn't. Twice in one night, she'd held the business end of her gun against his skull. He fought with his uncooperative respiratory system. *Breathe, damn it!*

A flashlight flared, shining in his face.

"Sam?" Polly said, as if she'd forgotten he'd been there. She spun, sweeping the room. "Where'd he go?"

At last, his body relaxed allowing him a glorious sip of air. He wheezed, "Out the front."

Glass and wood crunched as Polly stormed across her living room, down the hall, and out into the night. A minute later, the click of the front door closing echoed. He sensed, rather than heard, her reenter the living room.

"He's gone," she said. "There's a murderer loose in the Cove. Again."

Chapter Thirteen

S am sat on the pile of busted-up coffee table—the ragged wood digging into his ass, the faint smell of gunpowder and charred wiring lingering in the air. Though he couldn't see her in the pitch-black, Polly's footsteps echoed as she crossed the room, crunching over glass shards. The lights blossomed to life for a second, casting twisted shadows across the ruined space. But the overhead fixture burst in a shower of sparks.

The world plunged into darkness once more.

She cursed in what sounded like Italian and stomped off. The garage door slammed. She must have reset the breaker because the sconce lights mounted to the wall flared to life. She returned to the devastation of what had been a tranquil, comfortable living space but now resembled the aftermath of an Avengers movie.

Polly marched over, knelt, and inspected his wounded arm. She snorted. "You'll live."

She stood and began searching the house, concern etching her features. "Saundy!" She hurried to the kitchen, calling her dog's name.

Sam checked the wound. The bullet had only grazed his triceps. As per Polly, he'd live.

From his position on the pile of coffee table ruins, he could see into the kitchen—where the faint glow of the sconce lights reflected off the stainless-steel fridge, casting a warm sheen over the floor. A lower cabinet door flew open with a bang, and Saundy bolted out, her nails skittering across the tiles.

Polly held open her arms.

The dog sailed into her mistress' embrace, a blur of fluff.

"I'm so glad you're okay." She kissed the little dog's head and nuzzled her face.

The energy singeing Sam's nerves abated, and the pain in his arm snarled to life, a fiery pulse that throbbed with every beat of his heart. Blood trickled from his nose, warm and sticky. He slowly stood, wincing as he brushed wood splinters and glass from his body.

A quiet relief settled in his chest at seeing Saundy safe. "She was hiding in the cabinet?"

Polly glanced in his direction. "She's just a little dog. There's nothing she can do to stop an armed intruder. I trained her to hide in the cabinet when she feels threatened."

Polly continued to gush over the fluffy furball. "Mommy's so relieved her little girl is okay. Do you need to go potty? Come on! Let's go." Saundy jumped to the floor and scampered out the front door. Polly raised the Beretta and followed.

"I'm okay. No. Really," Sam said to the empty house, his voice echoing in the vacant space. Sighing, he tore a strip of hem off his shirt with a sharp rip and tied it around his triceps, wincing as the pressure of the fabric sent a fresh stab of pain through the bullet wound. He looked around the devastated living room, the sconce lights casting a dim glow over the chaos—shattered glass, the air thick with the acrid scent of burnt wiring. Searching for the intruder's gun, he scanned the floor, but it wasn't anywhere obvious. He got down on his knees, peering under the couch. The cold of the hardwood seeped into his palms and tiny splinters pricked his skin.

A few minutes later, Saundy's nails clicked on hardwood as she flew back inside with her usual enthusiasm, her tiny paws pattering like a drumroll. Polly bolted the door with a heavy thud, went to the kitchen, and poured a bowl of kibble.

After setting the dog's food on the floor, she returned to the living room. "What are you doing?"

"Looking for the guy's gun," Sam said, his voice tight with focus as he swept his gaze under the couch, hoping for a glint of metal. After another minute of fruitless searching, he gave up, a bitter knot of frustration tightening his chest. He sat back on his heels, wiping sweat from his brow.

"I guess he——" Polly's breath hitched. Her gaze snapped to a box in the corner, its edges crumpled. The lid torn off and lying on the floor like a roadkill squirrel, smeared with a faint streak of blood—likely Sam's from the fight. "No!"

"What?"

Polly stumbled to the box, her hands trembling as she picked it up and shook it out. A few scraps of paper fluttered to the hardwood like dried leaves. "No, no, no!"

"What is it?"

"I had copies of all the printouts, my laptop, and the phone in here," she said, her voice hollow, as if the intrusion had gutted her. She threw the box down and knelt in front of the armoire. She seemed to angle her back intentionally so Sam couldn't see what she was doing. After a muted click, a hidden drawer popped open. As she rifled through it, her shoulders drooped in defeat. She cursed.

A secret stash, Chet observed.

As a cop, she probably got into the habit of having several places to hide weapons and other things she didn't want found. It's not out of the ordinary.

True. It's just one more piece of the Polly puzzle.

"It's all gone," she said unnecessarily. "All our evidence."

"I still have the copies you gave me... Shit!" Sam ran out to the front porch. His bag—along with the printouts and his notes—was missing, of course. After relocking the door, he returned to the living room. "My bag's gone."

"What? What bag?"

"I had my copies of the printouts and a bunch of notes I wanted to go over with you. But when I got here the first time, I thought you might be in trouble, so I dumped the bag on the porch to free up my hands in case I had to fight."

"What first time?"

He explained how he'd come to the house before she'd summoned him to the clinic.

"You lost your copies," Polly said, slamming the armoire drawer shut. "The phone that had the photos, messages, and GPS data on it is gone. And the printouts I'd had are all gone too. We don't know who murdered Phil and Trooper Lane, and we don't know who broke into my house. The long and short of it is...we have nothing." She jumped to her feet and booted the box. "Nothing!"

Maybe you should have locked up critical pieces of evidence in your super-secret drawer if it was so important instead of leaving it in a goddamned shoe box?

Polly snorted, anger turning the green of her eyes dark, her jaw clenching so tightly Sam could see the muscles twitching. "You know, we might have stopped him if you hadn't been so preoccupied with incapacitating me."

"I... What? Incapacitating you? No, I was trying to——"

"*I* had the gun. Did you forget?" Her voice was a low growl, her hands balling into fists at her sides.

"Forget?" he spat. He pressed two fingers to his temple, mimicking her weapon. "It was pressed to my head. What the hell?"

She glowered at him, her chest heaving. "What the hell indeed! I could have dropped that guy. But you had to play the hero."

Is this chick for real? Chet asked.

Seriously.

"I wasn't trying to be a hero," he bit back. "I risked my——"

"And because you tackled him, I couldn't shoot him without hitting *you*. I should have just shot you both. It would have saved me a lot of hassle."

Nothing to say to that. She claimed she didn't want to shoot him accidentally, yet she avoided explaining why she'd kept her Beretta pressed against his head.

Polly harrumphed with disdain as she surveyed the broken coffee table, that familiar anger rolling off her like radiation. As Sam braced himself for a wave of her wrath, her shoulders slumped, and the heat in her simmering gaze cooled.

She ran a hand through her mussed hair and sighed dejectedly. "It's not your fault. Yes, I'm annoyed that you think I need protecting—and make no mistake, you push me down like that again for any reason, I'll shoot you myself." She waved at the box. "But I'm mostly mad at myself for making such a stupid mistake. I should have protected the evidence. It was such a rookie move."

Relieved that Hurricane Polly had chilled from a category five to a mild tropical storm, Sam said, "I'm sorry about that. The pushing you down part, I mean. Won't happen again. It was just instinct. The bullets were flying, and I didn't want you to get hit."

Polly nodded. "I know."

They fell silent for a minute.

"You know," he said eventually, "I read through your notes about four or five times today, and I've got a pretty good memory. What about you?"

She furrowed her brow. "Yeah, at least that. Maybe more."

"Well, there's no getting the actual photos back, but we could reconstruct most of the notes and write up descriptions of the pictures."

Polly scratched her cheek and gave a slight nod. "Alright. I'm willing to give it a try." She whipped out her cell phone, clicked a few buttons, and ordered a large "Cahill Special" from Michelangelo's Pizzeria, the only place in town still delivering at this hour.

Sam arched a brow at her.

She hung up and, without explaining what a Cahill Special was, said dismissively, "We need to fuel our brains. Besides, violence, especially when combined with getting my ass handed to me by some unknown jack wagon, makes me hungry."

Polly cracked her knuckles and rolled her shoulders. "Alright, let's get to work."

Chapter Fourteen

Burnt gunpowder still hung in the air. The jagged splinters of the coffee table had scattered like fallen soldiers on a battlefield. "Let's start with the bastard who broke into my house," Polly said. Sitting on the floor amid the apocalyptic scene that had been her living room, her back against the couch, she opened a blank note page on her tablet. "Did you get a look at him?"

Beside her, Sam closed his eyes. Pushing aside the dull throb in his arm—an ache that pulsed with every heart-beat—and the sharp sting in his face where the man had punched him, his nose still tender and crusted with dried blood, he concentrated on the fight.

When he'd collided with the interloper, the impact had been unyielding—more like hitting a brick wall than a human being. They'd wrestled, trading blows. Then Sam had the gun and had pulled the trigger. The echoing ex-plosion had been as loud as a bomb, the recoil jarring his injured arm. He paused the mental replay, focusing on the image fragments captured during the milliseconds as shelled powder flamed. A fleeting glimpse of the man who'd nearly killed them. The outline of the perp in muzzle-lightning flash.

"Tall. Bald. Muscular. Tats, though I couldn't make out the details."

She typed the description into the tablet. "Not a lot to go on, but it's better than most of the descriptions I got when I was in Boston."

Sam opened his eyes, pretending not to know what she meant. "Boston?"

"In another life, I was a cop with the Boston PD."

She'd just downplayed her former career. Why? On the surface, it didn't seem to matter, yet he felt this omission was significant in a way he couldn't yet see. She could be trying to find out what he knew. If he corrected her, that would reveal he'd been investigating her, so he didn't say anything.

"Anyway," she continued, "maybe the description will match whatever footage the sheriff and his deputies find. If they find any at all."

While Polly didn't seem to notice the mess, the glass shards and splinters of wood were distracting him. He could dictate notes and clean at the same time. Sam went into the kitchen, grabbing the garbage can and a broom. Returning, he began sweeping up broken coffee table bits.

Leaning back against the sofa, Polly typed while he recounted what he remembered, with her filling in her own details.

After they'd rebuilt most of the documents, supplementing them with an account of the intruder breaking into her house, she set the tablet aside and helped him clean up. "That was pretty smart thinking," she said. "Recreating the notes, I mean."

As he dropped a pan full of shards from the broken light fixture into the trash, the glass clattering, a cloud of dust blossomed from the can like a small mushroom cloud. He coughed, waving a hand in front of his face. "Thank you. I'm sorry about what happened to your house. I can help pay for the damages."

She waved it off. "The money's not the issue. What really irks me is that this is my safe space, you know? I shouldn't need to be on alert or have beefed up security in my own home." She kicked a splintered piece of coffee table; the wood skittered across the floor with a hollow clatter.

Sam nodded. They fell into a comfortable silence as they worked.

After a few minutes, he asked, "Back in the clinic, was there anything else about the scene that stands out to you?"

She snorted. "Other than the senseless violence against two innocent men?"

"Aside from that, yes."

Polly's expression turned to stone as she thought about the crime scene. "Nothing...aside from murder, of course. Why?"

"They were looking for something."

"I agree," she said slowly. "The body. Which they took."

Sam brushed off his hands, facing her. "The place was torn apart. Cabinets, doors, everything. At first, I thought it was because they were looking for the morgue keys. But why go through the hassle? They were clearly able to pry the drawer open."

"The lock on it isn't great," she agreed. "Blasting the place to shit with automatic weapons was overkill since just about anyone could bust it apart in a couple of minutes. We didn't invest in better security because crime sprees usually involve banks or jewelry stores, not morgues." Polly seemed to consider. "They were looking for his phone."

"You said the bagged evidence was gone. The phone was hidden in the cigarette case, so they must have found out about it after they'd thrown him overboard."

"That seems like a logical conclusion." She thought for a second. "How did they know to come here?"

"Could they have gotten your address from the computer?"

"It's not likely. There's a lot of security because of HI-PAA regulations. I suppose it's possible though."

Or they tortured the information out of Phil, Sam thought, but did not say. Polly had been through enough without tossing unsubstantiated guilt onto her shoulders. "I'm hoping they came here first and didn't tear up the chief's house too."

"He's been at the clinic since the deputy found the body. He might be in for a nasty surprise when he gets home."

A sudden dread filled his gut. "Is the chief married, or does he have anyone living with him?"

She shook her head. "Lifelong bachelor. No significant other. But I see what you're thinking. His wife, if he had one, could have been killed if our perp broke in. No one is in danger, per se, but maybe we should warn him?"

"I don't think that's necessary." He pointed at the fragmented remains of the Investigative Wall. Pushpins still anchored scraps of paper. The sheetrock scraped and marked where the intruder had ripped everything down. "If the perp went to the chief's first, the place would already be a mess. Going there after coming here would be a waste of time since he already has the phone, your notes, my notes, your computer, the body, and the evidence bag. There's nothing more. If we told the chief, all we'd be doing is distracting him from the crime scene. His house is either torn up or it isn't."

Polly didn't look convinced, but she also didn't pull out her cell phone and start making calls.

"We'd also have to tell the chief what happened here and what was taken."

"True," she said. "That would be a pretty uncomfortable conversation. Palmer wasn't a cop in a former life,"——her gaze found his for a heartbeat——"or even military, but he's got a good nose for bullshit. Even if we spun a pretty convincing story, he would most likely sniff out the stink of it."

"The guy got your computer. Is there anything on it you're worried about?"

She shook her head. "No. It's got about five layers of security. My guess is that they already tried to get in. The computer turned itself into a brick, and they tossed it into the gutter."

That seemed paranoid even for a former police detective, but he kept that opinion to himself. "I suppose that's a good thing. Unfortunately, they got the phone, which was probably the most damning piece of evidence," Sam said. "Frank was building a case against them. Except, the trooper would have no way of knowing about it because we didn't log it into evidence."

"*You* didn't log it into evidence," Polly corrected, a sharp edge to her voice. "And you stole it."

Sam didn't remind her that she'd been a willing participant in the theft. They hadn't traded barbs in about thirty minutes, and he didn't want to start now.

Polly let out an exasperated sigh. "Except I also didn't return it, and I held onto it all night. I'm pretty sure that any lawyer worth their salt would charge me with being an accessory after the fact, if not a coconspirator."

"We broke the chain of evidence," Sam said.

"Like a piece of kindling." She pantomimed snapping a stick over her knee. "And when the trooper claimed he didn't know about it, they didn't believe him."

"Hence the torture. They didn't want us to see what was on it."

Polly took the broom from him. Sam moved aside as she swept up the diamond-shards of glass. "What I don't understand is why kill Frank and throw him overboard *with* his phone?"

"Maybe the murder itself was spur-of-the-moment, and they somehow found out about it later."

"Perhaps. As you pointed out, there was no indication that they'd tried to weigh him down to hide the evidence, so I guess that makes sense. How though?"

He held the dustpan as she swept the pile into it. Another cloud of dust made his nose itch, a sneeze threatened. He dumped the pile into the garbage. "How what?"

"How did they know about the phone *afterward?* They never would have dumped him if they'd known he had pictures and documented evidence."

Great point. "Maybe they had some kind of surveillance system on the ship. They reviewed the footage and saw him taking pictures."

Leaning on the broom handle, Polly furrowed her brow. "Maybe. The problem is, criminals don't like evidence. And surveillance video footage would be the most damning."

Their eyes met.

"A snitch," they said in unison.

They stared at one another, unified for once. The light in her eyes reflected the excitement he felt—a rare moment of alignment.

The doorbell rang, a sharp, jarring chime that sliced through the quiet and broke the spell.

Polly held his gaze for another beat before looking away. "It's probably the pizza," she said, her voice low and edged with caution.

She retrieved a small revolver taped to the bottom of the dining room table, the adhesive peeling away with a faint *rip,* and handed it to Sam. He took it, the cold metal heavy in his hand, surprised but not really surprised that she had a gun stashed within easy access. Polly must have had a dozen weapons hidden throughout the house.

He might have called her paranoid, except someone had broken in and almost killed them. The old saying, *it's not paranoia if you're right,* seemed apt.

She pulled a pair of twenties from her back pocket and, resting her hand on the butt of the Beretta tucked into her waistband at the small of her back, went into the front hall.

Sam moved to the inside of the doorway next to the hinges, hidden from view. He held the revolver at the ready.

Polly cut her eyes in his direction.

He gave a sharp nod.

She unlocked and pulled the door open.

Through the crack along the jamb, Sam saw a pimple-faced kid in an orange Michelangelo's-embroidered polo shirt and matching hat. "Hey, Polly," he said. "Got your usual."

Though her fingers never left her weapon, she said, "Thanks, Tom." Sam could hear the smile in her voice. They exchanged the flat box for the money. "Keep the change," she told him as she closed and bolted the door.

As she carried their late-night snack into the dining room, the aroma of cheese and spicy meats trailed her, reminding Sam of the coastal pizzerias he and his brother had frequented when they'd been teens. She dropped the pizza onto the table and cracked open the lid, which boasted in a looping font *Piping Hot or it's Free!* A wave of steam accompanying the heavenly aroma wafted up. Turned out a "Cahill Special" was pepperoni, sausage, and mushrooms. She folded a slice in half and took a large bite.

Sam's stomach grumbled. He was suddenly famished. *Maybe Polly was right about there being a link between getting your ass handed to you and hunger.* He set the revolver on the table and picked up a slice.

The restaurant had delivered on the promise printed on the lid—the dripping grease almost burned his fingers. He blew on the cheese to cool it off a few degrees and bit down. As the epic cacophony of tastes exploded in his mouth—salty pepperoni, savory sausage, and mellow mushroom melding with the zing of marinara—stringy mozzarella drizzled down his chin. He wiped at it absently with the back of his hand.

Polly grabbed a couple of beers from the fridge and handed him one. The cool glass soothed the almost-burnt skin of his fingertips. Holding the pizza slice in her mouth like Saundy might hold a bone, Polly twisted off the cap and set the bottle down. She pulled the slice from her lips.

"Frank trusted someone he shouldn't have," Polly said, picking up the conversation where they'd left off.

He continued the thought. "They sold him out, but maybe they didn't tell the others about the phone until later."

"It fits."

"Yes, it does," Sam said, "but what happened tonight doesn't."

"What do you mean? They wanted to get the phone because it contained evidence against them."

"Not that," Sam said around a mouthful of crust. "Frank. They find out he's an undercover cop, beat him up, kill him, and dump the body in the ocean. They didn't bother to weigh him down or anything. Then, a few days later, they take a huge chance to steal the body back. Why?"

Polly's brow furrowed. "Another good question."

Sam let out a frustrated sigh. "Unless we catch these guys, we'll never know. They got the body and have most likely taken it back to their ship. They're halfway to Australia by now."

"What are you talking about?" Confusion rang in Polly's voice. "What ship?"

"The *Vengeance*. I think it's here."

"What?! How do you know?"

He told her about his conversation with Savannah, emphasizing how much the boat reminded him of the *Vengeance*. "It's what I came to tell you earlier."

Understanding registered on Polly's face. "You think these guys are from that ship?"

"It's a fair bet. But, like I said, they're long gone by now." He didn't believe they'd left yet, but he wanted to make the situation sound urgent to help move Polly along. To get her on board, he'd have to convince her that the two of them should investigate the ship, while letting her believe she'd come up with the idea. She needed to think that bringing in the Coast Guard involved a lot of time-wasting red tape.

She arched a slim brow. "I hardly think so. Our deputies might be inexperienced, but RU isn't. We're as trained and organized as the Green Berets. There's only one bridge in or out of town. The deputies set up a roadblock. They're inspecting every car."

Sam pretended to consider this new information. "So if someone needs to leave the Cove, they'd have to go by boat."

"Right. We have our folks at both marinas, and we have boats patrolling the shore."

Before he could throw out the idea of investigating the ship himself, he needed to present her with rational options she'd never agree to. "So, we send in RU or the Coast Guard to investigate this mystery ship."

Polly hesitated, a range of expressions crossing her face.

"What?" he asked.

"First, we don't know this is the same ship," she said. "It only *might* be."

"I don't believe in coincidences——"

She held up a finger, stopping him. "Second, we can't send the Coast Guard without probable cause. We might have been able to sway them with Frank's phone and the printouts, but those are gone."

Without probable cause? Chet scoffed. *Someone killed two people, snatched a body and the evidence that washed up with it, broke into Polly's house, and stole Frank's phone and Polly's computer. You couldn't have more probable cause if they set up a lighted sign that says: We kill cops. Come arrest us.*

Right?

"Third," Polly said, "I'm not sending RU to investigate a ship that could be Russian Mafiya and getting a bunch of my people killed."

I didn't think you could pull this off, Chet admitted. *I gave her fifty-fifty odds she'd have RU check it out. She's right though. Her people, trained or not, would probably get killed. But alerting the Coast Guard felt like a slam dunk.*

She still hasn't shared her true motivations. Not all of them, anyway. She's trying to keep this as low profile as possible, but it's getting bigger than she'd anticipated.

Well, my gut says your lady friend here believes this is our boat but isn't interested in sharing the love.

My gut instinct is listening to his gut? Surreal.

Just saying, Chet said, *she won't be including a third party.*

Any idea why?

None whatsoever. But keep going, and you'll get her aboard your sortie. No pun intended.

Polly retrieved the tablet from the living room and began pacing while devouring a fresh slice of pizza and taking notes. "Tell me about this ship Savannah saw. Any idea how big it was?"

Sam replayed Savannah's words in his mind. "It didn't sound like she got near it. I'd guess she wasn't any closer than a mile. But she thought it looked old and rusty."

"Did she catch the name on the hull?"

"No. She never got close enough."

"So, it wasn't huge, like a cargo carrier, but it also sounds larger than a fishing boat. I'm going to guess somewhere between a hundred fifty and three hundred feet. An old vessel, not in decent shape, and factoring in the size, could cruise at roughly fifteen to twenty knots on average."

"What are you getting at?"

"We need to know if the ship Savannah saw was even capable of traveling long-term and long distances on the ocean. Savannah is a bit of, what we in the Boston PD called, an unreliable witness. She didn't even see the ship's name. If we waste a lot of time investigating it, we might miss the real perpetrators."

"I see," Sam said. "Based on her description, it sounds like it could be Frank's boat."

"Alright. Let's assume for a moment that this is our tub. I still don't see why they'd come back to get Frank. Seems like their best course of action is to beat feet to the other side of the Pacific and get lost in traffic."

"I might have an answer to that," Sam said. "First, I have a question. Are there any limitations to ship-to-shore communications?"

"What do you mean?"

"I mean distance-wise. Are there dead zones that are too far away to talk to the mainland?"

She thought it over for a moment. "A few years ago, the old two-megahertz systems would have been limited to near-shore communication. But the new high-frequency kilohertz systems all the new ships are rigged with allow for worldwide connectivity."

"That fits," Sam said as he factored this information into his hypothesis. "Let's say our Russian friends have been cruising around the ocean, picking up drugs and black-market Ford Fiestas. They discover a traitor in their midst and work him over. Only someone gets an itchy trigger finger."

"And blasts him when normally they would have forceful-ly *encouraged* him to tell them what he knows," Polly added.

"Right. Our guy had some signs of being beaten up, but he should have looked a lot more like the trooper and janitor. Alone, in the middle of the ocean, with all the time in the world and no one to hear him scream, they could have taken him apart piece by piece. Instead, he's shot and dumped."

Around a mouthful of pie, Polly said, "Okay, I think I see where you're going with this. Carry on."

"So," Sam said, "after they did the deed, they probably had to call in to some pit boss and tell him or her what just went down. But, for argument's sake, let's say they still have one of those old two-megahertz jobs."

"Meaning they have limited communications capability."

"Right," Sam said. "They dump the body, then some-time later—maybe a day or two—they're close enough to shore to radio home and tell the big Russian kahuna what happened. The boss goes apeshit because they basically dumped two hundred pounds of evidence into the ocean. Then it washed up on shore here. The sheriff notifies the state police. But the ME is conveniently 'too busy' to come collect the body. Instead, they send some noob to sit on it."

Polly added, "Then the goon squad shows up to collect."

"Right."

Sam could almost see the wheels spinning in Polly's head. She said, "This leads to some very unsettling conclusions."

He waited for her to complete her thoughts.

"First, they would have no idea of where to look for Frank or that he'd even washed up on shore. For all they knew, he was still floating around in the Pacific."

"But they did know," Sam said.

She held up a finger. "Yes. Meaning that someone—either one of our local boys, the LAPD, or one of the staties—got on the horn and made a report to the big kahuna." She scrunched up her lips as she thought. "The idea of the deputies or the sheriff calling the Russians doesn't sit right in my head. Not enough connections."

"Except you have to remember the Alabaster Cove Rumor Mill," Sam reminded her.

"Shit. Savannah was spilling the beans two minutes after she found out about the murder."

"Meaning everyone in town is a suspect."

Polly let out a long breath and shook her head. "No. Still doesn't work for me. There's just not enough that happens in the Cove to warrant paying an informant to sit here and twiddle their thumbs."

"Okay. Point taken. So, we've limited our suspect pool to the LAPD and the state police."

She shook her head again. "I didn't call the LAPD because I didn't know it was one of theirs. And the sheriff told me he only called the staties."

"Could the staties have called the LAPD?"

Polly shrugged. "Could be. I guess it's not unreasonable to think that the Russians would have someone from either or both forces on the payroll. But..." She paused. "I don't know. There's so much visibility with what just happened. These hypothetical cops on the take would have to be high on the food chain. They'd have to delay both the investigation and the ME. Totem pole bottom dwellers don't have that kind of pull."

Someone up the ranks at The Agency had sent him to kill Monica to save a drug lord. The two chains of events looked parallel. "It could be the ship was already out searching, but it's a pretty big ocean. When Frank washed up here, the sheriff called the staties, who contacted our kahuna."

She frowned. "This ship shows up thirty hours later. The timing fits. Even if it's not the *Vengeance*, it could be related."

"Right. They were in the area and thought they'd come in and help a fellow drug lord by cleaning up their mess." Sam let a couple of beats pass before dropping the bait he hoped she'd find too enticing to pass up. "But all of this is mere speculation. We need to prove it."

"Well, like I told you, I'm not sending my people in to get killed," her voice firm. Her decision final.

"And if we can't send the Coast Guard, that just leaves one option."

Polly arched a brow, the question obvious, her green eyes searching his with a mix of skepticism and curiosity.

He knew the risks in what he was about to propose. But this was their only shot at answers, and he'd be damned if he'd let these bastards slip away again. "You and I need to get on that boat."

Chapter Fifteen

Sam expected Polly to say something like, "Have you lost your ever-loving mind?" Or "You got a death wish, Bradford? You really want to go into the lair of the beast?"

Instead, she just nodded, as if spying on Russian Mafiya ships were as commonplace as getting ice cream on a sultry Sunday afternoon.

She had dismissed his suggestion to send RU to investigate—purportedly to protect them from being killed. While that seemed like a legitimate concern, she'd then claimed they lacked sufficient probable cause to report the ship to the Coast Guard. *Bullshit.* Sam had spent his youth on the ocean, and while not a maritime law expert, he'd heard of suspected drug runners being boarded off the coast of California all the time, and he doubted warrants had been issued in all those cases.

Clearly, she wanted to do this on her own, though Sam still didn't understand why. If she sought to balance the scales of justice, why exclude other capable, well-prepared, well-equipped resources?

He tried reading her expression, searching for fear or hesitation, but only determination filled her vibrant green eyes. Their intensity a raging forest fire. Unyielding. Fierce. Polly had no intention of backing down, and Sam couldn't help but feel a flicker of admiration for her unshakable resolve.

Gotcha.

"When?" she asked.

"Time's wasting," he said. "The longer it takes us to narrow down our list of suspects, the harder it will be to catch the man who butchered Trooper Lane and Phil."

Would this push her over her limits?

Polly tossed her half-eaten piece of pizza back into the box and brushed off her hands. "I have my own gear, but not enough for the both of us."

Evidently not. Did she even have limits? Based on what he'd seen in her police record, maybe not. *Guess we're doing this.* "I have my own," Sam said. "But since someone broke into your house, I'm going to borrow this"—he picked up the revolver from the table—"to go get it." The small handgun wouldn't deliver the same thug-killing punch as his Sig, but it was a hell of a lot better than a weaponized Buddha statue.

"Fine," she said. "Bit of advice."

Here it comes, Chet said. *The moment we've all been waiting for. What are you talking about?*

Every woman you've ever known senses what a broken, disastrous wreck you are. They may not understand all the ways in which you're messed up, but they all want to help. No-boundaries-girl here has a background in police investigation and a never-say-die drive to see justice served that you could only dream of. She's smart, intuitive, and loyal. As such, she senses that you're waffling on your dedication to our great nation, your convictions, The Agency, everything.

I'm not waffling. My relationship with The Agency is just complicated.

Chet ignored his excuse. *If I had to guess, her advice will be for you to get out of the spy business. Your lack of dedication makes you a liability.*

Not every woman tries to give me advice, Sam said. *Some of them... Okay, a lot of them do, but not all.*

Bro.

Also, this bit of unpleasantness with the Russian Mafiya aside, I'm not in the spy business. He paused. *Okay, technically, I spy on people all the time. But that's just so I can learn their secrets, manipulate them, and kill them. That's my job.*

Is it? I thought you were giving it all up to smoke out with the hippies.

I don't know, Sam snapped. *We have this case and then we'll see.*

Chet arched a brow as if Sam had conceded his point. *You're either all in or you're all out.*

I'm all in on this case. We'll see about the rest later.

Spartacus, for the record, your cream-filled spine is getting old. I deserve a more stable, less psychotic gig. How do I bail on Ship Bradford and join Team Cahill? He tapped his chin as though thinking. *Who do I know that's adept at Vulcan mind melds?*

No. I——

Chet barreled over him. *The problem is you still see yourself as being on some gallant mission. A crusader riding in on a white stallion to rid the world of wickedness. But you're not Bellerophon. He never gave up his Pegasus or his hunt for the Chimera. And, while you claim to be getting justice for a fallen Marine, the only thing your lack of conviction is going to do is get you and your partner killed.*

I don't need to justify my choices to you. Some of the asshats we've taken down have been more destructive than a fire-breathing monster with a chest cold. The Greeks romanticized a fictitious character to symbolize evil, but in the real world, things are more complicated.

Chet scoffed. *I stand humbly corrected. You clearly have your priorities straight. Maybe you and Taylor Swift can become a song-writing duo. She can sing about good love gone bad. You can croon about good partners gone dead.*

I'm not going to get Polly killed. I told you I'm all in, I just haven't... Sam stopped his fruitless discussion with his inner conscience when he realized Polly was watching him with a curious, inquisitive expression.

Sometimes, when he got into the thick of it with Chet, he would lose a minute or two. Maybe he should see a shrink? Perhaps bantering with his inner conscience—which was really just himself—might be a sign of a cognitive problem. Sam wouldn't be surprised to find out he had an emotional disorder or had suffered a psychotic break.

But as long as he kept that mess locked away, he functioned just fine. Besides, only the weak wasted their time yammering about their problems.

"You here?" Polly asked.

He let out a long breath. "Just mentally packing my bag."

Yes, Chet said, *your emotional bag.*

Sam ignored him.

"Anyway, like I was telling you before you checked out of Hotel Reality," she said, "Abby is my friend. She generously let you rent that house for a song because you're

Max's friend. I know it isn't the Taj Mahal, but please try not to get it all shot up."

"Funny."

She closed the pizza box and tucked it into the fridge. Still holding her beer, Polly left the dining room. A few seconds later, Sam heard the closing click of her bedroom door.

He took that as his cue to head home. Polly had dropped her flashlight onto the table. He grabbed it and left.

While mentally keeping his radar tuned for threats stalking him in the night, he made his way through the quiet city streets, vigilant for the murderer who still roamed free. Every shadow a potential ambush. Every nook and crevice a potential hiding place.

Polly had accused him of having a hero complex. Funny, since when they'd found her front door ajar, she'd instructed him to stay out on the porch and then gone in by herself. At the time, they'd had no idea what nastiness awaited them. Had they entered together, they still might have been outnumbered, but as a team, their odds of success would have been significantly better.

Her behavior reminded him of a lecture from back in his Agency academy days. His professor, Dr. Wergent—the brainiac behind the *122 Rules of Psychology*—had spent an entire day discussing the theories he'd created around *defensive projectionism*.

Rule #34:
Defensive Projectionist - Redirect and Double Down.

Individuals temporarily functioning outside their moral or rational norms—especially in extreme instances—might project their unacceptable behaviors, thoughts, and motivations onto others as a type of self-defense mechanism. Their inability or unwillingness to change their misconduct may have a myriad of underlying causes. No matter the reasoning, casting blame absolves the subject of any responsibility or wrongdoing. Furthermore, instigators often go on the offensive and attack their victim's character. Make no mistake, the subject, on some level, understands completely what they are doing yet are in a state of such severe self-denial, they will go to extremes to prove their innocence. Calling them on their self-deception will only lead to vehement, even hostile, recrimination.

Note: In this state, the subject has transferred their power to their target. They want to do whatever actions they claim to disapprove of. Through careful handling, individuals can be controlled and manipulated into performing even more aberrant behavior. Optionally, if the situation warrants, doubling down on their accusations might break the cycle and cause the subject to back down.

—122 Rules of Psychology

The professor would have held up Polly's picture as a prime example of defensive projectionism. Infiltrating the

Russian Mafiya single-handedly was so outside her self-defined behavioral norms, Polly had rid herself of wrongdoing by casting her own vigilantism onto him.

And by going along with her, he'd become her enabler. Sam had worried when he suggested they investigate the ship that she might back down. But she hadn't. If anything, Polly seemed even more determined.

Sam needed to decide what line he wouldn't cross. At some point, he might have to create boundaries because, clearly, Polly could not or would not create them herself. Personally, Sam didn't know how far he'd go. That, he'd have to play by ear. But professionally, he had to be very careful.

Josha had instructed him to not "go off the rails again." What constituted pushing his Josha-granted latitude too far? Did sailing out to investigate what could be the *Vengeance* fall under the umbrella of being Polly's consultant, or would his handler interpret his actions as ignoring orders—an offense that might result in him being relocated to a cell in some forgotten federal prison?

More disturbingly, his handler always had access to a lot more information than he let on. Did Josha already know about the link between the Russian Mafiya and Frank Boreman's death? It seemed unlikely he wouldn't. Since he probably did, how far into the mob did his handler want Sam to go?

Sam wanted clarity, but, as usual, the murky waters in which he swam teemed with sharks, piranhas, and whirlpools that threatened to suck him under and never let him resurface.

He parked these swirling, distracting eddies as he paused in the shadows across the street from the rental house. He waited, studying the humble structure, searching for signs of unauthorized entry. From his angle, the door appeared secure, and he didn't see anyone moving behind the windows.

Sam crossed the street, avoiding the yellowy pools cast by the overhead streetlamps. On the porch, he ducked under the window as he sidled along the front of the house. He didn't know how anyone could have discovered the connection between him and Polly, but making reckless assumptions could be costly. Best act as though they knew.

He held Polly's revolver at the ready. Since he never locked his door——a decision he might reconsider going forward——when he turned the handle, the latch released. He pressed the business end of the flashlight against his leg and clicked it to life. Sam took a breath and pushed through the front door. He waved the light and gun back and forth, sweeping the room as he sought a target.

Only silence and emptiness awaited him. After clearing the bathroom, he switched on the overheads.

He winced as he dropped to his knees on the hardwood floor——the dull throbs in his back, his shoulders, and his joints a reminder of the night's earlier violence. He accessed the compartment hidden beneath the floorboard, the wood creaking softly as he pried it open.

Sam fastened the pancake holster and Sig Sauer P229 to the waistband at the small of his back, the leather cool against his skin. As he slid the weapon home, his body relaxed as if he'd just received a massage from the goddess

Rati—whose sensual, talented fingers caressed every knot, tense muscle, and electrified nerve. He felt fully dressed for the first time in months, the weight of the gun a familiar anchor. Letting out a long sigh of relief, he turned to the other items in the hidden compartment.

Shedding his torn, bloody shirt, he donned his Chameleon bodysuit—covering it with a pair of tactical pants and a clean shirt—then tucked his supplies into the various compartments in his waterproof, Kevlar-insulated backpack and hiked back to Polly's.

He tried the front door. Locked. Sam rapped his knuckles on the heavy oak, the sound echoing sharply in the quiet night. The door flew open.

Sam froze as he came face to face with the barrel of Polly's Beretta. Again. Clad in combat pants and a tech-hoodie, with her hair in a tight braid running down her neck, Polly held the gun in a two-handed grip, her finger on the trigger.

That's the third time today, Chet noted. *Either this is some severely twisted foreplay, or she's trying to tell you something.*

Polly took a deep breath, irritation crossing her face. She slowly lowered the weapon. "Are you trying to get yourself killed?"

"I knocked. How did you expect me to let you know I was here?"

Polly snorted. "It's like you want to see if I'll shoot you." She grabbed her bag from the floor, shouldered it, and pushed past him. "Come on. Let's go find that ship."

Sam followed. His disturbing conversation with Chet pinged in the back of his mind. Could it be he wasn't truly all in? He thought he was, but his inner conscience hadn't been harassing him for the sake of being an asshole. His job was to warn Sam of potential danger before Sam was aware of it.

Could his unstable relationship with The Agency be a symptom of a larger problem? He didn't think so, but he wouldn't want to go into battle with a soldier who had half their mind back home and half on the upcoming war. The intruder breaking into her house aside, until this point, he and Polly had been playing amateur detective. But this shit was about to get real. He either needed to bail or he had to fully dedicate himself.

Pushing aside his questions about The Agency and his future, Sam doubled his resolve as the distant waves crashing against the Cove's shore echoed in his ears, a haunting reminder of the perilous waters they were about to navigate. He was one hundred percent in on this mission and nothing else.

He had to be. The price of failure was more than not getting justice for a fallen Marine. It could cost both him and Polly their lives.

Chapter Sixteen

Slivers of moonlight sliced the sinister night clouds like an assassin's blade, casting an eerie glow that made Sam's skin prickle with unease. He gazed through the windshield of the boat, studying the undulating sea all around them. Slashes of lunar rays twinkled off the varnished ocean, glimmering as though molecularly infused with burnished obsidian. Incandescent froth, as white and fragile as tulle lace spun from spider's silk, edged the misting breakers. But the peaceful, sloshing waves proved to be a misleading subterfuge. Somewhere ahead of them, hidden in the lakes of darkness between moonbeams, floated a ship of murderous criminals with vicious savagery pumping through their veins and souls as black as crude oil.

Beside him, Polly kept the *Finders Keepers'* throttle pegged, driving the twenty-five-foot white powerboat over the unstable water. The hurricane-velocity wind, blasting around the edges and over the top of the front window, chafed Sam's cheeks and numbed his forehead—while the strain of gripping the rail sent a sharp twinge through his injured arm.

With a pointed bow and aerodynamic lines, the black-bellied *Finders* was everything Savannah had bragged it to be. Even with the additional weight of a jet ski mounted on its rear swim deck, the powerful inboard engine propelled the vessel's sleek hull, skimming across the waves.

The engines roared as they lost their grip on the disgruntled sea when the *Finders* sailed across a fissure and slapped dramatically on the opposite side. The storm that had delivered such epic surfing conditions on shore had also created canyon-deep crevasses and oceanic hills whose peaks sometimes stood as tall as the boat itself.

According to the GPS, they still had a little time before arriving at the random patch of ocean where Savannah had spotted the *Vengeance*, so Sam retrieved a pair of lined windbreakers from his bag, slipped one on and offered the second to Polly.

She shook her head, keeping her focus on what lay beyond the bow of the boat. "My suit's insulated," she shouted above the growling engines, the water shushing against the hull, and the whistling air.

So is mine. But evidently not as well as yours.

Fifteen minutes later, she eased off the gas, slowing the *Finders* to an easy canter.

After locking the steering wheel in place, Polly knelt and rifled through her bag.

Despite his best efforts to remain focused on the tasks ahead, Sam couldn't help but admire the way her black, skintight top and pants hugged her gentle curves. He'd heard through the grapevine Polly spent considerable time in the gym, working out and practicing Krav Maga. Based on the way her lean, limber muscles flexed beneath the fabric, he didn't doubt it.

Dude, Chet said, *this woman would rather put a bullet in your brain than go down that path with you.*

I have no intention of going down that or any other path with her. But you can't admonish a guy just for looking.

I see what you mean, Chet admitted, *but remember, you need to keep your head in the game. What's that old spy saying? You must first deal with the terror before you can have the fairer.*

No one says that. It barely makes sense.

Chet shrugged. *I just did. You can quote me. People might actually think you're smart.*

Polly pulled out a pair of binoculars, complete with a set of hands-free mounting straps. When she pulled the contraption over her head, she looked ready for a bird-watcher's expo.

Oblivious or not caring about her comedic aesthetic, she fussed with the focus and zoom buttons for a few minutes. Once satisfied with the settings, she flipped them up so they sat on top of her head and turned her attention to Sam. "We go dark from here on in. Sorry, I only have the one pair of binoculars. You'll be blind, but I'll give you a play-by-play of what's going on."

Sam unzipped his backpack and pulled out a pair of night vision goggles and a baseball cap. "No problem. I brought my own."

Polly scoffed. "I don't know what you think you'll be able to see with those crappy little opera glasses, but when I cut the lights, it's going to be pitch black. With the clouds rolling in, soon there won't even be moonlight. My binocs are infrared illuminated, thirty-two magnification with up to sixty-four digital enhancement, two-twenty FPS, ten-eighty P, and a four-hour memory chip."

"Huh," Sam replied. "I'm sorry you have to work with such outdated equipment. Mine are IR illuminated combined with thermal imaging, auto-focusing, one-twenty-eight digital enhancement, with radar overlay, and they are ATN capable, so they'll sync with my rifle scope. Also,"——he pretended to hide his smirk as slipped them on——"they're so light, I don't need special straps." The goggle frames, not much larger than a standard pair of eyeglasses, looped over his ears and connected to the compact circuitry neck band that held them snugly in place. "Unlike some people, I don't look like I'm wearing a giant jockstrap."

Polly huffed and cut the lights on the boat without comment. She revved the engines. After a few minutes, she yelled loud enough to be heard above the clamor of piston, cam, and water. "As long as we keep our distance, they won't be able to visually spot us, but this boat isn't exactly stealthy. They're going to hear us a mile away. Literally. And a ship that size is going to have radar. They'll know we're out here. Until we get too close though, I'm hoping they'll think we're just part of the offshore patrols. But if they smell a rat, they might do something drastic."

Sam leaned into her ear so she could hear him. "Then *drive casual*."

She glanced at him. "Casual?"

"Yeah, you know, like we're just out on a date or something. Just two lovers tooling around the Pacific. If you can make them believe we're on a romantic cruise, they might not get suspicious."

In the green glow of the infrared goggles, he watched her pinch her lips together in disapproval. "Seriously? That's your plan? '*Drive casual.*' It's almost two in the morning and forty degrees out. There are a dozen patrol boats cruising the shore, and we're running without lights."

Sam shrugged. "Maybe they'll think we're shy."

Polly turned her attention back to the ocean. A few minutes later, a small dot appeared on Sam's display. He pressed a button on the side of the goggles, zooming in. The image pixelated for a second as the internal computer worked. In the night's murk, a ship shaped like an upside-down cockroach materialized on the surface of the ocean.

He touched her shoulder. "Hold on."

She throttled back the engines. "I don't see anything."

"It's still a few miles away." He restarted the *Finders'* GPS and entered the coordinates reported by his goggles. An icon appeared on the map.

Sam hit a button on the side of the glasses, toggling the measurement system. "It's about two hundred feet long, with a ten-foot freeboard."

"Thirteen miles from the coast," Polly noted. She slipped her binoculars off to study the map. She pointed at the screen. "There's a knoll right there, which explains how they anchored offshore. Otherwise, the water's too deep."

"It's also conveniently just outside the US jurisdiction." He zoomed in with the goggles. Though magnified, the image provided no new clues as to the ship's identity. It might resemble the pictures Frank had taken, but differing perspectives and distance made connecting the two sets of prints difficult.

The ancient ship appeared to be more mystical apparition than man-made oceangoing vessel of steel and steam, its rusted hull swallowed by the creeping fog. It seemed to float through time and space, raised by a deity of unimaginable dark power from the bottom of the ocean after being sent to the murky depths on a wave of violence. The spirits of the long-dead captain and her crew timelessly manned the boilers, held vigil in the crow's nest, and steered the helm.

He shivered as a foreboding dread formed in the pit of his stomach. Pushing the sensation aside, he said, "There's no name on the hull. At least not on this side. Might be one on the other or on the stern."

After pulling her binoculars back on, Polly revved the engines, though not as hard as before, heading in the general direction of the ship. As they drew nearer, Sam scanned it from bow to stern, then sent a few pictures, including the boat's dimensions, to his and Polly's cells. He pulled out his phone and ran an image search, hoping to get an ID.

"It's not flying a country-of-origin flag," he noted. His cell buzzed. He glanced at the screen. "According to this, it could be one of a dozen classes of ships. From 1960s Russian icebreakers to Leninsky Komsomol cargo carriers to World War II patrol boats repurposed as fishing vessels. There are fleets and fleets of ships this could be. From this distance, they all more or less look the same. What kind of ship did the captain of Frank's boat, Levka something, have?"

"Belikov. Levka Belikov is the captain's name." She thought it over. "It was a Russian icebreaker. But I don't want to make any assumptions without facts to back them up. That leads to tunnel vision."

Interesting. Polly more or less had just quoted Rule #38 about assumptions being misleading. To her credit, that rule would be a valuable trait for an experienced detective. While Sam didn't disagree, at some point they would need to make some assumptions to help move them forward in the investigation.

"Regardless of what make it is," Polly said, "it's an old ship. My question is why the hell would anyone park a twentieth-century tub in the middle of the Pacific?"

Though he suspected they already knew the answer, he refrained from saying, "Stealing a body and committing murder." Instead, Sam followed her lead, trying to remain as impartial as possible. "Could be they're waiting for a rendezvous. Or maybe they're having mechanical problems. Something that old probably breaks down a lot."

He stared through his goggles. Sam's skin prickled as though the thickening, mystical fog enshrouding the boat wasn't fog at all, but the poisonous breath of the hydra who had accompanied the vessel's ascension from its grave beneath the frigid fathoms of the sea. Deep in his marrow, Sam sensed Death piloting the wheel from within the rusted bridge. It beckoned with long bony fingers to come aboard and join its eternal, toiling crew.

His heart gave a hard thump against his breastbone.

Suddenly exasperated with himself for letting his imagination run away, he took a deep breath and pushed aside the ridiculous images conjured up by the night and a little foul weather. Grateful Polly couldn't read his expression in the dark, he told her, "My gut says it's here for less-than-legal reasons and it's tied to Frank and the two dead men."

Polly shook her head. "I'm not surprised your other organs are giving your brain a badly needed assist, but I only work off *facts*. Investigation 101: Withhold drawing conclusions based on unsubstantiated information. We don't know this ship has anything to do with Frank, Trooper Lane, Phil, or the person who broke into my house. We also don't know if they've committed, or intend to commit, anything illegal. This is why we couldn't send in the Coast Guard. You need to learn to gather valid, indisputable evidence before making accusations."

Something a little too hot to be called irritation knifed through Sam's heart. She'd dismissed and lectured him like some rookie cop. Sam bit back a thousand sarcastic remarks. Arguing with his partner wouldn't further the case. It was no wonder she and the Boston PD had parted ways. A tongue that sharp could never be an ambassador for those tasked with the arduous responsibility of serving and protecting.

"You said there were lots of these types of ships, meaning there could still be a lot of them around," she continued her lecture. "It could have legitimate business out here. Whatever its original intentions, it may have been repurposed to haul cargo."

Though she'd said the words—the good detective trying not to draw conclusions without supporting evidence—Sam could hear in her voice she didn't believe any of it. Like his gut, Polly's instincts had already tried and convicted the crew of this vessel as murderous pirates. She just couldn't get past her legal upbringings to admit it.

Polly cut the engines and turned on the dome light. From this distance, the ship wouldn't be able to spot the weak illumination. Without momentum, their boat sank and rose in the rough swells, but they didn't dare get closer or risk being detected by the ship's radar.

"I don't see anyone moving," Polly commented as she stared at the two hundred-foot freighter. "But the fog's rolling in, so it could be hiding the heat signature of anyone aboard. There's a crate on the bow, and it's hard to tell for sure, but it looks like there might be one on the stern as well."

"That's consistent with the pictures Frank took."

"Perhaps. If it is the same ship, why didn't they put them in the hold? There's been a storm out at sea. You wouldn't want to risk losing valuable cargo. My guess is they're planning to offload them soon. The weather reports call for cloudy skies but no rain for the next few days, so they might have just found it easier to keep them topside."

It was a good point. It seemed unlikely they'd leave something like that to chance. "I don't see any weapons. Though I doubt they'd have them out in the open." The infrared had given him a headache. Sam turned off the goggles and dropped into the seat beside her. "Okay, here's what I'm thinking. I'll take the jet ski and go around to the far side of the ship to see if there are any markings——"

She folded back her goggles and held up her hand. "Hold on, Captain Nemo. First of all, we aren't going to risk them detecting us. This boat is loud. That jet ski will be even louder; plus the heat of the engine will light up their radar like a stick of dynamite. That thing's as subtle as a Nazi admiral in a Jewish deli."

Sam shook his head. "It's not a problem. The ski's electric. It'll run quiet, and if there's a heat signature at all, it'll be minimal."

Polly furrowed her brow. "How do you——"

"That"——Sam pointed to the stern——"has no exhaust system, and it's plugged into one of the boat's outlets. Noticed it when we came on board. Also, if their communication system is as old as we suspect, then their radar might be as well. In that case, the ski will be too small for it to pick up."

"It would be a risk to make such a wild assumption about the age of their gear, but I don't disagree that the electric ski would be more difficult for them to detect, no matter how modern their system is. Given that, what makes you think you're the one going out? This is my jurisdiction."

He refrained from reminding her they were thirteen miles off the US coast. They weren't in anyone's jurisdiction. Instead, he said, "True. But if we get caught, there's a potential for the owner—if they aren't who we think they are—to call in the Coast Guard."

"If they aren't who *you* think they are."

Sam ignored her and kept going. "Depending on what we're charged with, the crime could be considered a felony. For me,"——he shrugged——"I would only need a legal team to help me stay out of jail. But I don't have anyone or anything at risk. It would be just another black mark on my name. If you're caught and brought up on charges, you could lose your paramedic license and potentially your position within RU."

"Then we won't get caught. I'm more than capable of——"

"Yes, I know you are. But it isn't worth the risk."

She looked about to object, but he didn't give her the chance. "It's simple. I'll go around to the port side, see if there's a name, maybe get a few up-close pictures we can match to the ones Frank took, and be back in thirty minutes. No muss, no fuss."

She sighed resignedly. "Fine. But at the first sign of trouble, you need to bail. Legal issues aside, just because we can't see any weapons doesn't mean they don't have any. And if you're caught,"——she thumped his chest with her index finger——"I don't know you or why you came out here."

Nice.

"And don't forget that electric skis aren't silent, just quiet. They might still be able to hear you."

"I noticed a paddle mounted to the swim platform. I'll go in slow. If I get too close, I'll use it."

"You shouldn't get that close. We're over a mile away, and your super goggles seem to work just fine."

"Yeah, but not even my supers can see through fog. I might need to move in for shots of the bridge and bow."

Polly did not look pleased, but she also didn't argue.

He peeled off the jacket, shirt, and pants covering his bodysuit.

"Why did you wear a gray suit?" she asked. "Black would blend into the ocean and background better."

"It's a Chameleon."

"What? No. Those are just science fiction."

He smirked. "Not anymore. This is made of a copper-woven fabric that can change the color of the integrated pigments. Microsensors embedded along the sides, back, and front detect the patterns and colors around it and program the fabric to match. There's a flexible battery in the seams that powers it." He pointed at the thin lines running up the insides and outsides of his legs. "It can also be programmed to a single color." He pressed the end of a flexy controller on his arm. The suit changed from gray to black. "This way I'll match the ocean."

"That doesn't hide the jet ski," she pointed out. "It's white and bright blue and about as visible as a spotlight."

He nodded. "Yeah. I wish I had thought to bring the Chameleon blanket from my LA apartment. We could have covered most of the ski. But I think the fog will help hide it." Sam rummaged around in his backpack, dropping it to the deck when his search came up empty.

"What's the matter?"

"I can't find my gloves." He must have left them behind.

"Your hands are going to get pretty damned cold," she observed.

"Don't suppose you brought any extra?"

"What?" She mocked dismay. "You don't want my old-fashioned gloves. They don't have any specialized embedded wires and color-changing pigments."

"Fine. I can go without." He pulled the baseball cap with the affixed goggles back onto his head.

Polly tsked, reached into her bag, and pulled her gloves out. She slapped them against his chest.

He held them up, inspecting them. "These are——"

"My magnetic grippers." She retrieved something else from her bag and handed it to him. "You'll need the kneepads too."

Polly's gloves and accompanying kneepads—also known as geckos—would allow her to scale the vertical face of a metal wall. Such as the hull of a ship. "Were you planning to climb some metal mountains?"

"Unlike you, I came prepared. I didn't expect to have to board the ship, but you never know what could happen."

He arched a brow but made no comment.

"Be aware," she said, "the glove batteries last forty minutes, fifty tops. The pads are half that. Then you'll drop like a rock."

"Got it." He snapped a waterproof pouch around his waist and slid his Sig Sauer inside. After clipping his phone to the pack's embedded retractable cable—allowing him to use it while also keeping it attached to his body—he released the phone. The slim wire retracted into the micro, spring-loaded pulley, snugging the phone to a magnetic plate on his pouch. He slipped on Polly's gloves, which stretched to fit his hands, and pulled on the kneepads.

She gave him a radio with an earpiece, a twin of her own. They synced the frequencies and tested them out.

Returning to the stern of the boat, they pivoted the Taiga electric jet ski on its ramp and unwound the pulley holding it in place. While Polly finished sliding it into the water, Sam dug around in a nearby bin until he found a long rope.

Polly saw him winding it around his arm. "What do you need that for?"

"My father always taught me the number one rule of boating is to *always* have rope." He grabbed the paddle and climbed onto the bobbing ski, stowing his supplies in the front storage compartment. Even collapsed, the telescoping paddle—now the same length as a walking cane—proved too long for the cubby. He sat on the blade, leaving the handle sticking out behind him like a stiff tail.

Polly watched without comment, though he could practically feel her criticism.

The lump under his ass would get uncomfortable really quick, the paddle's edge digging into his thigh like a dull blade. Hopefully, he wouldn't need to leave it there for very long. Without a word, Sam gently twisted the throttle. The Taiga hummed softly beneath him as he gave Polly a sharp salute. He headed out into the foggy night, the ocean's icy breath wrapping around him like a shroud.

He was only going to snap some pictures of a ghost ship most certainly full of criminals and killers. Out in the middle of the ocean. At night. In low visibility. Alone.

What could go wrong?

Chapter Seventeen

Feeling like Charon—the mythological ferryman of the underworld who carried the souls of the recently deceased across the waters of Hades—Sam eased the jet ski through the dark fog, the motor humming quietly beneath him. The Pacific was as black as rotted flesh and exuded the same desolate aura as Acheron, the river of woe, its waves whispering mournful cries that echoed through the misty night. A shudder so deep it seemed to originate in the underworld traversed the cosmos and rattled through the marrow of Sam's bones. He shivered at its intensity.

In Sam's version of the Greek tale, the restless spirits—already trapped in a land of misery and pain—threw themselves again and again against the ocean's surface, seeking a freedom and mercy that would never be theirs. Their desperation, he imagined, caused the sea's violent undulations. As if the evening needed more drama, Charon was the son of Nyx, goddess of night, and Erebus, god of darkness. The kicker? That last name—Erebus—was also the name of the killer Sam had put in the ground three months earlier.

Normally skeptical of coincidences, Sam paused, wondering if the universe was trying to tell him something. If so, he'd received the message; he just didn't understand it. Warning, premonition, or a billboard flashing neon to hightail it back to dry ground? He didn't know.

Why did I insist on taking this mission?

Trying to keep his spinning mind from drawing any more parallels between ancient Greek mythology, doomed destinies, and his present situation, he kept the Taiga's pace slow and the perimeter wide so the ski would blend into the radar's white noise background. The sluggish cadence would keep the motor cool while his Chameleon suit hid his body heat, further camouflaging him from electronic surveillance.

While his plan had seemed logical and sound when he'd started, it had also given his imagination too much time to wander and misbehave. Needing a distraction, he checked the embedded micro watch on the cuff of his sleeve. Time to phone home. Sam pressed the radio's transponder button. "Checking in, Polly. I'm north of the bow."

Her voice came back in his earpiece. "You said thirty minutes. It's been over twenty, and you're telling me you haven't even reached the far side of the ship yet?"

"Negative. I'm exercising caution. Giving it an extra-wide berth and a low speed. Plus, visibility is limited."

Polly paused for a heartbeat. "Maybe we should abort and wait for better conditions?"

Could that be a note of concern in your voice? Surely not.

Sam had already considered postponing this leg of the mission. But as eerie as the night had become, the conditions actually proved ideal. The choppy ocean masked the slight whir of the ski's motor, and the thickening fog hid him from the prying eyes of any lookouts. He conveyed this to Polly.

"Understood. Keep me apprised and watch your six."

Despite her concern, he'd still expected some kind of disparaging remark. None came. Maybe in their short time apart, she'd realized just how fond she'd grown of him. Yeah, and maybe pigs could learn to fly if he handed them a pair of feathers.

At last, Sam came around to the far side of the vessel. The soupy fog curtained the ship in an impenetrable white mist, obscuring the name on the hull, if one existed at all. Needing to get closer, Sam revved the throttle. He tried to ignore how the whine of the ski's motor sounded like the scream of a tortured spirit. He now understood how sailors of the past came home with fantastic tales of monsters and ghosts. An hour of isolation, mystical fog, and a moonless night had sent his imagination on a drug trip as crazy and full of twists as Alice's journey through Wonderland. He couldn't fathom being alone for months at sea, in uncharted waters, with little to no understanding of the science behind tides, nighttime lights, and the weather.

A quarter mile off the ship's bow, he still couldn't see its hull. Someone might very well be able to hear him no matter how quietly the ski whispered. Sam cut the motor and pulled the paddle out from under his butt, wincing as the icy ocean spray stung his face. After extending the handle, he dug into the water.

The rough ocean fought him like a contender for the MMA title, yanking him back and forth, tossing him around like a rag doll. He felt like a bull rider going for the gold buckle. His pulse pounded in his ears, and his limbs trembled from the effort. In his night vision goggles, the ship remained stubbornly distant, its silhouette a faint green ghost in the swirling mist. Despite his efforts, it seemed to drift even farther away. Sam paddled harder, his breaths coming in ragged gasps. As he battled the current, he couldn't help but wonder: with humankind's ability to drive buggies across the surface of Mars and deliver piping hot pizza to his door in under thirty minutes, why hadn't they invented a pair of lenses that could see through fog?

He would have to talk to Josha about this oversight.

Provided The Agency hasn't put a hit on you, Chet said. *In which case, griping about how your night vision goggles came up short during an unsanctioned operation is kind of a moot point.*

Yeah, well. There's that. If you'll recall, I got his blessing to help Polly.

I think you know this goes way beyond the spirit of his permission.

He did know.

At last, the ship materialized from the mist. No name broke the monotonous black surface of its rust-spotted hull. He snapped a couple of photos with the goggles, then clicked the radio button, whispering into the microphone. "I'm here."

"It's about time. I was starting to think you'd decided to go on a cruise or something. Sitrep."

"Everything's quiet. I practically had to drive up the ship's ass to see through this fog, though."

"And?"

"Nothing. The hull's blank."

Polly cursed. "Alright. Come back in. We'll regroup and make a new plan."

Sam stared at the ship for a full minute.

"Bradford? You hear me?"

"Yes," he said quietly, "I read you. And that's a negatory on returning."

"What do you mean?"

"I mean, I came all this way. The crew's asleep. I'm going aboard to gather intel."

"Um, no. You're not. I'm ordering you to return to the *Finders*. Immediately."

Sam almost laughed. "Well, in case you've forgotten, you're not my CO. I'm a volunteer. I work for me."

"Then your commanding officer is a fool," she bit back. "A fool who's going to get you killed. You need to return. Now."

"I will...right after I get the information we need."

In the resulting silence, Sam imagined Polly sitting in the captain's seat, swearing a blue streak.

She came back over the earpiece. "According to the images you sent to me, the ship's got a ten-foot freeboard at its lowest point. From the waterline to the top of the railing along the bow, it's more like seventeen feet. There are no embedded ladders on this side of that tub, so unless there's one on your side, how did you plan to climb a vertical wall of steel?"

"You gave me your climbing gloves."

"To keep your hands warm! Jesus. That's the last time I do anything nice for you."

"I also brought my rappelling gear."

"Of course you did. Might I remind you that you're on a jet ski and in rough waters. Successfully connecting to a moving ship from that position is a million-to-one shot."

During the war, he and his men had been forced to scale buildings in enemy territory. While both the climber and the structure remained stationary—unlike the jet ski he rode or the ship bobbing in the ocean—the Marines still had to stay alert for IEDs, snipers, and a host of extremists trying to stop them. "I've been in worse conditions. At least no one's shooting at me."

"Not yet," she scoffed.

She's got a point, Sparky, Chet said.

Sam didn't reply to his inner conscience. "Going silent. Will radio when I'm aboard."

"Ten-four," Polly said dejectedly.

He stared straight up at the side of the ship. In the images he'd taken earlier, ten feet from the waterline to rail hadn't seemed far. But from this vantage point, he seemed to be staring at the side of a skyscraper. To add that extra spice he loved so much, paddling the last quarter-mile had been a lot harder than he'd expected. His back ached, and his arms felt like rubber. The wound on his arm, where he'd been shot, throbbed. Polly was right; this was going to be tough.

Sam retrieved the grappler launcher from his backpack. After strapping it to his arm and attaching it to the body harness he wore under the suit, he pulled the rope from the ski's cubby and looped one end around the Taiga's handlebars, the other around his fanny pack. He would tie it off on the ship to keep the jet ski from drifting away.

He'd been about to take aim when a large wave smashed into the ski, pushing it into the side of the ship. Sam's heart leapt as he stuck out his hands, shoving back as hard as could. The ski scraped against the *Vengeance's* steel hull with a grating screech. Grabbing the paddle, he forced the Taiga away from the ship, his chest tight with the realization of just how close he'd come to biting it.

When he arrived at what seemed a safe enough distance, he stowed the paddle, gave his body a minute to rest, and took several deep breaths to calm his hammering heart. The jet ski bobbed up and down in the heavy chop, dipping into deep troughs and riding high on peaks.

Had he crashed into the side of the *Vengeance*, the jet ski could have been destroyed or him killed. Sam reconsidered following Polly's advice and returning when the conditions were less volatile.

Except that opportunity might not come.

Josha could pull him from the mission. Or the Mafiya might decide, with the murders and the police and the patrols, that things had gotten too hot and weigh anchor. By this time tomorrow, they could be halfway to Nicaragua. This might be Sam's only chance to find Frank's killer and get justice for the death of a fellow Marine.

Retreating was not an option. He had to push forward.

As he stared at the mist-shrouded ship, it occurred to him he might have trouble returning to the Taiga after he'd gathered the intel. As was so often the case with his missions, he'd have to deal with that problem when the time came.

Trying to coordinate his shot with the rise and fall of the ski, he aimed the launcher at the railing and hit the trigger. The grappler flew. It pinged off the ship's hull with a loud *clang* and plopped into the water. Sam cringed so hard his butthole puckered. He reeled in the line, alert for the scream of an alarm or the shouting of guards. When all remained quiet, he raised the launcher again, this time aiming higher.

He hit the release button.

The grappler sailed off into the night sky and onto the deck of the ship. Sam yanked back. It caught.

Ha! Million-to-one shot! Too bad you weren't here to see it, Polly.

Keeping the tension on the cable, he toggled the retractor. In a sudden jolt of momentum, he flew off the ski—the harness biting into his ass and thighs. If he survived the night, he'd probably have harness-shaped bruises all over his butt and legs in the morning.

With the velocity of a suicidal fighter jet, Sam sailed through the misty air. As he closed in, he reached out and caught the rail. Rusted metal bit into his gloved palms as he absorbed the impact, narrowly avoiding a collision with the vessel's hull. Feet planted, gecko gloves gripping the cold, slick steel, he clung to the side of the ship. The distant creak of the vessel's frame echoed through the night as he waited, once more, for the cry of alarm.

Nothing.

Peeking over the rail, he scanned the deck. Only the rolling fog awaited him.

He pulled himself up and slipped over the railing. As he silently landed on the balls of his feet, Sam removed the gloves and retrieved his Sig Sauer from the pouch, while crouching low to blend into the shadows. He touched the radio's transmit button. "I'm on board," he whispered. "Still no movement."

"Try not to get killed," Polly replied. "I already have enough paperwork to do."

"Nice."

"Can you tell, based on Frank's pictures, if this is the *Vengeance?*"

Sam studied the bridge, double-stairwell, and bow. Though he felt certain they had found the right ship, he wanted time to explore. "Maybe. It's hard to know for sure. There are a lot of these boats, and Frank wasn't exactly Annie Leibovitz."

"Okay. Get what we need and get out," Polly instructed.

"Will do. Sam out."

He tied the ski's rope to a deck cleat. He'd been about to run to the bridge when a sharp crack split the night. Sam dropped and rolled. He came up, kneeling behind a crane, certain someone had shot at him. But the lights remained dark, and no voices broke the shushing sea.

Another crack resounded—sharper this time—slicing through the air. He recognized the sound: fiberglass against steel. Returning to the railing, he peeked over the side, his night vision goggles casting the scene in a sickly green glow. The Taiga's white hull battered against the ship's rusted belly. Though he'd paddled a fair distance away, the ocean must have pushed the jet ski back. Tossed by rough waves, the two vessels smacked together in a steady cadence. From his position, it sounded loud.

Well, that's less than optimal, Chet remarked.

Hopefully, distance and the hull will muffle the noise.

Hope? Chet scoffed. *That's your plan? It'll work, unless a patrol comes around to this part of the ship, or you're spotted by a lookout, or a thousand other possibilities.*

Well, there's nothing I can do about it.

Except leave. This doesn't need to be a one-man show.

Polly doesn't want to call the Coast Guard or anyone else.

His inner conscience gave him a "You've got to be kidding" look. *You understand that she doesn't have a monopoly on using the phone to call in the cavalry. Last I checked, yours worked just fine.*

Look, you've been pushing me to get back into the game. To protect the country I swore an oath to protect. This is what that looks like.

Chet sighed but made no reply.

Sam took a deep breath. Time to enter the Lion's den.

Chapter Eighteen

North of the cargo cover, at the tip of the bow, a chin-high crate had been strapped to the deck. According to Frank's images, there should have been twin boxes mounted on the back corners of the squared-off stern. The roiling mist shrouded the rear of the ship like a curtain of tarlatan lace, preventing Sam from confirming their positions. He considered skipping the unmarked pine box and heading straight for the bridge, but instinct prodded him to take a closer look.

He moved behind it and squatted, hoping it would hide him from anyone looking down from the bridge. After disabling the infrared of his goggles, he snapped on its mini lamps. A pair of LEDs no larger than pen lights but as focused as space lasers shone from either side of his lenses.

The sun and salt air had bleached the box's wooden surface to the color and porousness of old bone. Though ropes crisscrossed the sides and top, the hemp proved to be ornamental. The varying short lengths of gray, ragged braids served only to mislead onlookers into believing the container had been lashed to the deck. In reality, a series of brackets and bolts anchored its wooden base to the steel floor. A heavy, rusted padlock, secured to a clasp, prevented a hinged side panel from opening.

Despite its appearance, this was a permanent fixture. A Trojan horse, whose clever camouflage probably hid a cache of weaponry no less deadly than a secret Greek army. He had seen similar cargo containers during the war. The crates' strategic positions on the bow and stern allowed the crew—who might only have minutes to arm themselves—quick access to munitions in the event of a boarding.

Sam snapped a few pictures with the goggles, then stood back, mentally calculating how much weaponry a container of this size could hold. He didn't like the results of his back-of-the-napkin math.

Suddenly, it didn't seem so ridiculous that Polly had refused to send her people to investigate. If RU had attempted to board, they may have been cut down in a hailstorm of bullets, their simple search turned into a bloodbath. Even the Coast Guard might struggle against determined, well-armed men.

Sam glanced around. Ships with hidden caches of guns never left their flanks unprotected or their perimeters unpatrolled. No matter how quiet things appeared, shoot-first-ask-questions-later security prowled the decks. Somewhere. So far, he hadn't bumped into anyone, but his fortune could change in a blip. Eventually, they'd notice him, and if his suspicions proved correct, he'd be outgunned and outmanned. He needed to get to the bridge, get the intel, and get out.

Sam was about to snap off the goggle's micro lights when Chet spoke up. *Wait. You need to look inside.*

No. I need to get moving, Sam replied, glancing around for signs of life. The soupy fog rolling across the deck made detecting movement difficult.

I disagree. As long as you're careful, you have time. There's probably only a single guard on patrol. I believe most of the crew is asleep. Note the keyword "most."

This is important. Anyone not involved in security will be below deck. Down in engineering and maintenance. Stay out of the engine and subsystem rooms, and you should be fine.

Sam almost ignored Chet's advice, but his gut had saved his ass too many times to doubt it now. He ran his hand along the box's seams. Recessed handles held the top and sides together. He unlatched the ones securing the side panel, but the clasp and heavy bolt kept it from opening.

Electrified nerves twinging and muscles tense, Sam tucked his Sig Sauer into the pack on his waist and pulled out the pick kit, his breath fogging faintly in the cool night air. Inserting the rake and tension wrenches into the lock's keyhole, he worked its tumblers while keeping his ear attuned for predators lurking in the night. He tuned out the splash of the ocean and the repetitive knocking of the jet ski against the hull—damn, was it loud—focusing instead on any telltale rustling of a guard: the clearing of someone's throat, shuffling of boots on the steel deck, the cocking of a gun...

The simple lock should have been easy, but its metal bearings suffered from element exposure. Rusted stiff, the mechanisms resisted his efforts. Despite the cold and

Chet's assurance he had time, beads of sweat peppered Sam's face as he pushed, pulled, and raked the lock's pins.

He wished like hell he could draw his gun and blast the bloody thing to bits. Except, of course, the satisfying shot would have every member of the crew up his ass in about two seconds. He could use the silencer. However, the decimated lock would evidence his transgressions. Sam embraced the old outdoor enthusiasts' adage about leaving no trace. A practice that had saved his bacon more than once.

At last, with an irritated, rusted grumble, the ancient tumblers relented. The shackle popped open. He removed the lock. Hinges creaked as he lowered the box's side.

Sonofabitch.

Ordinarily, the alluring aroma of lubricating oil and gunpowder would have delighted him the way another man might savor the smell of fresh-baked bread. But he barely noticed the divine scent—his eyes were locked on the crate's contents. The waterproof-lined box held a militia's worth of AK-47s, flares, rocket-propelled grenades, ammunition, and even a tool kit.

But these were merely the potatoes and carrots to the main course. Bolted to the steel deck stood a 25mm autocannon, mounted on a collapsible, pivoting tripod—its chipped and worn barrel glinted ominously in the LED light. He didn't recognize the identification markings, but it looked like a variant of the US military's Bushmaster M242, a heavy-duty weapon used by the Navy, Marines, and Army in both defensive and offensive combat operations.

Now Sam understood what his subconscious had wanted him to see. A chill of dread snaked down his spine as he imagined the carnage this beast could unleash.

Though old, the gun had a clean, well-maintained assembly and barrel. It still looked like it could kick some serious ass. A stack of armor-piercing thirty-round belts stood next to a set of high-explosive round belts. With a range of over four miles, this cannon could decimate a boat the size of the *Finders* in about ten seconds.

Depending on where the ship traveled, certain parts of the world might warrant such powerful armaments as protection against pirates, mercenaries, and kidnappers. Possession of heavy artillery like this was illegal in most countries; though in some nations, inspectors could be paid to look the other way. That didn't fly in the United States. If this ship came within twelve miles of the US coastline, it would be subject to boarding and inspections. The weapons would be confiscated, and the crew arrested.

Sam had seen cheap AK knockoffs in Afghanistan, but these appeared to be the legit, more-expensive Kalashnikovs—terrorists' worldwide first choice for bulk murder. Unfortunately, the black market brimmed with the reliable, Russian-made automatic weapons. Anyone with the scratch could arm themselves with enough firepower to level a city the size of the Cove in an afternoon.

He picked up a gun, pulled the magazine, and inspected the well-oiled and maintained bolt and barrel. To keep them in proper working order, they would have to be serviced regularly. He snapped the full magazine back into the receiver. The stockpile of these Russian-made autos didn't prove the ship came from overseas, but if the owners had been western-based, they most likely would have had a cache of US AR-15s instead.

Sam snapped several photos with his goggles.

Though he and Polly had been thinking Russian Mafiya, this ship and her crew could still be Somalian, Indonesian, or even Nigerian pirates. Except, criminals from that part of the world rarely wandered this far north in the Pacific. Since the ship was parked off the US coast, they were likely drug or contraband runners.

This vessel—large enough to carry a profitable volume, but small enough to avoid classification as a cargo ship and thus evade maritime laws and regulations—could stop at ports that gave it favorable inspection reports for a few bucks. They could fill their holds to the brim, then transfer their wares for import into the US.

Methodically, Sam dropped the AK-47s and RPGs over the rail, the splash of their descent swallowed by the ocean's restless growl. He almost did the same with the flare gun, but at the last second changed his mind, tucking it into his pouch instead. He opened the ancient toolbox and picked through the rusted contents until he found a screwdriver of just the right size.

Sam shoved the business end into the muzzle of the autocannon and, as quietly as possible, tapped it deep into the barrel with a hammer. Each muffled strike sent a micro-jolt of adrenaline through his nerves as he braced for an alarm. He sat back and checked his handiwork. Without a thorough inspection, it would be impossible to see the blockage.

Whoever fired this gun was in for a very unpleasant surprise.

It turned out he'd be leaving a trace after all.

He closed and locked the crate. After retrieving his Sig Sauer, he turned off the LEDs and re-enabled the goggles. Sam hit the radio's transmit button. "There's a deck-mounted machine gun on the bow of the ship. High probability there are two more on the stern."

"What are you talking about? We scanned it and——" She broke off. Sam could almost hear the mental pieces fall into place as Polly made the connection. "The crates," she said after a pregnant pause.

"Right."

"You opened one?"

He relayed to her what he'd discovered, though failed to disclose that he'd committed sabotage or that the AKs and RPGs now rested on the sandy bottom of the Pacific. His impromptu plans tended to piss her off, and he didn't want her distracted.

"Remember," she said, "this is a covert op. In and out. No one knows we were there. Don't *mess* with anything."

Oops.

"Headed to the bridge," he said.

"Okay. If something happens, abort. If you think I'm going to turn over my coffee money as ransom to some pirate, you're delusional."

Nice.

"See if you can figure out the origin of the ship," she said unnecessarily. "Where do they call home? You're also trying to find evidence of Frank having been there. But while you're looking, see who they've met up with and what they're carrying. Also, see if there's something on the navigation system that says where they've been. But do not take any unnecessary risks. Copy?"

Maybe I missed something, but every part of your plan sounds risky. Instead of pointing out the contradiction, he replied, "Copy. Going silent."

She's a serious micromanager, he said to Chet. *It's kind of annoying.*

It's because she smells the incompetence on you. The stench is as rank as a dead rat in a hot outhouse.

Thanks for your keen observations, but I think it's just the way she communicates.

If it makes you feel better, go ahead and believe that. Someone as incapable as you must rely on all sorts of rationalizations to justify your ineptitude.

Sam dropped the subject. He needed to focus.

In a half crouch, he made his way to the deckhouse. Flattening himself against the side of the building, he sidled along the wall. Twin stairwells ran up each side of the structure, leading to the bridge on the third level. As lithe and quiet as a ballet dancer, he took the stairs, which were slick with condensation. When he reached the top platform, he ducked under the side window, crouching next to the door. He tried the handle. It turned with a soft squeak.

Sam pulled open the door and slipped inside. Waving the gun in each direction, he searched for a target. Other than the muffled protest of ancient steel as the ocean stressed the ship's superstructure, the vestibule was as silent as a crypt.

A pair of doors on either side of the bridge led to the external stairwells. An interior entrance probably led to the crew's quarters. A front wall of windows overlooked the bow. The old, wavy glass—its perimeter coated in grime—must have been extra thick to handle the stresses put on it by decades at sea. He might be able to shoot his way through it if he had to, but it would likely take several shots. Time he wouldn't have if he needed to make a quick escape. The only practical ways in or out were the doors.

He stared down at the deck three stories below. The ship appeared to be drifting through a sea of clouds. If he hadn't snuck on board in search of information about illegal activities ranging from smuggling to murder—and if there weren't guards that could come and slice him down in a barrage of hot bullets—Sam may have found the scene peaceful. Serene even.

He tore his attention away from the misleadingly calm vision to focus on the task at hand.

The bridge reminded him of an old, abandoned car he'd used for several days as part of a stakeout. Left to rot in a forgotten alleyway, mold had permeated the ancient Pontiac's foam rubber; fungus and stale water clogged the ventilation system and coated the floor; and dirty oil leaked through the rusted fire wall and dripped into the cabin. All these years later, Sam could still smell that car as he baked inside during a series of unseasonably hot Chicago afternoons.

The bridge might have been perfumed with what he'd coined Ode to Derelict Pontiac, with a dash of dead sea creatures thrown in for spice. If he could harness this aroma and bottle it, he might make a fortune selling it on Fifth Avenue to bored housewives with too much time and too much money.

In the center of the bridge stood a large steering wheel mounted on a dashboard dotted with dials, buttons, and readouts that might have been new in 1955. The labels, all in Cyrillic, could have been Russian, Ukrainian, or maybe even Czech. Sam couldn't tell the difference. A decanter of clear liquid sat on the dinner plate–sized compass next to the steering wheel. He removed the stopper and sniffed. Vodka.

The grungy dashboard was a wasteland of rusted switches, filthy dials, and waterlogged gauges. A subset of levers that must control functioning parts of the ship had been wiped clean.

Mounted on the surface of the dash sat a mid-1980's computer. When he tapped the screen, a circular display flashed to life. Radar. A series of yellow dots glowed alongside the mainland. More advanced systems kept a few hours of recordings and sometimes included integrated navigation. From what Sam could tell, this archaic piece of hardware simply displayed surrounding watercraft. On the screen, a nearby dot floated by itself. Though not an expert in reading radar displays, he recognized Polly and the *Finders*.

That's not going to do. Not at all.

He pulled out his pocketknife and sliced through the computer's cable. The screen flashed and then went dark. Nothing else on the bridge looked as though it had been built in the last five decades. Without navigation, the captain would have to manually calculate their position and route. Unfortunately, no electronic records logging their destinations and who they met with meant prosecuting them in any court of law would be a challenge.

Next to the far door sat a long desk. Sam sorted through the random piles of papers covering its marred surface. The night vision goggles were great for viewing things far away, but close-up reading in a dark room was murky at best. He squinted, trying to decipher what looked like an odd mix of Russian and English. It seemed unlikely they'd have kept records of drug, weapons, or contraband transfers, but maybe a clue lay in the jumble of sloppy handwriting floating in a letter soup of languages.

Worried that any recording made by the goggles would be blurry and indecipherable, Sam pulled his phone off the pouch's magnetic plate, the micro pulley system whispering the faintest of whines as it fed out the hair-thin attached wire. He quickly documented the pages. Using optical magnification and large sensors, the cell's camera amplified light the way the infrared goggles could only dream of. Hopefully, the images would be clear enough to read.

The paper, stiff from years at sea, crinkled as loud as a brass band in the quiet space. Each page flip sent a small electric shock traveling down his spine. After he finished, he sent the files to Polly and uploaded encrypted copies to a personal folder in the cloud. It wouldn't hide the documents forever from the prying eyes of The Agency, but it would buy him some time before he had to decide if he'd share them with Josha.

He then cleared the photos and stuck the phone back on the pouch's plate. If something happened and his cell ended up in the wrong hands, he didn't want anyone to know what he'd been up to.

Polly's quiet voice came over the headset. "The ship's Russian."

He hit the transmit button and whispered, "Is it? I couldn't tell. I'm not up to date on Cyrillic writing. You?"

"Besides English, I speak three languages. Unfortunately, this isn't one of them. But I know enough to generally distinguish between some of the Slovak-based dialects. I can't translate it, but I believe this is a mix of Russian and English."

The more he learned about her, the more the diversity of her background and her wide breadth of knowledge impressed him. Given her propensity to swear in Italian, he'd assumed she'd either taken some language classes in school, or maybe someone had taught her the fine art of international blasphemy. Given this new information, he reassessed that assumption.

Why hadn't the documents supplied by Josha mentioned her multilingual fluency? If they lacked something so fundamental, what else had The Agency either missed or chosen to withhold from him? And, more importantly, why?

"Bradford," Polly said through the earpiece, interrupting his thoughts. "There's a binder on the corner of the desk. Can you get a better image of it?"

He found the one she meant. It had Cyrillic lettering stamped on the front in a faded black font. He sent a picture of it to her.

"I don't know this word," he whispered.

A few seconds ticked by. Then Polly's voice returned, low and uneasy. "Jesus."

"What?"

"The word is *vozmezdiye*. It means *vengeance* in Russian."

A beat.

"Bradford... you found the ghost ship."

He glanced around. "Looks pretty damned not-sunk for a boat that's supposedly at the bottom of the Baltic."

"Anything to indicate where they'd been or what they'd been up to?" she asked.

Beneath the stacks of papers, Sam found some navigation charts so old, they might have been sketched by Magellan. He wanted to turn on a light to read them but didn't dare take the chance. There didn't appear to be anything relevant, but he scanned them with his phone anyway.

After once more sending the images to both Polly and the cloud then deleting the files, he looked around for anything else that might provide clues as to what sort of shenanigans—besides murdering an undercover police detective—the crew had been up to. He'd already ruled out the radar, and the radio looked as though it hadn't been serviceable in years. Without the proper equipment, how would an ancient chum bucket like this one rendezvous with a modern ship?

On a hunch, Sam went out the side door, returning to the stair landing. He gazed up. Through the drifting fog, he could just make out a tower mounted to the mast. It looked newer than the hodgepodge of rusted bits of metal sticking out every which way. There had to be a port that allowed something to be plugged into the antenna.

He went back inside, the door hinges squawking as he slipped through. Sam scanned the console but found nothing. A thick, grime-coated cord ran along the base of the compass. The cord's plug dangled—whatever it had been connected to was gone. Getting to his knees, he traced it to the bottom of the console.

The night goggles blurred the details. Sam was about to click on the penlights when the soft clomp of footsteps echoed on the stairs.

Sam froze, catching his breath.

The steps drew nearer.

Outside the door, he heard the unmistakable cocking of a rifle, followed by the squeak of unoiled hinges as the door creaked open.

Time had just run out.

Chapter Nineteen

The guard didn't turn on the lights, leaving the bridge draped in shadows. He paused just inside the door, waiting. Only the groan of the ship's hull under the ocean's pressure and the rasp of his labored breathing broke the tense stillness.

From half beneath the console, the icy metal floor biting into his shoulder, Sam could see a pair of feet in heavy boots outlined in the goggles' infrared. The ship's wheel and the waist-high compass with the decanter on top were all that lay between him and the guard.

Quietly, Sam unzipped his pouch and withdrew the Sig Sauer. He didn't want to kill this man—who, as far as he knew, had just been on patrol. A low-level lackey, conceivably an innocent deckhand, forced to take the late shift no one else wanted.

Someone—perhaps this guard, perhaps someone else—had killed Frank. If this man had committed that murder, Sam would deal with him in due time. But he shouldn't have to die simply for doing his job and stumbling across a trespasser.

Regrettably for him though, Sam wouldn't allow himself to be captured. Hopefully, he could just disable the man and slip out. Otherwise, Sam would do what he had to do to survive.

Silent as a spider, he moved out from beneath the console. Sam rolled up into a deep crouch, careful to keep low behind the steering column.

The infrared goggles blurred the man's outline, but Sam estimated him to be about six feet tall, two hundred ten pounds. Not huge, but big enough. The guard held an AK-47 at the ready as he swept his gaze back and forth.

Despite the guard's heavier firepower, Sam had the tactical advantage of surprise. And since the guard wore no night vision gear, he'd be nearly blind. If he could be dropped quietly enough, Sam might be able to slip from the bridge and make his escape. He pulled out a miniature flashlight, turning the dial to maximum. If LEDs were a gun, this one would be a .44 Magnum.

Sam laid the light on the dinner plate-sized compass. He disabled the infrared goggles and slipped them into the pouch. In one swift motion, he hit the on switch. The tiny but mighty army of LEDs flared to life like a sun gone supernova. Sam flew around the compass and helm in a half crouch.

The beam of light struck the guard in the face. Sam glimpsed shoulder-length dreadlocks and a long beard. As the man reflexively raised a hand to shield his eyes, he also raised the AK-47 and pulled the trigger. The deafening blast of automatic weapon fire echoed in the confined space like containerized cracks of thunder.

Bullets whizzed and ricocheted off the steel walls and ceiling. The decanter exploded in a spray of glass and vodka.

Using the ear-splitting cacophony as cover, Sam sailed across the floor. He leapt, driving his shoulder into the man's ribcage with a bone-jarring thud, knocking the sputtering AK aside. Despite the guard's slim outline in the goggles, his body felt as beefy and immovable as a tractor.

They dropped in a heap, Sam's body slamming against the unforgiving steel floor.

An alarm blared, its shrill wail piercing the night. Deck lights blazed to life, bathing the world outside the bridge in a yellowish glow——as though the sun had made an early showing.

Shit's about to get real.

Before the guard could get his bearings, Sam landed a blow to the man's nose. He pulled back for another punch, but the guard released the AK and caught Sam's fist with a vise-strong hand.

Disregarding his merciful plan of disablement, Sam aimed the Sig at the man's head.

Either sensing his impending demise or attempting to gain the advantage, the guard rolled to the side.

Sam's shot went wide. The bullet pinged off the metal floor.

With the adrenaline-infused strength of someone fighting for his life, the guard yanked Sam by the neck, pulling him down instead of pushing him away. The men flattened against one another like lovers in the night; the Sig pinned between them.

Sam brought his forehead forward, smashing the man's nose.

The guard grunted, his breath a tornado stench of half-digested vodka. His fingers slipped off Sam's neck.

Sam brought the Sig up toward the guy's chin, determined to finish this and get the hell off the ship. The countdown until reinforcements arrived had started the second this goon pulled the AK's trigger. Though he couldn't hear the crew's approach over the blaring alarm, he knew they would arrive shortly and in great numbers. As Sam slid the gun barrel toward the man's head, the guard grabbed his hand and forced it to the side.

Shit.

With one hand, the guard pinched Sam's throat once more while smashing the Sig over and over against the floor with the other. Sam's fingers popped open. The weapon skittered off into the shadows.

Sam pulled back his fist and smashed the guard's face. Once. Twice. On the third blow, the guard's stranglehold on Sam's esophagus loosened. He continued raining down punches until the goon, at last, went limp.

Shaking and out of breath, Sam got to his feet. Knees rubbery, he leaned against the shard-covered compass for support while his heart thundered in his chest. His throat felt as if he'd swallowed a handful of Legos. He needed to find his gun and get off this tub.

But over the screaming alarm, he could make out rattling footsteps on the internal stairwell. He was about to have company.

Sam bolted for the side entrance. As he yanked back the knob, the interior door slammed open.

A gun cocked.

Sam ducked.

The window above his head exploded. Another shot ricocheted off the steel wall, striking the huge bridge window. Though the glass had been designed to withstand the harsh punishment of life at sea, it hadn't been designed to absorb the kinetic energy of a slug traveling at Mach 2. The reinforced safety glass spiderwebbed as the bullet ripped through it.

Sam stumbled outside, pulling the door closed behind him.

Inside, boot steps pounded as their owner gave chase.

Sam yanked the 9mm Glock from his ankle holster and shot the lock. The handle erupted in a twisted mess of metal.

A loud thump inside the bridge echoed as his pursuer hit the floor.

Sam fired two more rounds through the broken window, encouraging whoever lay inside to stay put. He moved beside the door, waiting to see if the guy would give chase. If he let this thug get behind him, the gunman would cut him down before Sam could hide. But he also couldn't afford to stand out on the platform all night in full view of anyone on the deck. More goons were coming. Plus, he didn't have many bullets left. He needed to disable the bridge guy and get off the platform before someone spotted him.

Sam unzipped his pouch, pulled out the flare gun he'd taken from the crate on the bow, and fired through the window. The flare ignited in a blinding crimson streak.

He tossed the gun, turned, and raced down the stairs, leaping over the last five treads to the deck as the bridge bloomed into fiery life behind him. Smoke billowed from the open window, and someone screamed in anger.

Sam could have sprinted to the bow and the waiting jet ski, but that would've left his flank exposed to anyone rushing to aid the roasting goon. The fog might conceal him, but even firing blind, the gunmen would let loose with their AKs. Brute force and bad luck would be Sam's downfall.

At the top of the stairs, the door rattled as the man on the bridge, coughing and sputtering, tried to exit. But the handle's mechanism had been too damaged to function. Cursing, he gave up and moved inside, undoubtedly heading to the second external stairwell.

Sam slipped around the rear corner of the deckhouse, pressing up against the back wall. He considered blasting the man as he exited the bridge, but even with the extended magazine, the Glock only had four bullets left. Pissed that Sam had tried to sauté him, the guy chasing him carried a grudge, an automatic weapon, and probably several extra ammo clips.

Somewhere nearby, unoiled hinges squeaked. Not the bridge door, that was too far away and inoperable. Something at the deck level. Someone else had joined the fun.

He'd been formulating a plan when Polly's voice squawked through the earpiece, startling him so badly he almost squeezed the Glock's trigger. "Bradford!

What's going on? The ship's lit up like it's in a fucking Christmas parade."

He didn't dare reply and give away his position. He crouch-ran to the opposite side of the cabin and peered around the corner. Through the fog, he caught a brief glimpse of the bridge guard descending the stairs. The man sported red, scraggly, unwashed hair tied in a ponytail. Smoke drifted off his burnt clothes. He waved the AK's barrel back and forth, while his rage-filled, watery eyes searched for a target.

With Red on the left and at least one man on the right——both headed in his direction——Sam had seconds before being discovered. A dozen plans cycled through his mind as he sought options.

An AK's magazine typically contained thirty bullets and could unleash volleys of ten rounds a second. With four bullets left, Sam could catch one of the guys unaware. But their buddies would be alerted and come guns blazing. The overwhelming difference in firepower did not make for a hopeful situation.

He needed to hide, but he had nowhere to go. Except up.

He unzipped his pouch, slid the Glock inside, and slipped on Polly's gecko gloves. He pulled the mask down, covering his face, then pressed the integrated power button on the Chameleon bodysuit. If this didn't work, he'd have to come up with a Plan B real quick...assuming he survived long enough.

He faced the wall. He'd been about to start climbing when Polly's voice blared over the earpiece again. "Bradford! Report in!" He snapped off the radio. The men probably wouldn't be able to hear her even if she kept yelling, but he didn't want to take the chance. Besides, he needed to concentrate, and he couldn't do that with her babbling at him. The sitrep would have to wait.

Reaching up, he planted the gloves and his left knee and pulled. His right foot left the floor. Keeping his left hand and right knee in place to hold his bodyweight, he reached, planted, and pulled. Hand over hand, he repeated the movements, climbing the wall as fast as he could.

Keeping a sharp eye over his shoulder, Sam quickly scaled the three-story deckhouse while avoiding the few interspersed windows. He'd been hoping to make the roof before the goon squad arrived, but as he neared the top, Red came around the back corner.

Sam froze. With his cheek pressed against the cold steel, his gaze flashed to his hand. Unlike the Chameleon bodysuit, which had turned a gray streaked with rust to match the deckhouse wall, the gecko gloves and knee pads were black. They stood out like traffic cones, but hopefully from the goons' vantage point, they would blend into the background.

Wonder if Polly would consider this little maneuver an "unnecessary" risk? Chet asked rhetorically.

Sam didn't reply.

A second man with silver hair and sporting a long pea coat rounded the opposite corner. The goons came together, conversing quietly. Unfortunately, Sam didn't speak but a couple of words of Russian, so he didn't know what they were saying.

Don't worry, Chet said, *I'll translate.*

Please don't.

Red-haired Thug: Why is your face so hideous?

Gray-haired Thug: I don't remember. Mom says it was a proctology exam gone horribly wrong.

Ignoring the gallows humor, Sam waited, heart knocking. The bodysuit wasn't full-on camouflage. If they looked up, they would see him. His mind raced as he tried to come up with another plan.

He hung five feet from the roof. If they spotted him, he might be able to climb to the top before they shot him. Or maybe not.

Alternatively, he could drop. He knew how to land and roll to help his body distribute the force of the impact, but from thirty feet up, Sam would be traveling about twenty-eight miles per hour when he collided with the steel deck. Even if he landed perfectly, he had a pretty good chance of breaking a leg or his hips. And, say he survived and then took out the two goons with his remaining four bullets while they unloaded their AKs in his direction, he'd still be out of ammo and immobilized from busted bones. Sam would be a sitting duck.

His *only* option was to go up.

The two goons peered through the fog at the mist-shrouded stern below.

Sam spotted one of the two Trojan Horse crates loaded with guns. With the goons so close, he didn't dare pivot his head to try to find the second. Any movement might draw their attention. As he watched and waited, the fog seemed to thin. It hadn't been much, but the white mist had contributed to his camouflage. If these weasels didn't get on soon, he'd be even more exposed.

Red said something, went to the stairs leading to the lower deck, and descended. The gray-haired man walked to the opposite side and paused, looking around.

Red had been a mere thug. A meathead with a gun. But this older man's instincts must have alerted him that something wasn't on the up and up. He glanced back, searching the fog drifting over the empty walkway.

Time had become elusive. Sam had no idea how long he'd been clinging to the wall, but his shoulder and arm joints felt as though they were being stretched in a taffy puller. He'd kept his core locked to prevent telltale movements, but his muscles quivered and threatened to spasm. In addition, Polly had warned him about the geckos' short battery life. One way or the other, he needed to get down. Soon.

The last few feet to the roof now looked as far away as the peak of Everest.

The gray-haired guard faced the stern of the ship once more, scanning the deck. At last, he followed his comrade down the stairs.

Sam searched for a third gunman, but for the moment, he seemed to be alone. Letting out a relieved breath, he scurried down the wall, feeling a bit like Spider-Man. Dropping the final ten feet, he landed quietly. He shook his arms and shoulders, trying to get the blood circulating in his quivering muscles. He didn't have the luxury of time though. The hounds smelled prey.

Sam ran to the edge of the deckhouse and peeked around the corner. The coast was clear...for now. He crossed the narrow space and slipped over the rail.

If he'd missed anyone, this would be when they'd spot him. But no AKs rattled. No shouts of alarm.

He clung to the hull. The gecko gloves held, but the knee pad batteries must have drained because they no longer held his weight. *Great. Just great.*

Using only the gloves to support himself, he climbed down the side of the ship until he hovered just a few feet above the waterline. This position muted the howling alarm. At least it wasn't screaming in his ears anymore.

The good news: it would be difficult for anyone to spot him. The bad news: his muscles were shaking so hard, they threatened to drop him into the cold ocean below. He attempted to brace part of his bodyweight with his feet and miraculously found a position that gave his arms and shoulders a much-needed break.

As his heart rate settled, he made his way, hand over hand and feet planted, to the bow. Keeping his right hand against the steel belly of the ship, he unzipped the pouch with his left to retrieve the night vision goggles. Before he could pull them out, a wave slammed into him, driving him into the impossibly hard metal wall.

His hand slipped. Sam dropped.

Just before he plunged into the ocean, he caught himself with his right hand, almost tearing his arm from its socket. The wave receded. Dangling sideways and exhausted, Sam re-gripped the hull with his left hand and righted himself. He shook the stinging salt water from his eyes. His legs now submerged up to his knees, the ocean attempted to suck him under.

Sam hauled himself out of the churning surf. Thankfully, the waterproof suit had kept his body dry, or he might have been shivering uncontrollably and suffering from cold-induced muscle cramps. Likewise, his boots had kept the water out. But neither of those would do him any good if he had to take a swim. In fact, the boots would be a hindrance.

After doing a quick scan for more rogue waves, he reached for the goggles again.

The pouch was empty.

Well, shit.

With no alternative, he made his way along the hull toward the bow. Halfway there, he froze. Nearby, voices shouted and boots thumped.

Sam looked up, waiting for someone to poke their head over the rail and discover him. No one did.

As the voices faded, their owners headed for parts unknown, he continued moving. The closer he got to the front of the boat, the more the hull curved inward. The design helped it cut efficiently through the ocean, but the severe angle left his legs dangling. He could no longer brace his feet against the wall to help offset his bodyweight. His shoulders screamed, but he ignored the pain.

At long last, he reached the jet ski tie-off point. Unlike earlier, when the Taiga had banged against the hull, it was now——save for the splash of ocean against steel and the faint cry of the ship's alarm——silent. The ski must have drifted away. He reached for the rope but couldn't find it.

A fleeting image of the Taiga's fiberglass hull, split open and sunk, drifted through Sam's mind.

Trying not to dwell on the ramifications of losing it, he climbed, intent on retrieving the rope near where he'd tied it off. Just as he neared the rail, something brushed against the back of his hand.

It took him a few seconds in the dark to locate the object. When he did, he wished he hadn't.

In the yellow glow of the ship's halogens, Sam could just make out the cut end of the rope, its frayed fibers dangling like a severed lifeline. Only a few feet of nylon hung over the edge of the ship. Someone from the crew must have found it and sliced the line.

His lifeline cut, his ride gone, the noose of the ship's crew grew tighter by the second, and Sam had no escape.

Chapter Twenty

S am glanced around, searching for the Taiga—on the pitch-black ocean, under the moonless sky, in the fog, and without his night vision goggles. He may as well have been trying to find a black swan cruising an oil spill on the far side of the moon.

The *Vengeance* bobbed and rocked in the waves. With his feet dangling like a pair of bell clappers, his arms, back, and shoulders quickly grew exhausted.

Hand over hand, he made his way toward the stern of the ship. Once he'd gotten far enough away from the plow-shaped bow, he climbed down until he was out of earshot of anyone who might be nearby on deck but still high enough to stay above the raging swells. He braced his feet against the hull, relieving some of the pressure from his aching joints.

Sam had just reached for the radio, the device's plastic slick against his trembling fingers, when it occurred to him that if the walkie wasn't waterproof, the wave that had hit him earlier might have ruined it. With a thick dollop of trepidation in his chest, he switched on the dial.

Polly's voice blared in his ear mid-sentence, sharp as the night's chaos. "—the hell are you doing? So help me if you—"

Relieved, he clicked the transmit button, the faint crackle of static his lifeline. "Polly," he whispered. "I'm here."

"Bradford! It's about damned time." Her voice was a mix of irritation and relief. "What's happening?"

"I'm in a bit of a spot." *Talk about understating the obvious.*

"Where are you? The damned ship is so lit up, you could see it from Mars."

"I'm…" He thought for a moment. "Starboard, aft of the anchor. Opposite side from you."

She let out an exasperated sigh, which she didn't even bother to hide. "What about this being a covert op? In and out. No one was supposed to know we were there."

"Polly, you and I know criminals are fantastic at messing up the best-laid plans. The second I boarded that tub, I was shooting from the hip. You can't tell me your ops during your years on the Boston PD were any different."

She went quiet for a moment. "When you say you're aft of the anchor, do you mean you're on the *outside* of the ship?"

"Yes. On the hull about midway above the waterline. And let me tell you for the record, your gecko gloves have *really* come in handy. Literally a lifesaver."

"Sam, why are you hanging on the boat like some barnacle and not on the jet ski getting the hell out of there?"

"About that… They must have found where I tied the Taiga off because someone cut the line."

"So what?" she asked. "With your super special goggles, you should be able to see it. Swim."

"Well..."

"If you say you lost your goggles, so help me, I'll shoot you myself."

He took a deep breath and told her how he'd lost the goggles.

Polly remained quiet for a full minute, undoubtedly cursing his name.

She came back on. "Coming for you while they're on high alert is a lot less than optimal. In fact, it's suicidal. I'll never be able to outrun their autocannons or their AKs with the *Finders*. They don't know where you are, and I'm guessing they won't think to look on the side of the hull. Wait it out. I found an inflatable raft that will hopefully be less detectable by their radar. When things simmer down, I'll row in and get you."

"Don't worry about the radar. I took care of that. And—"

She cut him off. "What do you mean you took care of it?"

"When I turned it on, I could see the *Finders'* position. I didn't want them knowing where you were, so I cut the cable. By the time they fix it, we should be long gone."

"You are incorrigible. Did you even intend on going in-cognito, or were fireworks always the plan?"

"Of course I tried to go in quiet. The fireworks part is a longer story for another time that's not right now. Can we focus on the situation at hand?"

"Fine."

He glanced at the small indicators on the sides of the gloves. "Anyway, the geckos still have another fifteen minutes of power, so I'm good for a little while. The fog should hide the raft, but the swells are a lot bigger than I thought. They tossed the Taiga around like a piece of driftwood. A raft has a much larger surface area, so it'll be even more subject to the swells. I know you can handle it, but it's going to take a lot of time."

"Well," she snapped, her voice full of irritation, "I don't see where we have much choice. At least you're safe."

Chet piped up. *Don't say it!*

Don't say what?

"It could be worse," Polly said.

Chet's shoulders drooped. *That.*

A tremor ran through the hull of the ship, the steel vibrating like a volcano waking from a century of slumber.

What the hell?

Then he understood. Inky dread filled his gut, his pulse spiking as reality set in. He hit the radio's transmit button.

"Guess what? It's worse."

"Did they discover you?"

"No. Not yet. They started the engines. They're spooked and have decided to move out."

"It could just be a precaution. As long as they don't raise—"

A clang resonated from the bow, cutting off her words, followed by the whine of a motor and the *ching-ching-ching* of a thick chain rolling up into the ship.

"As long as they don't raise the anchor," he finished for her. "Except they just did."

"Well, that's a problem," Polly said. "How far do you think you could swim?"

Sam studied the ocean waves again. "Not very. It's pretty rough. And cold. Damn cold."

"Suck it up, Marine. Go straight out from the side. I'll come around and get in as close as the fog will hide me. You need to get as far away as you can. If they spot us, those autocannons are going to chew through this boat like it's a bath toy."

"About that," Sam said. "I disabled the gun on the bow and tossed the AK-47s and RPGs that were with it overboard. If you approach from the front——"

She cut him off. "Oh. My. God. What part of 'covert operation' do you *not* understand? You do whatever you want, whenever you want. It's no wonder you have a target on your back." She unleashed an exotic tapestry of curses as colorful and dirty as a hostel Turkish rug.

"I know you aren't happy," he conceded, "but the incognito ship—no pun intended—has sailed. We need to focus on the two advantages we have. The first is they don't know about *you*."

"Bradford, do you honestly think they haven't guessed that there's a boat out here somewhere? This isn't Star Trek. They won't believe you just beamed aboard. They're going to be looking for me. *That's* why they started their engines."

"I'm not convinced that's the case. It's dark and their radar is broken. Their cover is blown. They don't know who I'm in contact with. For all they know, I've called in the Navy. If I was them, I'd beat feet for South America."

"Well, you're not them. And don't forget, they still have a man on land. Do you think they'd just abandon him?"

Sam tried to put himself in Levka's shoes. Would a brigadier abandon one of her own? For profit or to save her own skin, maybe. But he didn't know how to factor in the extreme risk they'd already taken getting Frank's body and phone back. Not only did they have neither, but their crewmate posed another potential leak of information. If the authorities found him, they might get him to talk.

"I don't know," he admitted. "But that leads to my second point. As I said before, their radar is out of commission, and I sabotaged the gun on the bow. They're partially unarmed, though they don't know it, and blind."

Polly was quiet for a long time. Finally, she said, "Get off the ship and swim. I'll come around the front of the *Vengeance* as close as I dare."

"Thanks, Polly."

She didn't reply.

Sam peeled a hand from the hull. Dangling by one arm, he loosened the laces of a boot and kicked it off. Swapping hands, he repeated the process with the second. "Alright, I'm ready."

Polly said, "Since you lost your goggles, you'd better figure out how to see in the damned dark because you're going to have to find me. Now start swimming, jarhead."

Sam lowered himself to the waterline. The merciless ocean slapped against the cold steel, splashing him. Even through the suit, the spray felt like needles. He took a deep breath, bracing himself for the ice bath. With his feet against the hull, he prepared to launch off the side and gain some distance.

He pulled his hand free and pushed off with his legs. For a moment, he was airborne, soaring over the raging sea, the wind biting his exposed cheeks and forehead.

The landing was like plunging into the darkest pits of space—without a suit. The cold seized his body, a vice grip of ice that threatened to stop his heart. Though his instincts urged him to surface immediately, he swam as hard and as long as he could beneath the waves. When his lungs screamed for air, he finally popped his head up, letting his body float with the rolling ocean as he got his bearings.

He'd hoped the splash of his fall would be masked by the alarm—but he could no longer hear its high-pitched squawk. Maybe he'd drifted too far away?

Two men standing at the ship's rail snapped a spotlight to life, scanning the ocean near where he'd gone in.

Nope. Time to go.

Sam took several long breaths, then dove under and swam farther away. When he surfaced again, he hadn't traveled as far as he'd hoped, but he'd made it outside the area bathed in light. The beam roved back and forth, slicing through the fog until it flashed on the jet ski, illuminating its sleek form in the darkness.

The Taiga had drifted about a quarter mile—just a faint glimmer of hope in the blackness.

He was about to dive again and head toward the small watercraft when the unmistakable *rat-a-tat-tat* of automatic gunfire shattered the night. A crewman had broken down

one of the stern crates housing an autocannon. The stac-
cato braid of 25mm tracers flared from the gun's barrel
like tiny suns—white-hot beads stretching into thin, incandescent threads that devoured the darkness. As they arced
through the night sky, trembling ribbons of orange-red light
trailed behind like embers dragged across black velvet.

Lines of fire, beautiful in their violent power, blistered
the ocean—a relentless predator consuming its defense-
less prey. The streaks hissed and snapped as they found
their target. A chorus of mechanical pops and tears un-
dercut the chattering gun as the rounds cleaved apart the
watercraft's hull with almost surgical precision.

While the molten comets chewed through plastic and
fiberglass with a rapacious appetite, Sam could do nothing but watch in awed horror when a wave slammed into
his head. He stayed under for several heartbeats, the muffled thuds of the rounds reverberating through the water.
Then he resurfaced, gulping a lungful of cool night air.

The gun had gone silent. His gaze followed the arc of
the spotlight. Smoke drifted from what remained of the
Taiga—shattered fiberglass and twisted metal—before it
slipped beneath the ocean surface.

So much for his getaway car.

Another wave crashed over his head. Sam sputtered,
spitting seawater. He needed to move. If they turned
the gun toward him, there'd be no escaping the inevitable. Fatigued from the sea's relentless punishment,
he took several deep breaths and dove, swimming until his lungs burned. He resurfaced, gulped a few more
breaths, and dove again.

His muscles flexed like clay, each stroke heavier than the last, his limbs growing numb as the ocean's chill seeped into his bones. Despite the effort, his body no longer felt cold—a deceptive calm that signaled danger.

Not good. Hypothermia had already begun to set in. If he didn't get warm soon, he'd be dead. Still, he repeated the motion again and again, fighting against the sea's merciless pull.

The fog swallowed the *Vengeance*. He should have been safe. If he couldn't see it, the crew couldn't see him. Yet he still felt its malevolent presence lurking in the gloom. With its anchor hoisted and engines thrumming, the ship prowled the night. Only stealth and distance could protect him from its sinister intent.

Treading water, he searched, but the *Finders* was nowhere in sight. Sam was stranded in the middle of the ocean—tired, freezing, and officially out of options.

Chapter Twenty-One

Sam floated on his back, the icy water lapping at his ears—a relentless weight pressing against his skin—as he gazed up at the night sky.

A haphazard breeze chased the restless mist, stirring it into roving, translucent waterspouts—ghosts of tornadoes haunting a pelagic graveyard. When the wind died, the fog settled, blanketing the ocean in a woolen layer as opaque as chowder.

Sam's slush-filled muscles refused to cooperate. He rose and fell with the churning swells, the waves' rhythmic slosh an eternal lullaby.

At first, he'd shivered almost uncontrollably as he drifted with the tide, but the quaking had relented. A small part—deep inside—urged him to keep moving, to keep fighting. That reasonable survivor realized that his body temperature had dropped too low to register the water's frigidity.

But he couldn't summon the will or the energy to swing his arms or kick his legs. It was much easier to float.

He was dying. From early adulthood—when he'd chosen the Marines and later The Agency—he'd understood that the frailties of old age, the loss of memory and porous bones, would never accompany him to the hereafter. Death would call in his chips by way of an assassin's blade, a hot slug tearing through his flesh, or the very violence he'd spent his life trying in vain to eradicate. Sam had accepted those terms, even if he hadn't known the particulars of the contract.

Still, as his final wish, he'd hoped to glimpse the stars before the custodians shut off his lights one last time. But the clouds had not relented their hold on the heavens. The fog's damp tendrils curled around him like a shroud, denying him one last view of the cosmos before he became a part of it.

Now and then, his ear broke the ocean's surface, and during those brief interludes, he thought he caught the deep thrum of the *Vengeance's* engines. They seemed to be staying put.

I should radio someone and tell them about the guns on deck. Don't want the RU team getting killed. His numb fingers fumbled with the walkie clipped to his waist until they found and pressed the transmit button. The earpiece didn't click to acknowledge the signal.

Oh well. Nothing I can do. Polly will warn them.

Polly. He'd almost forgotten about her.

He slowly looked to his left and right. Where had the *Finders* gone?

The boat could have been a dozen paces away, and he might not have been able to spot it in the patchy fog against the black ocean. Polly had told him to swim to her, but in the vast expanse, he hadn't been able to locate the small craft. If he'd been more careful with his night vision goggles, maybe he wouldn't be in this fix.

At some point, he thought he'd heard the *Finders'* engines—a faint burble harmonizing with the *Vengeance's* diesels. They revved, then faded until disappearing completely. Perhaps he'd drifted off course, making it impossible for Polly to find him. Or perhaps it had been nothing more than his hopeful imagination.

Sam drifted in a daze, half asleep, his mind slipping into a foggy abyss.

Some unknown time later, his eyes sprang open.

Startled, he found himself seated across from his brother, Jake, at a café table along a Malibu beach. He wore a loose-knit shirt and a pair of cargos, the fabric soft against his skin. The gloriously warm, humid air carried the tang of salt and sea life—a scent that transported him back twenty years to memories he'd tried to forget.

As the sun dipped into the tranquil blue water, the sky blazed the same orange and red as the tracers shot from the *Vengeance's* autocannon, casting streams of light like Chinese dragons dancing across the surface of the Pacific.

Jake gazed at him with an introspective, calculating expression. Sam had seen that look a million times before. His twin always had something on his mind, but wouldn't just come out and talk about it. Such deep thoughts required contemplative mulling. Sam would have to be content to wait.

A part of him marveled at the familiarity of the scene and how easily he'd slipped into it. His brother, though a decade in the grave, sat alive and relaxed in a hallucinogenic

Hawaiian shirt. Jake had an unending supply of obnoxious prints, everything from old cars, to toucans, to tacos. He had the demeanor of a man without a care and all the time in the world. His bleached, wavy hair, waterfalling to his shoulders, dallied in the breeze as though it too embraced the surfer's hang-loose pace of life.

Why wasn't he more bothered to be hanging out with his dead twin?

Except, in a way, Chet was the personification of Jake. They had the same sarcastic wit, the same disregard for the rules, and they both thought they knew better than Sam. In that regard, he and his twin had never truly been apart.

Nevertheless, Sam's heart ached at the sight——a ravenous grief so old, yet so familiar, it stole his breath. "You look good, Jake." That was understating it by quite a bit. His brother looked *exactly* as he had before the drugs had turned him into a scarecrow and robbed his eyes of their vitality. "I've missed you."

"I miss you too, little bro." His easy tone and husky timbre were as familiar to Sam as his own voice.

Feeling slightly foolish——what does one say to a dead man?——Sam asked, "How've you been?"

If Jake thought the question odd, he gave no indication of it. His twin released his trademark easy smile as though relishing a delicious daydream. "The waves are tasty, the girls plentiful, and the brews are cold. What else could a man ask for?"

What else, indeed.

Jake took a drink of his beer, beads of sweat dotting the outside of the bottle. "But I didn't depart from Kanaloa's playground to talk about me. It's you I'm worried about."

Sam frowned. "Me? I'm fine."

"Fine? If you're so 'fine,' then tell me your plan."

Sam, who until that second hadn't realized he too had been holding a beer, also took a drink. The sharp bubbles tickled his tongue in a way only the bottom of the barrel brews could. He never understood why more expensive IPAs and ales didn't have the same punch. He looked back at his dead fraternal twin. "I don't have a plan."

"Oh, come on," Jake scoffed. "The great Samuel Paxton Bradford *always* has a plan."

Sam shrugged. "I don't know. I've been thinking about retiring."

"From the job or life itself?"

Sam shrugged again. "I thought I meant the job, but maybe deep down, I meant life. I'll admit that enchilada has gotten cold since you've been gone. The cheese is stale."

Jake nodded as though the idea had merit. "Yeah. I can see that. Which is why you're just floating out in the Pacific and not doing a damned thing to help yourself." He seemed to consider. "It would be pretty great to hang with you again. And being dead has a most excellent benefits package." He waved his beer at the ocean. "Surf all day. Different girl each night." He cocked his head, a mischievous grin playing on his lips. "Or, in your case, just *one* girl."

Sam didn't take the bait.

"Anyway," Jake continued, "you've found yourself a peaceful slice of heaven on the edge of the continent." He took a slow drink. "Given that, I'd think you'd fight harder to stay. But despite your pathetic attempts to save your own ass, I'm pretty sure you're going to get out of this fix. And that's why I wanted to talk to you."

Sam waited.

"To your earlier point, you've been thinking about giving up The Agency gig and settling down. But before you go get a picket fence and have your national average two-point-five tax deductions, you should know a little something about your new heavenly church."

Sam held his dead brother's gaze. "Oh, yeah? What's that?"

"There's a devil congregation. You know who it is, you just won't admit it." Jake's eyes darkened, a storm brewing in their depths as he leaned closer. "Their priority is to turn you to chum and feed you to the sharks."

Sam chuckled. "Someone's got it out for me? Tell me something I don't know."

"I don't mean the usual anti-Sam brood. Someone is gunning for *you*."

Confused, Sam furrowed his brow. "Erebus is dead."

"Not him. Someone else. You need to watch your back."

A roster of faces—the proverbial who's who of Alabaster Cove—flowed through Sam's mind, but no one he could think of hated him enough to stick a knife through his heart. "How could you know that?"

The breeze tousled Jake's hair as though he were starring in a shampoo commercial. "Things are a lot clearer on this side of the island, little bro. Besides, you,"—he pointed at Sam—"already suspect it. You just haven't gotten around to admitting it."

"Jake—"

"Look, I know your job as a super-secret spy or whatever, requires you to lie all the time. But the person you lie to most often is *you*."

Sam tried to read his brother's face. To get at the secrets hidden behind the amused, charismatic charm. "Who is it?"

"What's the fun in telling you?"

"I don't know who you're talking about. Can you stop playing games and just be straight for once?"

"Fine. Fine." Jake took another sip of his beer and leaned in conspiratorially.

Sam leaned in too.

"You need to watch out for—" But instead of finishing the sentence, Jake drew back his fist and slammed it into Sam's chest, the impact a searing explosion of pain radiating through his ribs.

It felt like getting hit by a car—his sternum screamed in protest as his chair tipped backward. Arms flailing, he tried to catch himself on the table, but his fingertips only slapped at the wood, failing to grip. He crashed to the ground, his head smacking the sidewalk with a resounding gong. Stars edged his vision. As he rolled and tried to rise, Jake shoved him back down and straddled his stomach.

His dead twin brother dumped his beer over Sam's face. Though the bottle held only twelve ounces, it poured gallons of icy brew, flooding his nose and choking his throat.

Sam sputtered and gasped, unable to breathe under the onslaught. Jake tossed the bottle aside, raised his fist, and drove it into Sam's chest again, a sledgehammer blow that crushed what little air he'd managed to recover.

Sam wheezed, desperate for breath.

Jake leaned down so close, Sam could feel his brother's hot breath against his cheek. "There's a demon in the church, Sam. Find it!"

"I don't care," he replied. "I'm tired of fighting, Jake."

His brother glared into Sam's eyes. "Suck it up, Marine! I don't give a shit if you're tired. This isn't the Ritz, and you aren't on vacation. This is war. You goddamned skell. You can sleep on your own time. Move!"

Sam grabbed his brother's face and pushed him away. "Jake! What the hell?"

Except the face in his hand wasn't his dead twin's, it was Polly's.

Kneeling beside him, she peeled his grip from her cheeks and chin and leaned back, concern etched in her expression.

Sam gazed at her for a second. Where had she come from? Where had his brother gone?

Then he turned to the side and vomited up Lake Erie. A series of violent, wracking coughs accompanied the flowing water spewing from his core.

Lungs cleared and teeth chattering, he rubbed his chest. "Ouch. Damn. It feels like someone ran me over with a 1952 Studebaker."

Polly arched a brow. "That's oddly specific."

He wiped his mouth, half expecting to see blood or puke, but his fingers came away clean. "What happened?"

"What happened is you almost died. I was giving you CPR when you went all Jackie Chan on me. Then you pushed me away and called me Jake." She paused for a second. "We're even, by the way."

"What?"

"Three months ago, when Erebus blew up the pier, you pulled me out of the wreckage and saved my life."

In his fuzzy mind, he flashed back to that hellish night when the murdering psychopath had garroted a fisherman and turned the dead man's boat into a dynamite delivery system. He'd set it on fire and had the auto-nav maintain a course parallel to the shore. RU had done exactly what Erebus expected. They'd boarded the boat, doused the flames, and towed it to the pier—which had been crowded with onlookers. Sam had realized nearly too late what was happening. But he'd gotten almost everyone away before the boat erupted in a fireball.

Almost everyone.

Drifting plumes of acrid smoke, a hearty mixture of burning fuel, sulfur, and scorched flesh. Screaming, chaos, pain. Sam had found Polly under a pile of boards, pulled her out, and gave her CPR. "What about it?"

"Like I said, we're even now."

"I wasn't keeping score." Sam glanced around at the mist shrouding the small boat as the mist in his mind began to clear. He lay on the *Finders'* back deck, his legs dangling in the water. Overhead, a single star shone next to a thumbnail moon. The sight triggered a faint memory that he couldn't quite recall. Something about him sailing through the cosmos.

Amusement, and perhaps relief, lingered on Polly's face. "You'll live, Captain Ahab. But we need to get moving before your Russian buddies realize we're here."

Her gaze snapped sharply to something behind the *Finders*. "Shit." Polly jumped to her feet and held out her hand to him.

"What is it?" His head was so fuzzy, it felt like mentally wading through tar.

"The *Vengeance*." Polly pointed behind them. "It's coming."

Sam looked back.

The black ship emerged from a wall of fog, plowing through the ocean like an iron leviathan. Its engines emitted a low, predatory growl that vibrated through the water.

It was headed straight for them.

Chapter Twenty-Two

An image of the icebreaker's autocannon blasting the Taiga flashed through Sam's mind as he gripped Polly's hand.

She hauled him to his feet. "Get moving, Marine," she ordered and took her position in the pilot's seat.

Sam laboriously followed, plopping into the chair next to her.

Polly flung her radio onto the dash and glanced back. "Oh, shit."

Sam followed her gaze.

The crew had extinguished the *Vengeance's* running lamps, but a set of spotlights, one on the port, another on the starboard, and a third on the bow shone as though advertising a Hollywood premier. They raked the surface of the ocean with beams no less powerful than space lasers.

Polly pulled her Beretta from her bag and set it on the dash as she cranked the ignition. The engines came to life, growling beneath the floor. Polly nudged the throttle forward and spun the steering wheel. The *Finders* turned out of the path of the oncoming ship, sliding over the ocean swells.

She reached for the gun, but Sam grabbed it.

"Hey!" she said.

"You concentrate on driving. Our only chance, is to avoid them." He held up the Beretta. "This won't do us a lick of good."

Polly studied his face for a second, concern etching her features. He must have looked the way he felt, nearly hypothermic and half-drowned. She gave him a sharp nod and twisted her neck toward the ship behind them as she maneuvered the *Finders*.

Sam had expected her to open up the engines and take them out as fast as possible. A journey, under the onslaught of autocannon fire, they most likely wouldn't survive. Instead, as the large vessel bore down on them, Polly guided the boat out of the path of the approaching *Vengeance* and into a shallow patch of fog, the *Finders* sliding over the tall ocean swells.

She eased up on the gas. The breaker's heavy diesels masked the *Finders'* purring engines.

It was a smart move. One he might have thought of if his brain were functioning at a hundred percent. But the adrenaline pumping through his veins was clearing away the murk between his ears.

Side by side, they gazed through the mist as the *Vengeance* sailed past, spotlights scouring the ocean.

They glanced at one another, the hope he felt reflected on her face.

"Maybe they'll miss us?" Sam whispered.

As though the crew had heard him, someone yelled in Russian—the harsh, guttural command slicing through the night. A spotlight bathed the *Finders* in a stark yellow beam.

"Son of a bitch!" Polly jammed the throttle forward.

Motors screaming, the *Finders* leapt forward like a scalded cat.

Sam stumbled. If he hadn't been holding onto his seat, he might have been thrown overboard.

The *Vengeance's* stern-mounted autocannon barked. Glowing orange tracers streaked through the darkness like a swarm of vengeful spirits unleashed from their prison in Hell.

Polly drove hard.

Their wake churned as the 25mm rounds chewed the ocean surface trailing them.

The rear corner of the *Finders* exploded in a spray of fiberglass. Tremors rattled the floor and dash.

Polly swerved the boat out of the line of fire. She cranked the wheel back and forth, attempting to be unpredictable. The spotlight and gunner tracked their trajectory. Molten threads blazing from the autocannon seared ember paths through the night, each a visible promise of annihilation.

The *Finders* outpaced the *Vengeance* and was a million times nimbler, but it couldn't outrun the autocannon. They had to get out of its line of sight.

She straightened the boat, making a beeline for open waters.

The engines howled. The boat leapt from wave to wave. The wind screamed.

Taking advantage of their ballistic path, Sam aimed the Beretta at the closest spotlight. He pulled the trigger several times. But the jouncing *Finders* combined with their velocity made the shot impossible.

Polly glanced at him, then back at the ship. She yelled above the cacophony. "I'm going to stop. You take out that damned light."

He nodded. It was a calculated risk, but they had little choice. As long as the *Vengeance* could see them, they were only biding time until the crew got lucky.

She held up three fingers. Folding back one after the other, she counted down and jammed the throttle to full stop, throwing them both forward.

Sam regained his footing, held his breath, aimed, pulled the trigger. The Beretta's sharp crack split the night.

The nearest spotlight shattered with a satisfying pop— its light winking out like a snuffed candle.

Under the cover of darkness, Polly jammed the throttle full forward. The engines roared.

Sam gripped the seat. Grabbing a new mag for the Beretta, he jammed it home.

Fire blazed from the barrel of the machine gun, sputtering thirty rounds of hate and death per second. Unable to see them, the crewman raked the ocean back and forth. A line of rounds punched through the floor of the *Finders*.

Smoke seeped from the engine compartment.

Polly drove the stuttering boat into a fog bank. The *Finders'* previous litheness, like that of a young gymnast's, had faded. Now it limped like an injured seal stranded on the beach.

As they glided deeper into the cloud, the engines grumbled unhappily. A hacking cough rattled, once, twice, and then stalled, plunging them into deathly silence.

Polly cranked the ignition. The engines turned over but didn't catch.

They caught each other's gaze as realization settled in.

They were dead in the water.

Chapter Twenty-Three

S am and Polly dropped to the deck, each snapping back the latches securing the cover over the engine compartment. Thick smoke seeped around the edges, stinging Sam's eyes. Its acrid tendrils burned his throat and coated his tongue with oily soot.

He pointed over Polly's shoulder as he gripped the cover's handles. "Fire extinguisher."

She grabbed the red cylinder mounted to the cabin wall, pulled the pin, and aimed it at the floor. She nodded.

Sam yanked the cover back.

Through the cloud of smoke erupting from the engine compartment, flames danced across the engine block.

As Sam flung the deck plate overboard, Polly doused the fire, then grabbed a pair of flashlights from her bag, tossing one to Sam. They snapped them to life and dropped to their knees, assessing the damage.

She shone the narrow beam on a bundle of wires. "There," she whispered. "Ignition wires are damaged."

"And here." Sam had been tracing the puddle of burnt oil on the engine block responsible for the smoke and fire to a severed line.

Polly wiped at her eyes, leaving long gray streaks across her cheek. "We got lucky. If the engine hadn't died, it would have run out of oil and seized."

"Maybe we should call for backup?" he whispered. Though he'd posed the question, based on her Boston PD service record, he didn't believe former Detective Cahill would radio for help.

He wasn't wrong. Polly gave a sharp shake of her head, her gaze unflinching. "They can't get here in time. We made this mess. We need to get out of it. All we'd be doing is putting my RU team at risk."

He didn't completely agree with her, but he didn't argue. Her team. Her call. Move on. "Which do you want?"

"The oil line is damaged and the space to work on it is tight. I'm smaller, so I can fit better."

Sam went to the back of the boat. He found a toolbox in a bench seat and two spare quarts of oil. He brought the haul back and opened the box on the floor between them. "It looks like this is all we have to work with."

"Hopefully, it'll be enough." She dropped into the narrow space behind the engine.

Keeping an ear tuned for the rumble of approaching diesels, Sam used a pocketknife to slice open the protective insulation on the bundle of ignition wires. Each injector had two wires, sixteen total, five of which had been severed and four that had been damaged.

Polly was right, they had gotten lucky. A couple of inches to the left and the bullet would have gone through the engine block.

Holding the flashlight between his teeth, Sam stripped the insulation and reconnected the copper, wrapping each splice in strips of electrical tape. In the hazy yellow light, the sheath colors and patterns looked almost identical. He stared, trying to make out which wires to connect.

Polly hopped out of the compartment and rummaged around in the seat benches, pulling various rolls of tape and rags. She dropped the smorgasbord of crap onto the deck, catching his gaze for a heartbeat.

He could see the same question in her eyes that was raging through his heart. *Will this work?*

They had no choice. This *had* to work.

Polly rolled onto her back and slid upside down into the compartment.

Despite the cold, beads of sweat peppered Sam's face. He wiped at it with his sleeve.

The sound of the *Vengeance's* diesels grew louder. If Sam hadn't sabotaged their radar, they'd have already been discovered.

He returned his focus to the two sets of wires. In the weird light, he thought one looked pink, the other light red. Maybe. If he got it wrong, the system would short out. Taking his best guess, he spliced and wrapped, then slid the toolbox tray under the bundle to protect it from the heat of the engine.

From deep in the fog, someone shouted in Russian, the voice sharp and commanding, cutting through the mist like a blade. Not on top of them yet, but close. Too close.

"Done," he whispered. "What can I do to help?"

She held up her hand. "Phillips screwdriver."

He handed her the tool. For the next few minutes, he served as the assistant to the surgeon. For a second, he was back in Afghanistan, where he'd served the same role one night to the medic as she patched the leg of a soldier while blood poured and men fought.

"Done," came Polly's quiet voice from deep in the engine compartment.

Sam helped her up and poured the two quarts of oil into the fill tube.

Through the murk, the *Vengeance's* spotlights shined like malignant moons behind a thinning bank of clouds. The diesels thrummed.

They scrambled back into the pilothouse. Polly gripped the ignition key, while Sam retrieved the Beretta.

She looked at him. If they'd missed something and the engines didn't fire, they would lose their only opportunity to escape. The ship would find them.

"Do it," Sam whispered.

Polly turned the key.

The starter whined. The engines turned over but didn't fire. In the silence, the failed attempt sounded as loud as a rock concert. Polly grimaced and tried again. No luck.

A voice yelled in Russian—sharp and urgent. They must have heard. Even over the thrum of their own diesels, there was no way they could have missed it.

Sam leapt, sliding across the floor. He shined his flash-light into the open compartment. At first, he couldn't see anything wrong. Then his beam found it. A damaged bolt had allowed the fuel injector wire bundle to come loose from the ECU—the engine control unit. He jammed the wad of wires onto the adapter, wrapping it in tape to hold it in place.

He gave Polly a thumbs-up.

Two spotlights from high overhead blazed down on them.

Polly turned the ignition. The *Finders'* engine turned, turned, turned—then roared to life.

AK-47s barked.

She jammed the throttle to full.

Bullets peppered the *Finders'* hull as it leapt out of the water.

Sam returned fire from his prone position on the floor, aiming for the muzzle flash.

The *Finders* sped deeper into the fog bank and blasted out the opposite side.

Behind them, the *Vengeance* emerged from the mist like a mythological beast conjured from humanity's worst nightmares.

The autocannon rattled. Tracers flew, painting the ocean with fire.

The *Finders'* windshield exploded in a shower of glass fragments.

"Jesus!" Polly and Sam yelled together.

Besides the missing window, the 25mm rounds had chewed the dashboard to shreds.

Sam cringed, expecting the boat to slow as the engines once more died. To his amazement, the *Finders* continued flying over the rough waves.

Polly drove them into another thick fog bank. Visibility dropped to zero. Instead of slowing, she left the engines wide open.

Sam hated not being able to see. Though only the *Finders* and the *Vengeance* occupied this corner of the ocean, he couldn't help but feel like they might run into something hard and unforgiving at any second.

"They ruined the boat's radio," Polly yelled over the din.

Sam pointed at the tattered electronics at her feet. "Yours too."

"We're deaf and mute," she said.

They were on their own. Even if Polly changed her mind about calling for backup, they'd have no way to request for help.

A quickening breeze thinned the fog. Only minutes remained before they'd be exposed and easy prey once more.

Through the mist, Sam could make out the flare of the cannon's muzzle and the hungry, flaming rounds seeking their prey. He resisted the urge to return fire. Given their velocity, the bouncing boat, and the poor visibility, he had almost no chance of hitting his target. Best save their ammo.

Considering how outnumbered and outgunned they were, Polly had done a good job of staying ahead of the Mafiya crew, but they couldn't keep this up all night. They needed to change tactics.

Sam pointed. "Get in front of the ship. If we stay to the side, we're dead."

"Are you crazy?" she spat. "The only reason we're alive is because that gunner has a lot of obstacles between us and him. There's nothing in his way if he takes the bow gun."

He touched her arm. "Trust me."

The dim lunar glow seeping through the fog highlighted the war waging in her green eyes. At last, she nodded and yanked the boat hard to the left, guiding it out of the mist and into the path of the oncoming ship.

More shouts from the *Vengeance* as the spotlights found them.

She matched the larger ship's trajectory as though playing *Follow the Leader*. The *Finders* outpaced the old Russian icebreaker, though only by a handful of knots. Polly widened the gap between the two vessels.

The gunman abandoned the stern autocannon and sprinted across the deck. He unlocked the bow crate.

I tapped that screwdriver in tight...right?

At the time he thought he had, but facing the business end of a weapon that could turn the *Finders* into chum-coated shrapnel in less time than it took to say "chum-coated shrapnel" gave him doubts.

Tossing the box's pieces aside, the crewman revealed the 25mm deck-mounted machine gun. He paused for a moment, clearly wondering where the AKs, RPGs, and the rest of the ammunition had gone.

Sam aimed the Beretta and fired in quick succession. His shots missed, of course, but the bullets spanging off the hull relieved the gunner of his curiosity.

The crewman grabbed the heavy weapon's handles, bringing it to bear on the *Finders*. The eternal maw of the barrel pointed at them. There was no way he could miss.

Polly craned her neck, watching.

Even from this distance, Sam thought he saw the man give them a wicked smile.

He pulled back the heavy side handle, cocking the gun.

Polly cut her eyes to Sam. The two of them held each other's gaze for a heartbeat before returning their focus to the icebreaker and the machine gun aimed at them.

The autocannon erupted with a deafening boom, shrapnel spraying like a fountain and glinting in the spotlight's glow. Its operator flew back in an arc, landing on the deck in a smoking heap.

Polly and Sam looked at each other for a beat, then back at the *Vengeance* and the smoke billowing from its bow. They burst out in relieved laughter—the absurdity of the fried crewman and their brush with death morbidly amusing.

The *Vengeance* slowed as the bridge crew charged down the stairs, rushing toward their injured mate. Two men brandishing AK-47s opened fire on the fleeing *Finders*, but the distance proved too great.

Polly wiped at her eyes as her laughter faded and she faced forward, pushing the boat as hard as it would go. The *Vengeance* fell behind. The angry shouts of her crew faded into the night.

Though she kept her focus on the open ocean ahead of them, Polly said to him, "So, I hate to admit it, but you did okay, Bradford. It would have been better if you hadn't gotten caught at all, but that was just the right amount of sabotage." She held out her fist.

The lady paramedic just paid you a compliment, Chet observed. *Never in a million years would I have believed it if I hadn't heard it with my own ears.*

My ears, Sam corrected.

Yeah, yeah. Whatever you do, don't spoil the moment.

Heeding Chet's advice, Sam gave her a small grin, nodded, and bumped her knuckles with his own. "You did pretty good yourself, Cahill."

Polly's eyes sparkled, mirroring the excitement pumping through Sam's veins as the weight of what they'd accomplished sank in. They had defeated the Mafiya crew. Together.

The victory was small. The *Vengeance* still sailed. The empire still stood. But two people had made a stand—and come out alive.

Now that the weapons had been lowered and the score settled, if only temporarily, Polly and Sam had nothing to do but wait for the miles to slip beneath the *Finders'* hull.

High on endorphins and giddy with survivor's relief, they chatted and laughed. In their retellings, events became funnier, more exaggerated, more colorful than the originals. The gunman flew farther, the shrapnel blast was bigger, the smoke thicker, the crew more frustrated and bumbling.

During that journey back to shore, Sam saw more of Polly's dimpled smile than in all the previous time they'd worked together combined. Her infectious laugh made his heart swell, and something inside him shifted. A pivotal moment struck like lightning, leaving him in awe: for the first time in decades, he'd found someone he could rely on.

Trust had never come easy. It was a gift he hadn't bestowed on anyone in years. But aside from her saving his life—and the two of them saving each other by overcoming impossible odds—he understood, on a primal level where instinct ruled over logic and intuition triumphed over reason, that former detective Polly Cahill would always have his six. Her integrity, her strength, her ingenuity—these were pillars he could lean on. Put his faith in.

Though he had no idea what the future held for either of them, or who he'd be when they got there, the relief of having a true partner after years of solitude buoyed his spirits even more than the victory itself. For now, at least, the future would take care of itself.

About a mile off the coast, with the *Vengeance* safely behind them, Sam's mood soared. They'd nearly made it to shore—yet another win for the record books.

Then something cold washed over his foot.

He looked down.

His heart froze.

A thin layer of water covered the deck.

He rushed to the engine compartment, fearing the worst—and found it.

The *Finders'* inboard lay almost completely submerged. Before he could call out to Polly the engine stuttered and stalled with a pitiful groan. The boat lurched forward from the sudden loss of power.

"What the hell?" she yelled. She turned the ignition, but nothing happened. She looked back at Sam.

"Not going to work." He shone his light on the flooded compartment before meeting her gaze again. "We're sinking."

Chapter Twenty-Four

S am half expected the icebreaker to reappear in the dark, its menacing silhouette slicing through the fog. But the *Vengeance* had given up the chase. Its crew must have been unwilling to venture so close to the US and its border patrol, leaving the ocean a vast, inky void.

He slipped on Polly's infrared goggles, the lenses casting the world in shifting shades of green and black.

"What are you doing?" she asked.

"Looking for your RU boats. I was hoping one of them might come help." He refrained from reminding her that he'd wanted to call for help before their radios were destroyed as he scanned the surrounding sea. The empty expanse stretched endlessly in every direction.

"Well?" she prompted.

He shook his head and pulled off the goggles. "Nothing."

"Maybe there's a flare."

"We'd be letting the *Vengeance* know our position."

"They already know our position," she countered.

"Good point."

The invading ocean gurgled as it filled the *Finders'* hull. They rummaged through the bench seats, tossing everything helter-skelter.

A long tapestry of Italian curses flowed from Polly's lips as they searched. "Who the hell has a boat but no emergency flares?"

"I'll file a formal complaint with the owner."

"Time for Plan B," Polly said. "Get the raft."

"Where?" he asked.

She pointed behind him, toward the rear of the boat. "Near where the jet ski was docked."

Sam sloshed to the stern. As he unfolded the raft, his heart sank. "We have a problem." He held it up, revealing a series of puckered bullet holes in the heavy rubber.

"Great. Just great."

Frigid water splashed over his calves.

With no other options, Sam connected the raft's stem to the compact inflation tank. Polly came up beside him. When he nodded, she opened the valve.

Air hissed.

They both waited. More expensive, segmented rafts allowed undamaged tubes to inflate even if others had been punctured. If Savannah's ex had gone cheap...

They let out a joint sigh of relief as the intact chambers ballooned.

The *Finders* dipped lower, its deck shuddering beneath their feet as water surged. A wave broke over the side, dousing them in a chilling spray.

Sam mentally urged the tank to hurry as the nose of the boat inched into the ocean. Finally, the tubes finished filling. He pushed the raft overboard. "Ready?"

Polly nodded.

Cringing, Sam braced himself and jumped. He hoped his imagination had exaggerated his memory of the sea's sub-zero temperature.

No dice.

If anything, it was twenty degrees colder than he remembered. The icy grip of the Pacific seized his muscles in a vice, his breath stolen by the sheer shock of it.

Sam belly-crawled over the flattened half of the raft, pulling himself up onto a hard tube of air. His feet stuck out from the drifting floor. He looked back.

Polly shone her flashlight around the deck, its beam tearing through the darkness as she searched for something.

"Come on," he yelled.

"I can't find my Beretta." As she continued searching, the bow disappeared into the ocean, the superstructure creaking under the strain and picking up speed as it filled.

"Polly! Let it go. The boat's too dangerous. When it sinks, it could pull you under."

Growling in frustration, she removed her heavy utility belt and kicked off her shoes.

The pilothouse filled, submerging the steering wheel.

Polly hopped up onto the edge of the doomed boat's railing and dove overboard. She resurfaced a few seconds later and dragged herself onto the damaged raft beside him, gripping an inflated tube.

They pushed off from the *Finders Keepers* and began to kick.

Sam glanced back in time to see Savannah's hard-fought prize disappear beneath the waves. She would *not* be happy. If he didn't survive, at least he wouldn't have to face her with the bad news. Death or life, glass half full either way.

"Sorry about your Beretta," Sam said, kicking hard. "I lost my Sig back on the *Vengeance*."

"That was my lucky gun," she groused. "We've been through a lot together."

"I understand. I'm going to get my Sig back," he vowed.

"Oh yeah, Rambo? How?"

"No idea. But there's going to be a reckoning."

They fell silent as they took up a steady rhythm. Despite the heavy waves, the tumultuous current seemed to assist them.

As the shattered raft crept toward shore, heat blazed through Sam's limbs from relentless effort, even as the night air turned his face and hands to popsicles—his body waging war between fire and frost.

After what felt like days, they neared the breaker's edge. He'd tamed thousands of waves, most of which were larger and more violent than those they faced now. But on a half-deflated rubber raft, and without his board, there was no chance of an elegant reentry.

They would wipe out.

Sam looked back, trying to predict the approach of a smaller wave.

Polly too stared at the turbulent sea, evidently thinking the same thing.

He kept one arm wrapped around the tube and gripped Polly's freezing fingers with his free hand.

She met his gaze, holding tight to his hand.

No matter what happened, they wouldn't let go. They either both made it, or they both died.

They faced the ocean, waiting. When a moderate wave approached, he glanced at her.

She gave a sharp nod.

They kicked, building momentum. Frothy white water seized the raft, its raw power dragging them behind it. Would they be able to ride it in, or would the ocean claim them?

With a resounding crash the wave broke, driving them beneath the surface, the salty water a crushing weight. Sam clung to Polly's hand as their lifeboat tumbled, shoving them deep.

Holding his breath, Sam let the current carry him, flowing with it as it pushed them toward shore.

His feet found the sandy bottom, and he surged upward, bursting from the neck-deep water. Gasping for air, he hauled Polly with him, refusing to let go. At five feet and change, the ocean was still too deep for her to stand. He pushed hard, yanking her above the surface just as another wave pummeled them.

Sam had seen it an instant before it had struck and had braced himself. Polly hadn't had a chance to prepare and was sucked under again. In an adrenaline-spiked burst of strength, Sam pulled her to him. Slipping his hands under her armpits, he rocketed them both upward. They broke the surface like a leaping shark.

She gasped. Wiping her eyes, she frantically scanned the ocean for another wave.

They had seconds before the next one.

He carried her inland until she touched bottom. Still holding hands, they slogged to the shallows. Once they stumbled beyond the breakers, they fell to their knees, then collapsed into the sand, side by side.

Chapter Twenty-Five

Polly and Sam lay on the sand, gasping for air.

"I feel like a beached orca," he wheezed between breaths.

"You look more like a manatee."

"I'll take that as a compliment. Manatees are cute."

She gave him a half-hearted smile. "Only to chubby chasers."

Sam let out a waterlogged chuckle. "That's not exactly politically correct, Cahill."

"In the last hour I've been shot at, saved your dumb ass, nearly drown, and I lost my favorite gun. You're busting my chops because I'm being insensitive?"

"When I quote you in my press release, I'll be sure keep your name out of the papers." Sam rolled onto his back, the sand coating his body like a Shake 'n Bake drumstick and studied the empty ocean.

Polly followed his gaze. "Looks like we lost them."

He dropped his head back. "Thank God. I don't have the energy to fight a disgruntled koala right now."

"Do you always compare yourself to animals, Bradford? I hadn't pegged you for a tree hugger."

"I'm more of an environmental crusader," he replied.

"A rose by any other name."

"I haven't checked my pits lately, but I'm thinking they don't smell too sweet."

Beside him, Polly let out a little laugh. "Yeah, I'm thinking I'm pretty ripe too."

"At least we're still alive to smell each other's stank."

She raised her fist. "Halle-frickin-lujah."

Sam lifted his arm, which seemed to weigh as much as the manatee she'd just compared him to, and bumped her fist.

Letting out a long breath, Sam stared into the black night sky. The fog and clouds had once more released the moon from its incarceration, its pale light casting ghostly shadows on the beach. *Thanks for waiting.* The crescent hung in the inky blackness of space as though lording over the quilt of stars that stretched from horizon to horizon.

Unlike the offshore breezes, the onshore air draped warm and humid, wrapping him like an electric blanket, chasing away the chill in his bones.

Sam fumbled up onto his elbows. His muscles flexed with the limberness of taffy; his core twinged from exertion. A sharp, smoldering ache from Polly giving him CPR antagonized his ribs. Each inhalation an effort as though his lungs had the same efficiency as that of a coal miner with a pack-a-day habit. She hadn't broken any of his bones, a testament to her skills as a paramedic.

Polly, who didn't look as if she felt much better, struggled to her hands and knees. She rested a moment before slowly standing, her back popping as loud as a cap gun. Despite her earlier observation that they'd lost their pursuers, she looked around, her expression troubled, as though expecting Levka the Lion and her merry band of gun-wielding scallywags to storm the beach at any second.

Logically, they both knew the Mafiya probably wouldn't follow them to shore tonight. Probably. But making assumptions about an enemy's tenacious dedication to criminal fuckery was a good way of getting blindsided.

Anything ping your radar? Sam asked Chet.

No. We're alone. But your lady friend isn't so sure.

A cop's instincts never die.

His inner conscience paused. *I don't sense anything, but don't hang out either.*

Roger that.

When no one ravaged the beach but the salty waves, their rhythmic crash a deceptive calm, Polly offered him her hand. "We need to go."

Even in the subdued light, he caught the hard edge of anxiety in her eyes. Her sand-covered body was tense, electrified for war. Sam let her pull him to his feet, and, without a word, Polly set off down the beach.

He fell into step beside her.

They slogged through the rough sand, each step a fight against the shifting grains sucking at their stockinged feet. After stumbling more than once, they slung their arms over each other's shoulders, bracing themselves with the stubborn resolve of survivors.

Their trek along the coast made Moses' desert crossing look like a stroll through Central Park. But finally,

Polly's glass-walled house came into view, glowing against the night. The lights burned behind the thick curtains. If someone waited inside, the heavy fabric kept them hidden.

Kneeling behind a dune, Sam and Polly surveyed the house. No shadows moved. No curtains rustled. No indication anyone waited for them.

For what it's worth, Chet said, *I don't think anyone's inside.*

You sure?

Not a hundred percent. No. But I'm not seeing anything that says "perps be lingering here."

Sam didn't reply to Chet the Pirate. Instead, he leaned into Polly's ear. "Anything?"

Though her eyes remained troubled and fixed on her house, she gave a quick, single shake of her head.

They threaded a jungle of beach grass. Sam pressed his back to the wall next to the door. His sandy clothes grinding against the siding. Polly knelt and pulled a plant from the narrow flowerbed, revealing an underground pot. Inside the terra-cotta bowl lay a .38 revolver sealed in a plastic bag. She dropped the false daisy back into place, unwrapped the gun, and checked its cylinder.

She flattened herself against the wall next to him.

He could see the former cop working through a mental plan to clear the house. She looked into his eyes. He thought she'd tell him to wait. An order they both knew he would ignore.

Instead of giving him the hand signal to stand down, Polly got up onto her toes and whispered into his ear, her hot breath tickling his skin. "I have the gun, cowboy. If there's someone inside, no heroics. I'll drop him. You touch me like you did last time, and the next round will go into your balls. Got it?"

Message delivered.

She patted his cheek, giving him a smile as sweet as vinegar. They swapped places, so she had point nearest the door. Using tactical hand signals, she gave him the breach plan. She'd go left into the kitchen. Sam would follow. Polly arched a brow, wordlessly asking him if he was ready.

Entering a potential hostile location unarmed yet again was like chewing broken glass. But he'd lost his Sig back on the *Vengeance*. That was on him. He just hoped they didn't pay for that mistake now. After creating his own mental plan—one that didn't involve tackling her no matter how many bullets flew—he gave her a sharp nod.

Polly typed the code into the electronic lock. The whine of the retracting bolt announced their presence as effectively as the blare of a trumpet. She pushed open the door, dropped, rolled. As the sand from her clothes scattered over the hardwood, she came up sweeping left then right with the small revolver.

Sam followed low, closing and locking the door to keep anyone from following. He went to the opposite side of the hall, his gaze searching for potential threats. No Buddha statue weapons this time. He'd stick with his bare hands.

When no shots rang out and no one attacked her, Polly slid into the kitchen, Sam right behind. He scanned the space and the room beyond. Other than Saundy watching them from her bed in the corner of the dining room, no one waited.

Polly knelt in front of the sink, slinked an arm into a cupboard, and tossed Sam a Glock.

Damn, that's sexy.

He checked the clip, the whisper of steel-on-steel deafening in the hollow silence. A quick press of the slide gave a soft click loud enough to be heard on the far side of the moon.

Round chambered. Game on.

They invaded the living room.

Nails clicked on the hardwood behind him—Saundy trailed them with bright, curious eyes.

Good.

If someone had broken in, she'd be hiding, not tagging along. Another sign they weren't walking into an ambush. Not a guarantee. But something.

They moved through the house leaving a light trail of sand in their wake. His senses, razor-sharp, devoured every creak, shadow, and scent.

Move. Sweep. Clear.

This was who he was.

He needed this—the rush, the danger, the clawing teeth of death at his heels.

Sam had died tonight. When Polly resuscitated him, she hadn't just restarted his heart—she'd resurrected him. Pulled him from the brink of extinction. Of obsolescence.

The truth hit him like a .45 slug: he needed this. Needed danger snarling and snapping at his heels, a gun in his hand and death waiting around the corner, its cold breath on his neck. To feel alive, Sam needed someone trying to kill him.

A touch on his arm.

Polly studied his face, brow furrowed. A question he couldn't read. Maybe she sensed the shift in him—one warrior's heart recognizing another—or maybe she just thought he'd gotten distracted.

Whatever her musings, the mystery remained locked behind those sharp green eyes.

After a beat, she seemed to find her answer—or gave up trying. They pressed on. Side by side, they finished securing the house.

Chapter Twenty-Six

After they checked the locks on the doors and windows, Polly retrieved a pair of towels, tossing one to Sam. The worn fabric was as soft as down. He'd been freezing in the ocean, but the heat of the evening and the adrenaline rush of clearing the house had jacked his internal thermostat, leaving him flushed.

The Chameleon bodysuit sucked away perspiration like a champ, but its embedded camouflage technology robbed the fabric of the breathability his advanced neoprene wetsuit had, trapping a layer of heat around his body. Sweat dotted his brow; a bead trickled down his temple.

He unfastened the pouch from his waist, dropped it onto the table, and partially unzipped the suit's chest, allowing cool air to wash over his skin. He felt ten degrees cooler in an instant.

Polly returned to the kitchen and pulled the leftover pizza out of the fridge. She tore open the box like a pilfering raccoon. Her teeth sank into a slice. Her jaw worked as she leaned against the counter, staring unseeingly into oblivion.

Sam's stomach gurgled, and he followed Polly's lead. The pizza tasted even better than it had earlier. Near-death experiences—or in his case *actual* death—didn't just enhance the flavors of food, they made them explode in your mouth. "I have a question for you."

She seemed to drag herself back to the here and now, refocusing on him.

He talked around a mouthful of cheese and crust. "When I was unconscious on the back deck of the *Finders*—"

She pulled a couple of bottles of water from the cupboard and handed him one. "You mean when I pulled your ass from the ocean, thereby preventing you from drowning and hypothermia, and then gave you CPR because you had no pulse and had stopped breathing? Oh, and you rewarded my efforts for saving your hide by pushing my face away and calling me Jake."

"Yeah, that."

Her dimples made a grand reappearance as a slight grin tugged at her lips. "What about it?" She took a long drink while watching him with amusement in her eyes.

"I was having a dream about my brother."

"Kinda figured."

Sam sorted through the fuzzy memories, stretching his mind to recall a conversation he couldn't quite grasp. Giving up, he said, "Jake and I were having drinks at this café in Malibu. We were sitting around talking when Jake tackled me and dumped so much beer over my face I couldn't breathe. That was probably my brain interpreting my lungs full of salt water."

"Probably."

"And then he hit me in the chest over and over."

"That was me giving you CPR," she confirmed.

"Right. I was half in this world and half in dreamland when it got really weird. He screamed at me. Something about not being at the Ritz."

She shrugged. "Me again. I needed to get your attention. I think I told you to wake up because you weren't at the Ritz. That's not exactly it, but something like that."

"Did you call me a skell?"

She let out a little laugh. "Oh, yeah. I suppose I could have called you a pussy, like your fellow Marines do, but that's an insult to pussies. You're insinuating they're weak, which is completely false. Pussies are tough sonsabitches."

Sam let out a surprised chuckle. "That so?"

"Not that you'll ever experience it firsthand, but if mine had arms, it could bench three-fifteen and pin Hulk Hogan in a single round."

Sam chuckled. "I'd pay big money to see that."

"Bet your ass," she replied, and they clinked water bottles.

He focused on devouring the cold sausage, mushroom, and pepperoni pizza. After a beat, he said, "Of all the things that went down this evening, there are two moments that keep going through my head."

"With your mind that busy, I'm surprised I don't smell something burning." She waved at him. "Please, share with the class. This is a safe space."

"Obviously. The first is the way that guy sneered at us right before he pulled the trigger on the front machine gun."

"That douche got exactly what he had coming. What about it?"

Sam chuckled. "He thought he had us dead to rights. Lined up for the kill shot. When bam!"

She giggled. "He flew through the air like the star preacher at a pagan's rave."

"And—" Sam laughed harder. "—when he landed, his clothes were smoking. I don't know why that's so funny, but it is."

"I'll tell you why. It was instant karma. Sometimes bad things actually happen to bad people. It doesn't happen often enough, but when it does, it's as sweet as grandma's cookies."

He laughed again at her metaphor. "One of my Marine buddies, Collins, used to say after we gave the enemy an epic beatdown, 'When Commie Joe goes to Hell, the devil asks him, *What was the last thing that went through your mind when you bit it?*'"

Polly yelled the punchline, "My ass!"

They burst out laughing.

After everything he'd been through, after all that had happened the last few months, it felt good—good, damn it!—to let his hair and his guard down. Never would he have guessed it would have been with Polly Cahill. But sometimes life threw a curve ball.

Around her lingering chuckles, Polly took a drink. "So, what's the second thing you keep thinking about?"

"How adept you were at fixing the *Finders'* engine."

"Hey! Just because I'm a girl doesn't mean I don't know my way around a six-point-two liter, V8, fuel-injected, three-fifty horsepower Ilmor."

He held up his hands as though in surrender. "It's not that you're a girl. It's that nowadays, that's a pretty rare skill."

"Sad, but true."

"Where'd you learn to work on engines?" he asked.

"Aside from having to perform minor mechanical surgery on the RU boats, I have an eighty-four Bronco."

He whistled. "Nice ride."

"And I don't see the point in owning a classic vehicle if you can't do the work to keep it up." She shrugged. "Cars were simpler back then. Don't need a lot of computers and equipment to keep them purring."

"It's almost more artistry than anything else," he agreed. "How'd you land it?"

"It was my brother's."

Sam thought back to her dossier. Feigning ignorance, he asked, "Why'd he give it up?"

Her face and voice grew sober. "I inherited it when his convoy ran over an IED in Syria."

"Marines?" Sam asked.

"Liam was an army corporal."

He nodded. "Your brother was leading a team."

It wasn't a question, and Polly didn't reply, her silence louder than words. The far-off look in her eyes told him all he needed to know.

He let a few seconds drag by. "When Jake died, it tore me and my parents apart."

She looked up at him, a silent question in her eyes.

"Drugs," Sam said. "It was a long, ugly road. He just couldn't kick the monkey. In the end, it kicked him."

Her gaze drifted back to that distant place where life stomped through the picnic, took a dump in the potato salad, and used the family's blanket to clean itself up. She drew a long breath. "Dad never found out. About Liam, I mean," she said, her voice low and thick. "Two days before Liam, my dad died in the Geneva bombings."

"Jesus," Sam said, playing dumb. A pang of guilt struck him. Treating her like a mark felt dirty. Pretending he didn't already know her scars wasn't just a lie, it was a betrayal. If they were going to stay partners, he owed her more than that.

Someday he would tell her about the background check—though that conversation led to The Agency, and sharing anything about his employer was tantamount to treason. Honesty in his world was a loaded gun. So he said nothing, swallowed the guilt, and kept playing his part.

"Why was he there?"

"He was security detail for the Speaker."

"Wow." Instead of saying something like "I never would have guessed"—a lie she might have detected—he asked, "And your mom?"

Polly let out an ironic laugh. "Mom... That's a whole other shit show. Let's just say that she didn't approve of me joining the academy."

It sounded like they hadn't been able to bridge their philosophical chasm after all.

Polly glanced up at him. "What about your parents?"

Sam finished his second slice of pizza and grabbed another. "Dad died not too long after Jake. Heart attack." He paused, putting up an emotional blast shield to keep the memories from busting his dike. "Mom couldn't handle being alone and took a bottle of sleeping pills."

He didn't share his past often, but when he did, people usually offered their condolences and their sympathy, mostly because they didn't know what else to say. The insincere platitudes were people's way of dealing with the darkness of death.

Instead, Polly summed up the world in three words. "Life's a bitch." Having gone through something similar, she knew no words offered comfort or would bring back the dead.

"Amen to that."

Leaning against the counter, side by side, their shoulders pressed together, they ate in silence. Most of the sand had fallen off their clothes, but they still created a small puddle of grains, and he wondered if Polly would have to refinish the floor to undo the damage.

"You handled yourself pretty good out there," Sam said around a mouthful of pie. "For a paramedic."

She gave him an amused look. "So did you. For a jarhead."

Their gazes locked for several heartbeats, the air thick with things neither dared say. Her breath was warm and close, a new softness flickering in her green eyes.

For an instant, he saw it—an impossible dream. The two of them living a provincial life in this little town, playing Mr. and Mrs. Smith. Scouting scumbags by night. Killing bad guys on the weekends. Vacation missions up and down the West Coast, waging their own war against the Mafiya. Together.

A deep part of him recognized the absurdity of the vision. He had a clean-up job to do with The Agency. If he straightened that mess out, they wouldn't allow him to stay. Deep cover meant alternate IDs and solo infiltrations. No partners. No exceptions. If he failed, they wouldn't just fire him—they'd bury him in a hole six feet deep. Either way, there was no future here. No roots to plant.

Even as the hounds of reality tore the throat of his little dream, for right this minute, a flame of hope burned bright—as though foretelling a future that *could* be.

He'd just been considering leaning in for a kiss when she held up a finger.

Her voice dusty, she said, "I don't know what I'm thinking, but I can't go there right now."

Sam arched a brow at her and, quoting one of his favorite lines, said, "So you're saying there's a chance."

She gave a small shake of her head and a little grin that engaged her dimples. "First, that's a *great* movie. Second, it's three in the morning. I'm exhausted, you're exhausted, and since I'm more than tempted, it means I'm sure as hell not thinking right. But until I figure it out, we need to keep on working the case." Polly paused. "Otherwise, things could get... complicated."

He gave a brief nod. She was right, of course. He was bone-weary and not thinking clearly either. In the morning, he would see what a foolish idea it had been.

She looked him in the eyes, holding his gaze.

His heart gave a hard thump. Despite what she'd just said and despite acknowledging it, he wondered if she'd changed her mind.

At last, Polly looked away, breaking the spell with an almost audible pop. "I'm going to shower. There's only one, so I'll let you know when I'm done." She scanned him from top to bottom. "I have some oversized sweats that will more or less fit you. You can put your clothes in the washer or take them home. I don't care which, but I want my sweats back *clean*."

"Yes, ma'am," Sam replied.

"I've got to be at the clinic at seven thirty, so when I'm done, I'm getting some sack time." She eyed him. "The only shower is in the master bathroom. After the night we've had, I won't ask you to go home, but you'd better not wake me up while you're in there, or I'll make your sortie to the *Vengeance* look like a Princess cruise vacation." Though her words sounded fierce, amusement and perhaps a challenge shined in her green eyes.

She inclined her head toward the Glock. "Keep that for tonight. But tomorrow evening, I expect to find it loaded and back in its rightful place under the sink."

Sam nodded again.

"Give me an hour at the clinic tomorrow to get the lay of the land. Unless I text you otherwise, come at eight-thirty, armed with coffee." Without waiting for him to reply, she snatched the last piece of cold pizza and headed toward the hall. She paused in the kitchen entrance, glancing back at him over her shoulder. "I meant what I said earlier. You did all right out there, Bradford. You suck at following orders, but even so, not bad."

"You did pretty good yourself, Cahill."

"I know. Don't forget, you have to tell Savannah about her boat."

He let out a little groan. Savannah. That conversation might be more heated than his run-in with the Mafiya. In the morning, he'd concoct a story about hitting a reef or something. He had money in his account; he'd make things right. "I'll take care of it."

"There are spare blankets in the hall closet. You know where the couch is." She hesitated, then added, "Who knows what tomorrow will bring?" With that, Polly turned and walked away, Saundy padding silently after her.

Who knows, indeed.

She'd warned him that if they crossed that line, things would get complicated. Polly had no clue how right she was. *Complicated* didn't even begin to cover it.

Her door snicked shut. The shower sputtered to life. Sam stood there in the oppressive silence.

The Agency. Polly. The Mafiya. A dead detective. Two murdered men. And himself—he'd died tonight, if only for a few minutes. His chest still burned with the phantom ache of Polly's CPR.

They said dying gave you clarity. Maybe it did. He knew he could never leave the life—the adrenaline and danger were as much a part of his DNA as the color of his eyes.

But he also knew he wanted Polly in that future. Somehow. Some way.

The idea seemed impossible, like snatching a distant star from a storm-clouded sky.

Sam drained his bottle of water, crumpled it in his hand, and dumped it in the trash along with the empty pizza box. He needed to focus on the case. Let tomorrow—and the future—take care of itself. No more what-ifs. No more dreams. He had a job to do.

The crew of the *Vengeance* had murdered Frank Boreman.

Time to bring them to justice.

Chapter Twenty-Seven

The red eye of the microwave clock mocked him: 3:15 AM. Sam had been up nearly twenty-four hours. Sleep beckoned.

His mind was sluggish, his eyes gritty. His body ached in so many places, he might've fared better spending the day in an industrial clothes dryer.

Taking the phone and Glock with him, he retrieved the blankets from the hall closet, tossed them over the couch, and collapsed into the cushions. The gun lay beside him while the half-eaten pizza slice drooped from his fingers like a wilted flag.

The exhaustion that had been stalking him since they washed ashore crashed over his body like a sneaker wave. Maybe the shower could wait until morning. So tempting to tilt his head back and close his eyes. He could sleep for a year.

But he couldn't rest. Not yet. He still had a decision to make—how much to tell Josha?

If he sent the *Vengeance* files and Josha decided Sam had crossed the line from consultant to operative, that alone could land him in a small cell deep in a federal prison. If The Agency was entangled with the Mafiya, they wouldn't send a cease-and-desist. They'd send an assassin.

Then again, that felt like a stretch. The Agency might be dirty—the Monica case proved something wasn't on the up and up. Maybe someone in the command chain had made a deal with drug lords. But the Mafiya? That felt like a different beast entirely.

Still, there was the matter of Polly's fake background report. The Agency had fed him disinformation, first about Monica, then about Polly. That was a troubling trend.

He didn't know why they'd done it. Maybe it had nothing to do with Frank Boreman's murder. Or maybe it had everything to do with it.

Regardless, the *Vengeance* needed to be stopped.

Polly didn't think they had enough evidence for a Coast Guard bust. She could be right. Maybe he could take down the ship solo. But if things went sideways, having The Agency's firepower behind him could make all the difference.

Stopping the *Vengeance* mattered more than anything else. Unless he found proof The Agency was compromised, Josha stayed in the loop.

Balancing the uneaten pizza on one leg, he unlocked his phone.

His vision blurred. His head bobbed. He considered sleeping first but dismissed the thought. Josha—perpetually awake, perpetually irritable—wouldn't appreciate the delay.

Focus. Get it done.

He started a new email, typing a rough summary of the night's events. Read it. Forced his mind to focus and his stinging eyes to stay open. Reread it. Then he attached the cloud-stored copies of the stolen documents.

His thumb hovered over the screen.

Josha had been clear: consult, don't engage. But Sam had done more than engage. He'd armed up, crossed the line, and kicked in the door.

Josha had to know that was always a possibility.

Right?

Still… Maybe he should wait. Sleep. Rethink and re-read his message when he wasn't coasting on fumes. But then he'd have to explain procrastinating.

"Tired" wouldn't cut it. Exhaustion was just an excuse. The rules were clear: complete all elements of the op. No exceptions. No delays.

Jaw tight, he tapped *Send*.

The message vanished—flashing away at light speed, along with whatever fresh hell it might bring.

After opening the phone's translation app, he uploaded the images, checking the boxes to have them translated and collated. Closing the program, he slid his phone under his leg and laid his head back. His eyes closed as he wrapped his fingers around the Glock's handle.

"Hey!"

Someone kicked his foot, startling him awake.

In a flash, his gun was up, leveled at his attacker before his eyes focused or his mind processed the circumstances. His heart thudded. Muscles tense and coiled for action.

Polly stood in front of him, her long hair damp and tied back. Fitted sweats hugging her body. Her gaze flicked to the barrel of the Glock, then returned to his face. "Calm down, cowboy. It's just me."

He lowered the gun to his lap, his hand shaking slightly from the surge of electrical impulses zinging his nerves.

She appeared unfazed to have been drawn on. "I called out, but you didn't answer. Just came to tell you the shower's free."

He wiped a hand down his face. "Okay. Thanks."

"Night." Polly turned and left the room.

"Night," he called after her.

He almost went back to sleep, but between the quick nap and being startled awake, it would take a few minutes to calm down. Just enough time to get clean. Coated in salt, dried sweat, and the grime of battle, he hauled himself up. Taking his gun and cell with him, he went down the hall.

Polly had left her door partially open, her nightstand lamp still burning.

Sam silently entered her bedroom.

Polly's slim figure was outlined by a heavy quilt. Her dark hair fanned out on the white sheets like a raven's wing. Her hand, tucked under the pillow, was probably wrapped around her revolver. Agency operatives and ex-cops found solace in bullets and steel the way a child might be comforted by their favorite teddy bear.

He entered the modest bathroom, closing the door softly behind him. The warm, humid air smelled of cherry blossoms, soap, and some kind of fruit—apples maybe—drifting on a gentle cloud of feminine strength and fortitude.

His head swam—whether from exhaustion, the intoxicating aroma, or both—he didn't know.

As promised, a pair of gray sweatpants and a navy shirt sat neatly on the counter beside an old, clean towel folded with such precision it would make a drill sergeant salute.

He set the gun and phone on the counter and fired up the shower. The Chameleon bodysuit had adhered to his body as though glued to his skin, requiring him to peel it off inch by inch.

The shower spray lacked pressure, but the glorious hot water scoured away the long miles of the day. He leaned against the wall for a minute, gathering his strength, then washed up.

A few minutes later, as he patted himself dry, he caught a whispered voice. Tying the towel around his waist, he creaked open the door.

Saundy slept in the corner of the bed, but the dog's owner was gone.

Crossing the room, he paused next to the entrance, angling his ear to the narrow gap between the ajar door and the frame.

Polly's quiet, aggravated voice floated in from the kitchen. "And what happened to Soren?"

Since no one answered her, she must have been on the phone. Who could she be talking to at three-thirty in the morning?

"It's not unsanctioned." Her sharp tone indicated irritation. "This was an Agency assignment. Soren himself asked me to—"

Though the caller had cut her off mid-rant, her words echoed in Sam's mind like voices in a cave. *This was an Agency assignment.*

No. No way.

All remnants of exhaustion evaporated. His mind snapped alert, working like a machine.

With an almost audible click, the pieces fell into place. Her disjointed history. Her preference to be alone. Her ability to clear a room, protect herself, and train a crew. She'd been a detective, but her skills had far surpassed what Sam expected of an ex-cop. Even a good one.

His mind flashed to the Investigation Wall and the impossibly detailed, impossible-to-get intel tacked to the sheetrock. She may still have connections in the department, but her primary source of information was...

The Agency.

It explained how she knew about Frank's undercover op. How she knew the inner workings of the Russian Mafiya. Everything.

Polly had gone silent for almost a minute. Then she said something that iced the cord in Sam's spine, "Yes, sir. I'll take care of him."

Sam could hardly believe his own ears. The Agency had just put a hit on him, and Polly Cahill——former detective for the Boston PD——was his assassin.

There's a devil in the congregation.

The words floated up unbidden from the murk of his dream.

Jake.

His dead twin had reached across the veil to tell him he was in bed with the enemy. Figuratively, anyway. Except a part of Sam already knew it. He just hadn't wanted to admit it.

Less than thirty minutes after emailing Josha the *Vengeance* documents, they'd already assigned an assassin to remove him from the gene pool. Either he'd crossed a line or The Agency was in bed with the Mafiya, and he'd gotten too close.

Except Polly knew what he knew.

Perhaps they planned to put a bullet in her after she'd done the same to him. She had to suspect, or at least worry about, their next move.

His body shook with a fresh wave of energy. Careful not to touch the door and alert her she had a witness, Sam pressed his ear to the opening once more, heart galloping against his sternum as though trying to break free from its ribcage prison.

Dozens of questions needed answering. For instance— what was the purpose of the investigation itself?

Why did The Agency—whose specialty was assassination—assign one of their own to investigate a police detective's murder? And why assign *him* to help her?

She wouldn't have included him otherwise.

He thought for a second, then revised the question.

Why did The Agency have *two* of their operatives digging into a detective's murder?

Also, what had they discovered that warranted putting him down? Had he really crossed a line—if so, their response seemed extreme—or was there something in the documents he shouldn't have seen?

"I don't know," she said. "Soon. But everyone in town knows we're working together. If he suddenly turns up dead, it'll look suspicious. Soren told me—"

She went quiet again.

"But my life in the Cove will be at risk if—"

Silence.

"Of course. I'll handle it right away. No one will know it was me."

He heard the distinct beep of the call ending.

Sam pressed his eye to the opening. Polly stood at the kitchen window, fussing with the small carved box on the sill. A phone stash. The box likely had a false back or bottom, maybe even an integrated charger.

I'll take care of him.

His mind still spun. The Agency had just green-lit the hit on one Sam Bradford.

Son. Of. A. Bitch.

Polly set the curio down and stared at the sink, seemingly lost in thought.

Just minutes ago, he'd been thinking... considering... the two of them... a life together...

His vision flashed red as he recalled her lecturing him when they'd first started working together. *If we are going to have any chance of working together, the one thing I'd ask is you not lie to me. I'd much rather have you say nothing at all than try to feed me your tired old BS.*

Look who's been lying to me this whole time.

He had trusted her. Believed in her.

Rage, betrayal, and disbelief thrummed through his veins.

Sam glanced at the Glock on the bathroom counter, then back toward the woman in the kitchen.

She wouldn't see it coming.

His trigger finger itched. His body urged him to move.

Before he did something he couldn't undo, Sam forced a deep, calming breath. Acting rashly was a good way to get dead.

He replayed the probable chain of events. The orders she must have received. Investigate Frank's murder. Befriend Sam. Kill Sam.

Had she known it would come to this?

Very likely.

Meaning she had probably disobeyed—or at least bent—those orders when she'd saved his life. If she'd been assigned to kill him, she wouldn't have bothered resuscitating him.

Or was that not always part of the original plan? Had the mission progressed or evolved to this final, inevitable objective?

Maybe he should vanish. Slip out the front door. In less than an hour, he'd have a new identity and be on the road.

Alternatively, he could confront Polly while she reeled.

Except he didn't know what came next. They might have it out in the kitchen—one walking away, the other bleeding to death on the floor.

Even if it didn't go south and she claimed she still had his back, he'd have to assume it was another ploy.

Lying came as natural as digestion to every employee at The Agency. He should know.

His third option awaited on the bathroom counter, one 9mm round in the chamber.

He'd still have to shed his name, and they'd send someone else. But removing Polly from the equation would buy him time.

Except… that meant running.

And Sam Bradford never backed down from a fight.

He wouldn't start now.

No matter what happened, he'd face The Agency—and Polly Cahill—head on.

They wouldn't know what hit them.

Not until it was far, far too late.

Chapter Twenty-Eight

Sam slipped back into the bathroom, carefully closing the door behind him. The faint click of the latch
echoed in the humid silence. As he finished drying off, the
lingering scent of cherry blossoms infused the air with the
fading dreams of yesteryear. He stared at the steam-dis-
torted man in the mirror.

The *mark* in the mirror.

He'd devoted ten years to The Agency—put his life on
the line countless times, sacrificed his individuality, murdered, cheated, and lied—all in service of an organization that had just decided to 86 him.

Chet had said they might put a hit on him. The two of
them had joked about it over the years. But Sam had never thought they'd actually do it.

If he hadn't overheard Polly's conversation, he never
would have seen it coming either.

His blindness to the truth, his blindness to The Agency,
his blindness to *her* only fed his boiling anger. What else

had he missed? What other truth mines waited to blow his legs out from beneath him?

His hands shook as he folded the towel and draped it over the side of the laundry hamper. He concentrated on slowing his pulse. Calming the storm raging through his heart.

Given your recent history with The Agency, this is not entirely a surprise, Chet said.

Yeah, I suppose. I honestly thought the worst they might do was drop me into a hole.

Chet admitted, *This does seem extreme.*

It explains the tone in Josha's voice. He knew he was passing on a false dossier. He knew Polly was an assassin with my name at the top of her list.

Chet replied, *We don't know that for sure, though it seems like a logical conclusion.*

You don't think he knew she had me on her list?

I think The Agency is one of the most compartmentalized organizations in the world. My guess is that Josha knew she was an operative but didn't know her mission.

Sam considered for a moment. *And since he couldn't divulge that she was an agent, he passed on the fake dossier.*

Yes, Chet said. *He probably assumed you'd figure it out and perhaps even make the logical leap to her being an operative.*

Sam digested Chet's theory, seeing if that made any difference in the way he felt. It didn't. He understood the hypocrisy of his feelings; he'd spent the last ten years lying and manipulating everyone around him. Yet, he couldn't help it. *I'm having a lot of trouble giving him the benefit of the doubt right now,* Sam admitted.

It's only a hypothesis. The truth is out there, though you aren't going to see it until you calm down.

Chet was right. He had to process as much as he could as quickly as he could. Emotions would only hinder his abilities and cloud his vision. Employing some of Zen Master Abby's meditation techniques, he took another deep breath. When he pushed it out, he also pushed away all thoughts about betrayal and loyalty and honor. Focus.

After a minute more of impromptu meditation, he let his mind off its leash. *Polly's been living a regular life in the Cove—either retired, or on sabbatical, or as a sleeper agent. They decided I'm too unstable, or rogue, or whatever, then reenabled and ordered her to take me out. It's kind of The Agency's MO.*

His inner conscience nodded in agreement. *But why did they make her wait?*

Exactly. She's had a lot of opportunities to "take care" of me. Hell, she saved my life tonight. She literally brought me back from the dead. Talk about an opportunity.

These are new orders from a new handler.

So her old handler, Soren, didn't tell her to kill me, Sam said. *At least not right away.*

The sequence of events fits.

Then what were her original orders?

To bring you in close under the guise of working on a case together, Chet said. *Milk you for intel, then put you in a situation where you could be conveniently killed without suspicion.*

What intel?

No idea.

Sam considered. *That can't be all of it. We're missing something.*

Chet shrugged. *Could be. But the ways of the Agency are as mystical as a gun-wielding paramedic with murder in her heart. The brass sometimes puts a hold on delivering final judgment. You know that. Get in position. Get close. Wait. We bide our time while the mucky mucks drink brandy and smoke cigars at the Casbah. Then, after the boys are done nursing their hangovers, they give the order to move forward.*

I suppose. He thought for a moment, trying to discern what bothered him. *It just seems too complicated.*

We've done cases that were more elaborate.

I guess.

Chet gave him a get-real look. *Does it matter?*

What do you mean?

You and I both know that the whys behind a hit are above our pay grade. If you want to live, you'd better pull your head out of your ass and start coming up with a plan.

Chet was right. Sam needed to stop trying to decipher The Agency's reasoning and focus on survival.

He pulled on Polly's sweatpants, which only hung to his knees, reminding him of knickerbockers worn by men in the late 19th century. He held up the sweatshirt, which didn't look big enough to fit Saundy. If reality hadn't just doused him in a rainstorm of shit, he would have suspected Ms. Cahill wanted him to remain shirtless because she longed to satisfy her sweet tooth with some Bradford eye candy. Now, he saw her motivations for what they were—just another way to erode his defenses.

He wrestled the shirt over his body, the fabric clinging like a banana peel, the tight fit amplifying the ache in his bruised ribs. Finger tight on the Glock's trigger, he draped his Chameleon bodysuit over the weapon to conceal that he held it at the ready. After snapping off the light, he waited—listening, giving his eyes a few seconds to adjust. The shadows sharpened into focus.

Muscles tense, Sam stepped into the bedroom.

Polly lay on her back, her hand once again tucked under the pillow. She and Saundy snored in unison—a deceptively peaceful rhythm that belied the danger hidden beneath the blankets. He studied her slim figure, tracing the contours outlined by the thick quilt. If she moved, she'd be in for a rude surprise.

But neither woman nor dog stirred.

For the first time, he felt like he saw her clearly. Beneath the lifesaving, RU-running paramedic lay the soul of an assassin.

Like him.

While Sam depended on charm and manipulation to get close to his marks, Polly's grace, strength, and beauty—combined with the ability to play whatever persona she chose—would easily disarm anyone. She was one hell of an effective operative. The Agency had trained him to smell deceit, yet she'd fooled him good. A mistake he would *not* repeat.

Sam left the room, closing the door softly behind him.

If he went home, securing the shack-like premises would be challenging. Too many potential breach points. It would also put distance between him and Cahill, giving her potential deniability if he turned up dead. Going to a hotel felt too much like running. Besides, with the wagging tongues of this town, word would get back to her, and he'd have the same security issues.

Also, leaving would tip his hand that he knew. He had to hold tightly to that ace.

Keep your enemies close.

His best option was to stay put. Maintain the ruse and secure his position.

Feeling like a man who'd suddenly found himself trapped in a dream, he passed the washer and absently considered dropping his clothes inside. But the sloshing of the barrel might mask the sound of her sneaking up on him. Polly could move as silently as a ghost, but he didn't want to make her job that much easier. He hung his grimy bodysuit on a hook beside the machine.

Glock in hand, he returned to the living room and settled onto the couch.

From this position, he could monitor both the hallway and dining room entrances. He reviewed other points of ingress and egress. If Polly slipped out a window, she could sneak around to the front or rear of the house, but not even she could undo the electronic locks without alerting him. The main door opened into the primary arterial hallway, which he had covered.

Sam turned off the lights and lay down, facing the front of the house. He tucked the Glock beside his hip, keeping his hand wrapped around its handle. His soldier's instincts awake and firing. If Polly attempted an approach—not likely, but always a probability—Chet would wake him.

For the moment, he was safe. He should catch some Zs. It had already been a hell of a long day. Tomorrow might be longer. He needed to keep his eyes sharp and his wits sharper.

But despite his exhaustion, he and slumber felt millions of miles apart. His mind whirled.

Mentally, Sam swapped their roles. As the assassin, what would *he* do?

He would have let her drown in the ocean, for one. That would have been the quickest and most succinct solution. But either she or The Agency had screwed up. Polly never should have let him live. Maybe the orders hadn't come through yet, or maybe she'd disobeyed them—unlikely but possible. Either way, he'd make them pay for that mistake.

His first reaction to her phone conversation had been to kill her. Put a bullet in her head and vanish. But he couldn't quite flip the switch from thoughts of a future with her to murder.

Though they hadn't talked about it in depth, when he'd almost leaned in for a kiss, he'd seen the desire in her eyes. *I'm more than tempted*, she'd told him. It hadn't just been physical, but a longing for connection. For partnership. For a life together.

Except that was shit. All of it.

She'd done what operatives did—lured him in, made him believe one thing while secretly plotting something else. He should know; he'd done it hundreds of times. Crushed hearts and dreams under his boot of indifference.

Under orders, just like hers.

But their budding partnership—fixing the *Finders'* engine together, evading the *Vengeance,* washing ashore side by side—not all of that could have been an act. Could it?

With a sinking feeling, the truth struck home. He'd trusted her, and she'd duped him. Made a fool of him.

And he'd fallen for it.

He raised the gun, pointing it toward the hallway, imagining Polly—The Agency mask gone, the killer beneath exposed—standing with her revolver aimed back at him.

His Glock bucked. A third eye bloomed in her forehead. As smoke drifted through the air, the familiar scent of scorched gunpowder and burnt ozone wrapped comfortably around him. Blood seeped from the hole in her skull, staining crimson the memories of warmth and camaraderie he'd felt just hours ago.

The hand holding the Glock trembled as the anger surged again. But this wasn't just about a bruised professional ego. Yes, her skills had bested his in this round. It happened when you went head-to-head with a pro.

Its roots ran deeper, striking a personal nerve that flared from betrayal. For the first time in over a decade, he'd let himself trust someone. Let himself believe life could be more than just one long solo operation. And while Polly had been the spark, the cataclysmic delusion had been his.

He'd let his guard down, and it had nearly cost him everything.

Sam had to get control of himself, or he might as well go underground and never resurface. He sent a silent apology to Abby—who always said emotions needed to be sifted through, not buried. But he had to do what worked for him.

He closed his eyes, centering himself—cramming his fury at The Agency for putting a hit on him, his sense of betrayal at Josha for not warning him, and his resentment at Polly for deceiving him into a little glass prison. As the box's sides blazed, the faces of those who had double-crossed him floated in an inferno of orange and red flames as hot and violent as the *Vengeance's* tracers, he sealed the lid shut.

Sam opened his mental vault, already filled with thousands of emotional boxes—the loss of his parents, his divorce, Jake's spiral as the demon drug consumed him, his dismissal from the Marines—and added it to the stack. He hefted the door closed and gave the lock a good spin, the metallic *whoomph* echoing in his mind. As the dial's clicking slowed and then stopped, he took a deep breath. Calm filled his soul.

Free of emotional distractions, he could work the problem.

While immediate survival had to be his top priority, even if he swallowed his pride and ran, fleeing wasn't an option. He and Polly had uncovered something much bigger than either of them had expected. Yes, he wanted justice for a fellow Marine, but the Mafiya angle had blindsided him. The bigger picture—protecting America—mattered more than his or Polly's lives. What they'd uncovered, he felt in his bones, was a cancer infecting his country. He didn't know how or why, but the certainty rang like the Liberty Bell.

He had to see it through. That meant working the case with Polly while avoiding the business end of her gun.

Back to his first priority: staying alive.

Polly wanted to keep her life in the Cove. That was her greatest weakness and Sam's greatest leverage.

Given that, her new orders, and their current situation, what would *he* do? He wouldn't shoot someone in his own home, where even an incompetent blowhard like Sheriff Austin could tie him to the murder. He'd put distance between himself and the mark. He'd want more than just plausible deniability. He'd want total absolution.

Which meant he needed to publicly tie himself to Polly Cahill. It was no secret they'd been working together, but that wasn't enough. He needed something more elaborate, more spectacular—and let the gossip mill do the heavy lifting for him.

To figure out the *what* and *when* of the hit, he had to decipher her orders. He replayed her conversation.

And what happened to Soren?

In his entire decade at The Agency, Sam had only ever worked with Josha. They had reassigned Polly to someone new. Her indignant and disconcerted tone said The Agency hadn't alerted, consulted, or warned her.

It's not unsanctioned, and this was an Agency assignment. Soren himself asked me to...

Whoever had replaced Soren did *not* approve of her investigating Frank's murder.

From what he could tell, her orders sounded disjointed. Uncoordinated. The Agency didn't investigate murders—they instigated them. They almost never put a hold on a hit, and they never swapped handlers. Ever.

Could the Mafiya somehow be connected to The Agency? He'd dismissed the notion earlier, but the timing was suspect. It seemed too convenient that just thirty minutes after he sent the *Vengeance* documents, his name landed on the hit list.

Something faint resonated in the back of his mind.

There's a devil in the congregation. You know who it is——you just won't admit it.

Jake had said that while Sam was dying and Polly was saving him. Had his brother said something else too? Something that might help him make sense of this whole mess? Sam fought to remember the conversation's details, but try as he might, the answer eluded him. Gnawing on that rag would only bring frustration, so he let it go——for now.

Despite the tornado of questions swirling in his mind, he found himself teetering on the brink of unconsciousness. The day's events had taken a toll. He needed to recharge his batteries.

But even as he neared the precipice of sleep, *I'll take care of him* and *There's a devil in the congregation* kept drifting through his mind.

He stared out the kitchen window, seeing but not really seeing the slivered moon. Unlike his thoughts, the fog and clouds had cleared. The stars shimmered, brilliant against a black velvet sky.

He could use a little of that brilliance right about now.

Though a hundred questions roamed his thoughts, Sam knew one thing for certain: The Agency could send a dozen operatives to put him down. He would turn the tables on all of them——including Polly Cahill.

Even if it meant killing her before she killed him.

Chapter Twenty-Nine

A buzzing like an electric chainsaw yanked Sam from sleep, the sound piercing the fog of his restless dreams. Blankets flew as he rolled off the couch, landing in a kneeling position. Sweeping the room with his Glock, he aimed at anything that moved.

Which was everything.

But instead of Polly or men in black suits bearing down on him, the heavy curtains trundled open, revealing the wall of windows. In the dining room, whining motors lifted the blinds, their mechanical hum echoing faintly through the stillness.

With a soft ping, the retraction cycle ended. Silence returned. Morning sunshine bathed the house in a dusty ember glow. Sam lowered the weapon.

He swiped at the beads of sweat peppering his temples and rolled his shoulders, wishing Polly had warned him about the curtains' automatic timers. Then again, given all the other secrets she'd kept, this barely registered.

He exhaled, nerves still taut, and reached for the blanket—only to freeze at the sudden beep slicing through the quiet. Glock up, he turned toward the sound.

A moment later, he recognized it—an alarm clock.

There was a soft thump, followed by the scratch of claws on hardwood. Saundy bounded down the hall and into the kitchen. Sam peered around the corner just in time to see the little terrier leap onto the counter, press her nose to a button on the coffee maker, and hop back to the floor.

On the return trip, she skidded to a halt. Cocking her head, she stared at Sam as if to ask what, exactly, he'd been planning to shoot. He lowered the Glock to his waist.

They held each other's gaze. Her ears pert, shiny black eyes inquisitive.

Polly's sleepy voice called from down the hall. In a flash of canine exuberance, Saundy bolted back to the bedroom.

Sam considered going home to get dressed but dismissed the thought. Every minute here was an opportunity to study, to assess, to prepare. The more he knew, the better he could predict her actions and reactions.

Accompanied by the quiet burble of the coffee maker, he lay back down on the couch, covering himself with the blanket. He had no desire to talk. Even engaging in small talk might be dangerous. He'd compartmentalized his feelings, but he still didn't know if he could keep the tension and resentment out of his voice or the anger from flashing in his eyes.

Agency Operative Polly Cahill had been trained to detect the subtlest changes in demeanor. If she suspected he knew about her or her true mission, she might be forced to escalate prematurely.

When they had their confrontation, he wanted it to be at a time and place of his choosing. Maintaining control over as many elements as possible would provide the greatest chance of survival.

For both their sakes, he pretended to sleep as Polly went about her morning routine. Though her footsteps were as silent as those of a prowling lynx, Saundy's claws tick-tick-ticked over the hardwood as she trotted after her owner, a virtual canine GPS. Following the sound of the terrier and tracking ambient noises—the soft clink of a coffee mug, the quiet whomp of the fridge door, the slide of kitchen drawers—Sam traced the assassin's movements on his mental map of the house. In his mind's eye, he watched her pour coffee, fill Saundy's bowl with kibble, and gather her things in preparation for the day.

He kept a tight grip on the Glock, ready to drop, roll, and fire at a second's notice. But if she intended to kill him this morning, she gave no indication of it.

Polly returned to her room, closing the door behind her.

Alone again, Sam stayed still—though his mind was anything but calm.

Staying alive and advancing the case remained his top priorities. For now, he didn't think she'd try anything. They were scheduled to meet at eight-thirty, and he'd show up armed with coffee as she'd asked. Unless she changed the location to somewhere isolated, the hit would come later. Just another day in the office.

By then, he'd have safeguards in place. What those safeguards were, he didn't yet know, but he'd figure it out.

He replayed her half of the early morning phone call, trying to piece it together. Aside from the likely kill order, it sounded as though she'd been told to back off the Frank Boreman case. The Agency didn't want the murder solved or the Mafiya investigated, proving there was more at stake than removing a rogue agent. It meant they were protecting someone—or something.

And what did all of this have to do with Frank Boreman? The more he thought about it, the less it seemed The Agency would be concerned over the death of an undercover cop, as opposed to the Russian Mafiya part of the investigation. If that were true, then Soren or someone else had already known there was a connection with organized crime, or they wouldn't have had Polly look into it.

No matter how Sam flipped this case around, everything circled back to the *Vengeance*. That ship wasn't just a clue—it was the fulcrum. The key that opened the entire investigation.

Telling Polly to back off only made it sound like they wanted to cover something up, which motivated Sam to dig deeper. He and Polly had touched a nerve. People overreacted when things got hot, and judging by The Agency's reaction, the pots boiled.

But what about Polly? What was her next move?

Despite everything, he still believed her blood ran blue—loyal to the law, to justice. Could she really let murderers and Mafiya thugs walk just because The Agency said so?

Not following a direct command felt like disobeying the law of gravity, but he didn't think she could let it go. If she was a good operative and dropped the case as command-ed, he'd push it forward anyway—even if he had to drag her with him. He needed to keep her by his side to prevent her from killing him. Also, taking down the Lion and her crew would require more than just a solo operative work-ing from the shadows.

He couldn't do it alone. Not this time. Only together did they stand a chance.

Polly's next move would tell him everything he needed to know. If she tried to let the ship and its crew slink away, she was just another pawn doing The Agency's dirty work. But if she kept digging—even after being told to stand down—maybe there was still hope for her. And if she told him about her orders to ram a dagger through his heart, maybe even for *them*.

The hope of them gave him pause. It was an unlikely perspective he'd not even dared to consider. Just as quickly, he shook it off. The case. That's what mattered. It had to move forward.

As he waited for her to finish getting ready, Sam men-tally replayed the night's events. The *Vengeance* crew's at-tempt to apprehend him hadn't been surprising. They'd caught an intruder red-handed, after all.

Yet, their reaction to the B&E after his escape was ex-treme—even for the Mafiya.

By following the *Finders* into the Territorial Sea—the twelve-mile oceanic perimeter where the US exercised full sovereignty—and unleashing their full arsenal of illegal weapons, so cleverly hidden, the crew of the *Vengeance* had shown just how far they'd go to protect their secrets.

Rule #57: The more one has to hide and the longer they've had to hide it, the more extreme their response to perceived threats.

Long-term stress as a result of criminal activity warps perceptions, erodes mental stability, and exaggerates the abilities, knowledge, and perceived threat of pursuers. Career criminals, who often start out as careful and pragmatic, will, after years or even a few months of sustained prosecutorial opposition—either real or perceived—oftentimes devolve to paranoia and impulsive overreactions.

Forming a relationship or partnership against a common foe can be a useful tactic to gain trust, manipulate, and control a degenerating criminal.

Note of caution: Though a potentially powerful ally, paranoia makes fugitives unpredictable and unstable. Align yourself when needed, but break off the relationship as soon as possible. It is not a matter of if they will turn on you—often with extreme violence—but when.

—122 Rules of Psychology

The Mafiya was desperate. The Agency was desperate. What exactly were they hiding?

Sam didn't know, but he sensed things were connected in ways he couldn't yet see.

He reviewed the events from the night before, one frame at a time—boarding, sabotaging, photographing, fighting. Then he'd jumped into the ocean. A literal leap of faith that his partner would come rescue him.

His memories at this point in the timeline grew murky. He'd swam for a while, then—too weak to continue—drifted. How long had he waited? He didn't know.

He pulled out his phone and did a quick web search. Using the approximate water temperature plus his list of symptoms—numbness leading to muscle fatigue, to no longer feeling cold, and finally loss of consciousness—he estimated that he'd floated in the ocean anywhere from fifty-five minutes to two hours.

The *Finders* had been parked a mile off the *Vengeance's* port. Even calculating for the rough seas, reduced speed to muffle engine noise, and a wide loop around the old ice-breaker to prevent the crew from spotting her, Polly should have arrived in his general vicinity within twenty minutes. Thirty tops.

That left anywhere from twenty-five to ninety minutes unaccounted for. Had she intended to abandon him? If she'd already had her kill order, this made the most sense. But if so, what had caused her to double back and save him?

He vaguely recalled hearing the *Vengeance's* diesels and the distant throaty growl of the *Finders'* engine at some point. Parked between him and the *Finders*, the *Vengeance* would have acted as a sound barrier, much the same way a concrete wall reflected the clamor of highway traffic away from a nearby neighborhood. Which meant that when he'd heard the speed boat, Polly had to have either been in front of or behind the larger ship and headed in his direction. But instead of growing louder, the rumble of the *Finders'* engine had faded until it vanished. The only way that could have happened was if she'd headed toward shore.

Of course, Sam had been borderline delirious by that point. The sounds might have just been his imagination. Or she may have come looking for him but been forced to flee before looping back.

Except that didn't feel right.

She'd spent five years working for RU and served as a paramedic practitioner for nearly as long. She understood how quickly the core temperature of the human body could plummet while submerged. In rescue operations, every second counted. Had she, as per her training and experience, come for him straightaway, she'd have made the journey—Mafiya ship or no Mafiya ship—in record time.

That meant she'd left him to die. Yet something had caused her to turn around. When he'd awakened on the floor of the *Finders*, Polly claimed she'd rescued him as repayment for saving her life three months back. Maybe that was true. Maybe not.

Sam could usually sniff out lies the way a hound could sniff out a rabbit hiding in the bushes. He tried envisioning her expression, the look in her eyes, her body language, and the tone of her voice. But in that moment, he'd been too busy coughing up half the Pacific to take a mental snapshot. The memories were too fuzzy to clarify anything.

She may have been telling the truth, but it was also possible Soren had called her with a last-second counterorder to *not* terminate—the equivalent of a governor staying an execution a minute before midnight. Sam had received a handful of similar calls during his career. The experience was always unsettling.

That also seemed improbable since she'd received yet another call a few hours later countermanding that order. The Agency sometimes reconsidered, but he'd never experienced such flip-flopping.

Her actions begged the question: Had Polly been following orders to save his life, or had she been acting on her own? Perhaps all those years in RU wouldn't let her allow someone to drown?

With nothing more to be gleaned from that line of thinking, he focused once more on the early morning call. Sam had received communications of one form or another in the middle of the night, but never one quite like this. It reeked of someone covering their ass.

Maybe there were mitigating circumstances that warranted replacing Soren. Sam couldn't know. But he did know the delicate operative-handler relationship required trust and respect. That first critical conversation was a time to build rapport. Instead, Polly's new handler had dressed her down like some rookie cop, told her to back off her investigation, and ordered her to immediately eliminate her target.

Polly had, of course, agreed. But she hadn't sounded happy about it. Could it be that she too harbored doubts about The Agency? If so, could she be swayed to disregard a direct order if it benefited the greater good? Her history with the Boston PD showed again and again her willingness to color outside the lines when the case warranted it.

But Agency Operative Polly? That remained unclear. Still, her tone during the call revealed a level of unease and doubt Sam knew all too well.

The click of Polly's bedroom door broke him from his thoughts.

He tightened his grip on the Glock.

Polly didn't seem to be hiding the sound of her footsteps as she strode down the hall and into the kitchen. She spoke softly to Saundy, telling her to be good and to hide if bad people broke in. The dog's nails click-clicked across the hardwood once more.

Through slitted eyes, Sam watched Polly slip on her shoes. After unbolting the front door, she paused, fingers on the knob, looking at him—her gaze so heavy it practically had mass.

An odd combination of emotions crossed her face. But the determination, calculation, and resignation he saw all took a backseat to something more significant. It took him a moment to pin it down.

Conflict.

A war waged inside her. A confrontation between Polly Cahill and Polly Cahill.

Where do your loyalties lie? With truth and country or The Agency?

Whatever her answer, it would shape the war to come.

His heart gave a somber thump. She hadn't flinched, hadn't moved, but somehow he knew—with absolute certainty—that she was aware he was watching.

The two of them stared at one another for several long heartbeats.

Snorting a short breath, she pulled open the door and left. The lock motor whined. The bolt sliding home echoed through the house like the cocking of a rifle.

Saundy lingered in the entryway as though hoping her owner would return.

Sam rolled off the couch and peeked out the front window.

Polly wafted down the driveway like a ninja—light-footed, but strong and capable. She turned left onto the street toward the clinic and disappeared from view.

Sam waited a few minutes to make sure she didn't return before retrieving his bodysuit from the hook next to the washer. He'd kicked off his boots before his extended swim in the ocean. Still barefoot, he wrapped Polly's Glock in the Chameleon and followed her out the front door.

Mr. and Mrs. Bryant had just exited their house across the street as Sam turned right at the end of the drive, the cool morning air biting at his bare toes. Gladis Bryant, the aging elementary school teacher, watched him with curiosity. As her husband fussed with the door, her gaze traveled from Sam's feet, to his knee-length sweatpants, to his ridiculously tight shirt, and finally to his face. She then swiveled her focus in the direction Polly had gone and back again to him.

Sam could almost hear her piecing together a scandalous tale worthy of an afternoon soap opera. She nudged her husband and whispered something.

Inspiration struck.

Sam smiled sheepishly and waved, as if he and Cahill had been caught doing the deed on the front lawn. He held a finger to his lips in the universal sign for secrecy—a gesture that all but guaranteed Mrs. Bryant would do the opposite. A slight disapproving grimace graced her lips, while excitement lit her eyes—an unvoiced promise of the gossip to come.

Let the rumors fly.

Savannah's not going to be amused when she hears about this, Chet said. *Don't you have a date with her today?*

It wasn't official-official or anything.

Well, it might be wise to get ahead of this thing before word of your torrid affair comes crashing down. If you don't, she might come crashing down on you.

Sam sighed. With all that had happened, he didn't have the patience to deal with whatever wrath came with Savannah's potential jealousy. Sure, he'd led her on, let her believe he was interested in something more—but it's not like they were in a committed relationship.

I'll deal with that later, he said to his inner conscience.

Back at his house, he swapped his clothes for a pair of loose khakis, a light button-down shirt, and tennis shoes. He slid his backup Smith & Wesson M&P .45 into the holster fastened at the small of his back. It wasn't his Sig, but it still felt damn good.

He'd been gathering his notes while wondering how far the rumors had already traveled when his inner conscience broke into his thoughts.

While you were busy wondering if your new girlfriend "liked" you enough to disobey Mom and Dad, I was hard at work, doing the heavy thinking. As always.

Oh yeah, Aristotle? Tell me about your profound musings. Sam wasn't in the mood for a Chet lecture, but it usually paid to listen.

It could be, Chet began, t*hat Polly didn't have a change of heart or a change of orders last night.*

Sam perked up. *Explain.*

Not only were the marina RU guards witnesses to your late-night excursion, but she might have been worried you'd blabbed about the two of you taking a midnight cruise together. She could've convinced RU you'd done something stupid to get yourself killed, but if you'd let it slip to Max, or——God forbid——Savannah, who, let's face it, is one of the most proficient gossips the Cove has ever seen, then the word would've already spread far and wide. No way to keep it in-house or explain the situation to the sheriff before the rumor mill did his thinking for him. The scheming tongues of this town would've had her tried and convicted of murder by breakfast.

I guess that's a possibility.

It's more than a possibility, Karen——it's highly probable. She's got a good thing going here. As you said, she'd need more than plausible deniability; she'd want irrefutable, total absolution. That's straight out of The Agency playbook.

Chet had a hell of a good point.

His inner conscience continued, *I'd recommend you don't read too much into her saving your bacon. That was as self-serving as it gets.*

Could "self-serving" be a word to describe Cahill? Sam didn't think so. But until last night, he hadn't known she worked for The Agency. Now he needed to reconsider everything he thought he knew about her.

Zach Ghinhart had claimed, *"You will never find a better, braver, more dedicated officer than Polly Cahill."*

A lot of water had passed under the bridge since she'd saved Zach's life, but in Sam's experience, people didn't change. She did—and would continue to do—what she believed to be the right thing. Which might include ending his life.

He understood, more or less. The two of them held dear the same principles—willing to sacrifice all for the greater good, which made her, in a way, an ally. A fellow soldier.

Still, he couldn't pretend Polly—a professionally trained and fully capable assassin—hadn't been ordered to put a bullet into his brain. Underestimating her would be a fatal mistake. Literally.

Regardless, he held an ace. Neither Polly nor The Agency knew he knew her orders. So, he'd proceed with the investigation as if nothing had changed.

He finished gathering his supplies, quickly flipping through a few of the documents they'd photographed last night. He checked the translator app. No results. Not surprising, considering he suspected the request had triggered The Agency to put a hit on him. It seemed probable that Soren's replacement had kiboshed it.

The Agency's corruption, Josha, Soren, the Russian Mafiya, the *Vengeance*, a slain detective, the dead cop and janitor, Polly's break-in, the hit on him—all of it painted an ugly, if circumstantial, picture of corruption, payouts, murder, and dirty politics.

Sam had to figure out how everything tied together. That meant continuing to work with Polly for as long as she stayed on the investigation. Heeding the old adage, Sam would be keeping Polly Cahill very close indeed.

Chapter Thirty

After stopping in at Sand, Surf, and Brew, Sam made his way to the clinic. The cool sea air held the promise of heat and humidity later in the day. For the first few minutes of the brief trip, the Cahill Heart Attack nearly burned Sam's fingers, forcing him to swap hands several times.

Yellow crime scene tape cordoned off the front entrance of the clinic. Two windowless vans—one belonging to the coroner, the other to the CSI team—sat amongst a smattering of state black-and-whites, the flash of their pompous bubble bars muted by the bright sunshine.

A small crowd of locals stretched their necks, watching the action. Except the "action" had happened yesterday, when someone had slain the two men. The crowd, probably having learned everything they knew about police procedures from cop shows, seemed unaware that this phase of the investigation—where CSI and the coroner collected and tagged evidence—was the thrilling equivalent of watching bridge construction. A pair of state officers stood behind the yellow tape barrier keeping the lookie-loos at bay.

Sam scanned the faces, the murmur of the crowd a low hum against the distant crash of waves. Mr. and Mrs. Bryant, not to be left out, had stopped by to see what all the fuss was about. Good. He might need them later.

Sam paused on a man with long red hair tied up in a ponytail. Forty-ish, he stood in the back as though attempting to be nondescript. But among the gaggle of shorts and flip-flops, his denim shirt, work boots, and heavy painter's pants glared brighter than the police bubble bars.

Didn't we leave Ponytail on the Vengeance? Sam asked.

Why do criminals always come back to the scene of the crime? Chet quipped. *What's that about?*

I don't know, Sam said. *Pride maybe? Technically, this isn't his crime scene.*

No, it isn't. But one of his associates committed a double homicide on behalf of the crew. In my book, that's close enough. Can't tell if he's carrying, but at least he had the smarts to ditch the AK-47. With all the police around, that might have been awkward. Chet paused. *You kept your face covered the entire time you were on board...right?*

Yes. I had on the Chameleon. He shot at me on the bridge, but it was dark, and we were both moving. Then I shoved a flare up his ass. The fumes and smoke would have made it impossible to see. The only time he had a chance to get a look at me was when I was clinging to the wall like Spiderman. He shouldn't recognize me.

How confident are you they didn't have surveillance cameras?

In his mind, Sam scanned the *Vengeance's* deck. He didn't see anything obvious. If there were cameras, they were small and hidden. *Pretty sure. Damn. I really wish I'd noticed him earlier. I could get out of his line of sight, but if I move, I'll draw attention to myself. He might look at me closer than if I just pretend to be another rubbernecker.*

Agreed. Stay put. Chet looked around at the gawking townsfolk. *There's the potential for a lot of collateral damage if this goes south.*

Sam kept his body relaxed and his expression passive. He pulled out his phone, staring at the little screen as if he'd just received a message, all the while watching Ponytail out of the corner of his eye. He calculated how long it would take to reach the man if things got hot.

Too long. Too many potential hostages. Too many opportunities for the situation to devolve into a shit storm of violence.

If he recognizes you, the crowd's going to get some excitement after all, Chet observed. *Just not the type they were hoping for.*

Ponytail's gaze slid from the clinic, to the police, to the crowd. It stopped on Sam.

The crewman could have easily concealed a pistol or two in the large pockets of his loose-fitting pants. If he went for a weapon, Sam could have his gun out of its holster in a second. While the two of them drew down, the crowd would scatter like frightened cats. Sam was fast, but maybe not fast enough to take out the perp before the *Vengeance* guard had grabbed himself a human shield. And what of the police? They would draw their service weapons, but who would they target? Could be either or both of them.

Sam's heart thudded heavily in his chest as he waited.

No sign of recognition lit Ponytail's weathered features. His attention returned to the clinic.

Sam let out a small, relieved breath. Tension he hadn't realized he'd been holding seeped from his knotted muscles. Aiming his phone at the front of the clinic, he used the selfie lens to take several pictures of the crowd behind him, getting a few close-ups of Ponytail.

As Sam tucked his phone back into his pocket, the *Vengeance* guard turned and wandered off into the park.

Sam considered following, but Ponytail hadn't come to the Cove to steal more bodies or murder anyone else. Also, the goon hadn't recognized him and therefore didn't pose an immediate threat. Polly, however, was a trained assassin with orders to kill. She was a threat that needed to be neutralized.

Sam turned to a trooper behind the yellow crime scene tape. The man, who barely looked old enough to shave, sported a square buzz cut beneath his sharp-brimmed Smokey Bear hat and wore an impeccably pressed uniform. His name tag identified him as Juno Bailey.

"Officer Bailey," Sam said, "I'm here to see Polly Cahill."

As Sam had expected, the trooper held up a hand. A slim gold wedding ring on his finger glinted in the early morning sun.

"I'm sorry, sir. Only law enforcement and authorized personnel allowed. This is an active crime scene."

A second trooper, his badge identifying him as Luca Hudson, wandered over, his fingers resting casually on the butt of his holstered gun. "Problem?"

"There's no problem." Sam gave both men a relaxed smile, making sure to keep his hands visible and his posture non-threatening. "This young officer is correctly explaining criminal investigation protocol, specifically regarding the preservation of a crime scene."

Trooper Bailey furrowed his brow. "Right. Mr...?"

"Bradford," Sam offered.

"Mr. Bradford said he was here to see——"

"Polly Cahill." Sam held up the large quad, non-fat, one-pump, no-whip, extra-hot, lightly salted mocha. The scalding heat seeping through the cup earlier had since cooled to a low simmer. "This coffee is for her." He frowned. "Though calling this 'coffee' is like calling rocket fuel lighter fluid."

Trooper Hudson began, "I'm sorry, sir, I——"

Sam interrupted. "If Ms. Cahill doesn't get her morning pick-me-up, there's apt to be another crime committed by a grouchy paramedic. This one of the 'disturbing the peace' variety. Capiche?"

The troopers glanced at one another.

Officer Bailey nodded. "I understand, sir. My boss is the same way if he doesn't get his morning joe. But I can't let you onto the premises."

Sam had been tossing out Polly's name like shark chum, and sure enough, the line tugged. Allison something-or-other drifted in for the kill, her gossiping tongue sharper and deadlier than a medieval knight's sword. As small-town fish went, this was a whopper.

Coated in enough hairspray to blast a hole in the ozone, her towering bouffant could have deflected bullets. A fake pearl necklace gleamed proudly above a wedge of leathery, fake-n-bake cleavage peeking from the placket of a bedazzled toucan-themed cardigan. A faux designer handbag—just big enough for her husband's testicles and matching credit card—swung from the crook of a stiffly bent elbow. She pretended to photograph the crime scene with her phone while inching close enough to eavesdrop without being obvious.

Perfect. Time to drop the first morsel.

Pretending as though he hadn't noticed Allison's tactical flanking maneuver, Sam gave the troopers a knowing smile. "I suppose from a certain point of view, you could say she's my boss. Or at least, my soon-to-be boss."

Trooper Bailey frowned. "Sir?"

Trooper Hudson wore no ring, so Sam focused on the younger officer. "She's my fiancée."

Allison let out a little squeak. In Sam's peripheral vision, he saw her body stiffen as if someone had pinched her bottom while her eyes turned to basketballs. She motioned energetically at someone in the crowd.

So far, so good.

"Soon-to-be-happy wife makes for a happy life and all," Sam said. "You know what I'm talking about, Officer Bailey."

"I...um...suppose so, sir."

Allison's bronzed-shouldered coconspirator—a younger clone of the gossiping warmonger—sidled up beside her. Hoop earrings peeked out from Dollar Tree hair extensions like marauding jungle explorers hacking through the synthetic underbrush. She wore canary-yellow capris and a hot pink, pupil-dilating tee paired with heeled Jesus sandals. A teardrop-shaped purple pendant, big as a cockroach, hung at her throat. Faux gem rings sparkled with cubic zirconia brilliance, flanked by bedazzled, Barney the dinosaur-purple press-on nails. Same pert nose, same broomstick figure, same lust for drama blazing in her brown eyes. Genetics did not lie.

Sam flipped through his mental dossier of townsfolk and came up with the daughter's name—Tabatha.

Still no last name. Earlier in his career, he'd have nailed it. Maybe in the last three months his skills had slipped? No more vacations.

The dime-store duo whispered to each other as if trading secrets vital to the survival of the rebellion, all while continuously glancing at him.

Chet slowly applauded. *Dude. I was skeptical, but I have to admit, you seem to be doing well despite your overwhelming incompetence.*

Sam gave his inner conscience a little bow. Pretending to not notice them, he lowered his voice to a whisper just loud enough the unofficial Alabaster Cove paparazzi could still hear. "Ms. Cahill is very *creative* when she's feeling feisty."

The troopers stared at him.

The two women fell silent, absorbing every syllable.

Make your point, Chet said. *Just don't go—*

Ignoring his inner conscience, Sam said to the troopers, "But, if she doesn't get her morning coffee, then that puts her in a not-so-great mood the rest of the day and takes her insatiable libi-do,"——he pronounced the last syllable as "due"——"to a libi-do-*not*, if you catch my drift."

Too far, Chet finished. He sighed.

Tabatha and Allison leaned in, practically perching themselves on Sam's shoulders.

Despite his stoic demeanor, a small smirk creased the corners of Trooper Bailey's lips before he recovered. Once more the unflappable lawman, he said, "Be that as it may, unless you are authorized, I cannot let you onto the premises." He considered for a moment. "I could deliver the coffee to your fiancée for you."

Sam gave the trooper his best men-of-the-world smile. "Would you? That would be great." He handed the lawman the hot paper cup. "You know, I wanted to follow in my father's footsteps, God rest his soul." Sam looked skyward for a second as if offering up a silent prayer. "And join the police academy. But I failed the physical."

"Vision problem?" the trooper asked.

"Narcolepsy," Sam deadpanned.

You just don't know when to stop do you? Chet snapped.

I died last night, got shot at, nearly drowned, was beaten up by my dead brother, and a trained assassin has my name at the top of her hit list. I'm in a mood.

Just don't let your mood blow your cover.

Trooper Hudson frowned. "Doesn't that just mean you're a deep sleeper?"

"Yep." He sighed. "Slept through my alarm and half the first day of training. By the time I woke up, it was dinner time. Fortunately, Polly was willing to marry me anyway."

Trooper Bailey blinked in consternation. With a slight shake of his head, he turned and headed toward the clinic.

Sam called after him. "Would you mind letting Polly know I need to talk with her?"

Bailey waved his hand in acknowledgement.

Someone tapped him on the shoulder. He turned, unsurprised to find Allison with daughter Tabatha at her elbow. They each had their hands on their hips and wore identical stern expressions.

Spooky, Chet said.

Right?

"Excuse me," Allison said.

Here it comes. Let the interrogation begin.

The troopers were the warmup, Chet said. *You'd better have some pretty good moves if you're going to dance with these divas.*

"Yes, ladies?" Sam said as though noticing them for the first time.

"Do I understand correctly that you and *Polly Cahill* are engaged?" Allison asked.

Sam offered his best slightly embarrassed smile. "Did you overhear me and the troopers talking, or did Polly tell you herself?"

Allison wrinkled her nose. "Polly and I don't run in the same social circles."

Of course they didn't. Sam already knew which circle this pair of juice jockeys ran in—but he played dumb. "Oh, that's too bad. Probably because her work schedule is so demanding."

That line hit home. Matching flames of suspicion lit up the dime-store duo's eyes. They hadn't heard any gossip about Sam and Polly doing anything more than working together—because there hadn't been anything to hear.

But Tabatha looked like she wanted to believe it. Badly. The hope was right there, flickering behind the scowl. Allison, meanwhile, looked offended not to be the first to know the biggest scandal since Pastor Brown got caught in bed with a male prostitute.

Neither of them was quite there yet. But they were close. All they needed was a little nudge.

Allison said, "The thing is, Mr... Um."

Now who's playing coy? You know exactly who I am. "Sam. Sam Bradford. Nice to meet you, ma'am."

Allison wrinkled her nose again, as though she found his choice in honorifics offensive. "Please, call me Allison. This is my daughter, Tabatha."

The younger woman offered her hand.

Sam's large fingers enveloped her small soft ones as he gave her a smile that he knew lit up his whole face. "Tabatha and Allison, then. Nice to meet you. Please, call me Sam. How can I be of assistance?"

Flustered at his formality, Allison said, "Mr. Bradford... Sam. We are what you'd call *tapped into* the community."

Oh, don't be modest. You're the biggest blabbermouths to ever grace the Cove.

"And, well, if you and Polly were dating, I'd have heard about it. In fact..."

Tabatha nodded along in agreement to her mother's line of reasoning.

Sam glanced around as though about to reveal the meaning of the universe. He leaned forward and dropped his voice. "In fact," he said, picking up her thread, "rumor is Polly doesn't like me very much."

The two women glanced at each other. Tabatha pretended to be embarrassed, but her face glowed with excitement. When she gave a slight nod, the hoop earrings swayed back and forth in the polyester follicle forest. "That's what folks have been saying."

"Can I let you in on a little secret?"

Identical big brown eyes glowed. They, too, glanced around as though making sure no one could overhear them. "Of course, Sam," Allison replied in a conspiratorial whisper. "Just between the three of us."

Right.

Mother and daughter stood cheek to cheek, fake jewels glimmering and matching ravenous-hound expressions bathed like spotlights by the West Coast sunshine. A fruity aroma, call it jubilant geraniums, and perfumed hairspray wafted off the duo like barn musk.

"The truth is," he said heavily, "Polly and I have a bit of *history*."

Mother turned to daughter. "I told you they had a past. Didn't I tell you?"

Tabatha nodded. "You did, momma."

They fixed him with their eager gazes.

"Go on," Allison urged.

"We were a bit of an item back when she was just a beat cop and I was active-duty Marines stationed at Camp Edwards. She got transferred for a bit of...well, let's just say some unnecessary roughness with a dirt bag named Four Strokes."

"Four Strokes?" Allison grimaced. "What kind of name is that?"

Sam shook his head as though the man's moniker filled him with dismay. "His name was just the icing on the cake. This guy was a piece of work. Stealing, drugs, you name it. He got caught and lawyered up. The evidence they had was circumstantial, and no one could get him to talk...except for Polly, who got a *confession* out of him."

This would align with the little they probably knew about Polly's Boston PD days. These nuggets, which helped satisfy their insatiable appetites for dirt to fill in Polly's blanks, would be the sugar that masked the bitter fake aspects of his story.

Sam added a chord of sadness to his voice. "Unfortunately, there was a lawsuit which the mucky-mucks wanted swept under the rug. So they transferred her. She asked me to come with, only I had two more years before I completed active duty. I tried to explain, but she was at a very vulnerable point in her life. It..." He pretended to choke up a little. "I broke her heart when I couldn't move with her."

Tabatha clearly didn't approve—though of the mucky-mucks, or what Polly had done, or him not following, Sam couldn't be certain.

"Anyway," he said, "we split up. I'm sure I don't have to tell you how many relationships are victims of ambitious careers. Only, I couldn't get her out of my head or my heart. When my tour was up, I looked for her. At first, I couldn't find her, but then, I heard she'd come here. So, I followed, hoping...well, you know."

The two women nodded in perfect unison as though they each knew very well indeed.

"As you noticed," Sam said, "she was still mad at first, but, like the old saying goes, there's a fine line between anger and love. Those old feelings just came marching back." He looked each in the eyes in turn, giving them a wistful look. "Anyway, we've been trying to keep it on the down-low because she's worried about her reputation as a paramedic practitioner. And I don't know if you've noticed, but there are people in this town that like to spread gossip." He glanced at the crowd as though micro-phone-wielding scandalmongers might invade their small circle of trust at any moment.

Tabatha clenched her purple pendant, as if she found the very notion of gossip appalling. "How long have you been together?"

"Besides the year or so back in Boston, a few weeks."

"And no one else knew?"

He tapped his chin with his finger as though giving the question serious consideration. "You know, I think Max has been suspicious for a while." The boardhead had hint-ed at that very thing during Sam's last shift. When the gossip vines buzzed with the new skinny, Max would say, "I knew it!" Feeding the flames of Sam's story.

He continued, "I've been staying at her place to keep out of the public eye. We were doing pretty good too, but last night we went for a romantic boat ride and stayed out too late. This morning, we overslept, and Mr. and Mrs. Bryant caught me leaving."

He looked earnestly into their matching brown eyes, as though imploring them to see who the woman he loved was down deep. "Polly's tough, but underneath, she has a heart of pure gold. She puts on a strong front, partially because it's difficult being a woman on the police force, and partially because being an officer—man or woman—is a hard job. You know she almost died in the line of duty?"

Tabatha gaped. "What? Really?"

Sam nodded. "A couple of times actually." He mentally scanned the pages of Polly's police record, quickly finding the entries he wanted. "You've probably seen the scar on her thigh and possibly those on her back—which is why she always wears a swim shirt over her suit."

Allison nodded.

"Knife wound." Sam pointed at his thigh and coughed as though about to say something he ought not. "God, she'd hate that we were even talking about this."

Tabatha whispered, "This is just between us, Sam. We won't breathe a word."

Right.

He held their gazes as though they'd become his new best friends and confidants. "Bullet wound on her shoulder. Courtesy of an insane meth addict."

Allison leaned into Tabatha and whispered, "I heard about that scar. Jessica saw it at the gym once."

That had been the final bow on their Christmas gift. They would, of course, confirm with Mrs. Bryant and probably Max too. But Tabatha's dewy face glowed as she allowed herself to believe Sam's story of love and loss and love rekindled. Allison glanced over her shoulder as though confirming that Mrs. Bryant hadn't left yet. She was locked and loaded.

"She hates her scars," Sam said, not quite ready to let them leave. "Thinks they're ugly. I tell her they're a beautiful reminder of how fragile life can be and to not waste a minute of it. Anyway, we haven't set a date or anything. We agreed to keep this quiet for now. But I'm just so excited, I accidentally spilled the beans to the trooper. Since you overheard, you're now in a small but trusted circle. If you don't mind, I'd appreciate your discretion."

As though they'd spent hours practicing, Tabatha and Allison made perfectly synchronized locking-their-lips-and-throwing-away-the-key gestures.

Touching each of their bony shoulders, he said, "Thank you." Sam gave them a little squeeze, then wandered over to a nearby park bench and sat down. He'd lit the kindling. Now he just needed to sit back and watch the forest burn.

Technically, Sam hadn't needed to carry it as far as he had, but he was pissed. Pissed at The Agency for rewarding over a decade of dedication with a target on his back. Pissed at Josha for either not suspecting, or—had he known—not telling him. And pissed at Polly for accepting an assignment to drop a fellow agent. She could have slipped him a warning as a professional courtesy. But she hadn't.

He crossed his legs as he waited. It wouldn't take long.

Thirty seconds later, Trooper Bailey came out, followed by Polly, who strutted like an enraged rooster down the short walkway and under the yellow crime scene tape.

Time to face his executioner.

Chapter Thirty-One

S am pointed to the cup in Polly's hand. "I see you got the coffee."

Heat lightning flashed in her green eyes. She looked like she might pull out her piece and shoot him right there in front of God, the troopers, and all the gossipmongers. The story of the paramedic practitioner that went berserk would live on in infamy for as long as the town was a town. "Why," she began through clenched teeth, "did you tell that trooper we were engaged?"

"Cover story."

She closed her eyes for a few seconds, as if he'd utterly trampled her patience. "Please tell me you didn't tell anyone else."

He shook his head. "Of course not." Polly would learn the truth in due time, but for the moment, he had to control her ire...or she really might shoot him.

"And why, exactly, did you say that to him?"

"You asked me to meet you here, and I couldn't get inside."

She gave him a look so heavy it felt like a punch. "So, naturally, you told him we were getting married."

He shrugged. "Like I said, cover story."

"For what?!"

"It's no secret that you're not a fan of mine." Sam nodded his head toward the squad cars. "Since the staties are here to take over, our official investigation is finished, negating our reason for being seen together. But thanks to our cover story, we can be together all the time, and no one will suspect we're really chasing the Russians."

Polly met his gaze, her eyes narrowing. He could practically hear the gears of her mind whirring.

She smells the deception on your breath, Chet said.

That's just toothpaste. Besides, an accusation of lying seems a tad hypocritical coming from her.

Just saying.

She rubbed the back of her neck as though trying to ward off a tension headache. Most likely she was wondering how she could kill him without the world putting her under a microscope. "You got me out here. What do you want?"

"I've got good news, and I've got bad news. First, the good. I spotted one of the guys from the *Vengeance* this morning."

Her eyes flashed with surprise. "What? Where?"

"Just a few minutes ago. In the crowd."

She glanced at the rubberneckers. A small gaggle of gossipmongers—Allison, Tabatha, and Mrs. Bryant—watched them. Polly sighed, understanding the significance of their attention. She looked back at him. "Why are you here spreading rumors instead of chasing after him, then?"

I had to make sure you weren't going to kill me. "I'm not worried about following him. I've got a pretty good idea where he's going next. I'm hoping he'll lead us to whoever murdered Trooper Lane and Phil. I came here first because I'd already gotten your coffee and didn't want it to get cold."

She ignored his ridiculous coffee comment. "What's your bad news?"

"Based on the way he's dressed and his scowly demeanor, he's practically got a glowing arrow above his head identifying him as an out-of-town criminal, yet somehow, he slipped past your RU patrols."

A fresh wave of irritation crossed Polly's face.

Not having a good morning, love? Me neither.

"Yeah, well, when the state police arrived this morning, the chief thought the patrols were redundant, not to mention expensive, and scaled back to a couple of guys monitoring the beaches." She took a long breath, clearly reining in her frustration. "But I have a bit of good news of my own. The deputies found a camera with a shot of the street, which caught someone leaving the clinic not long after the silent alarm was tripped."

This got Sam's attention. "Really? That is good news." Even better than the intel itself was that she still seemed interested in pursuing this lead, despite her new handler telling her to back off.

"Yes," she said. "Haven't seen the video yet, but I should be able to get a copy from the sheriff, who'll get me a copy as a courtesy."

"Guessing that the perp leaving the clinic is the same one who broke into your house."

"You think?" She took a sip of her coffee. "I still need a couple of hours. The ME is here to claim the bodies. I have some reports to fill out, and then we can go over everything. I'll message you when I'm done."

"Sounds good. Here, let me give you a visual in case he comes around again." Sam slipped out his phone. He stood next to Polly, leaning in so close he could smell the salted chocolate on her breath and feel the warmth of her skin against his cheek. From the crowd's perspective, it would look like their heads were together while having an intimate conversation. Holding the phone so no one else could see, he flipped through the pictures of Ponytail.

"Did he make you?" Polly asked.

"No. He never saw my face when I was aboard. And just a few minutes ago, he looked right at me. Nothing."

She considered, undoubtedly thinking about what would have happened had the man recognized him. "Send me the pics. I'll keep an eye out." She took a step away from him and nodded her head at the clinic. "I need to get back inside. In the meantime, please stop spreading rumors about me. You may be a drifter, but I live here. I see these people every day."

Polly had reacted exactly as he'd predicted. The cover story—what he'd have called a *double-blind* back in the Marines—wasn't just a distraction. It was a trap. A lie wrapped inside a more palatable lie. Recursive. Airtight. Impossible to unwind without unraveling her life.

Easy to swallow. Hard to trace.

He gave her a grave look, as though he'd agonized over the decision and landed—reluctantly—on the most rational path. "You get that I'm just trying to make it so we can keep working the case together. Given how vocal you've been about your dislike of me, the story had to be plausible. And what's more plausible than a forbidden romance?"

The jab was subtle, but sharp. This was her fault—at least partly. If she'd played it differently, maybe his actions wouldn't have needed to be so extreme. By sharing the blame, he softened his own responsibility. This mess? They'd created it together.

"You didn't answer me," she said, her voice tight. *Message received.* "Are you going to spread any more rumors about me?"

"Wouldn't dream of it."

He should've said something neutral, like *"The case doesn't warrant it."* But the smirk in his voice betrayed his satisfaction. He'd tied her hands, and she knew it.

The conflict she'd worn earlier still waged beneath the surface. As an operative, she was boxed in. Sam had played on her one weakness—her desire to protect the life she'd built. Now she had to juggle it all: keeping The Agency at bay, working the case, and maintaining her cover here in the Cove. All while the wagging tongues whispered her name and every eye tracked her every move.

He hadn't just spun a cover story—he'd weaponized it. And Polly was dead center in the crosshairs.

Damn, it felt good to be back in the game.

She gave him a sharp look, studied his face for a beat, then turned on her heel and strode back into the clinic.

Sam watched her go.

In the corner of his eye, he caught movement——several women had joined Tabatha, Allison, and Mrs. Bryant. His unlikely army toggled their attention back and forth between Polly disappearing into the clinic and him, like spectators at a heated tennis match.

From the outside, the scene had played perfectly: Polly angry at him for spilling their "secret," the two reconciling, her still upset but softening. Even an Oscar-winning writer couldn't have scripted it better.

Point. Set. Match.

You do recall you set up a date with Savannah, right? Chet asked.

Yeah, there's that wrinkle.

His inner conscience laughed. *Wrinkle? I'd say it's way more than a "wrinkle," my boat-wrecking, two-timing friend. First, you sank her favorite bathtub toy. Now you're engaged to her coworker.*

I'll just explain that things got a little complicated.

That woman's going to use your sack as a coin purse. There's a little nutty, bordering on psycho, behind those blue eyes.

Seriously? Sam asked. *That's what I said, but all you kept saying was I needed to do the horizontal waltz with her. Now you're warning me she's crazy?*

Chet tsked. *First, I told you to do the horizontal* tango, *then I said to do the* salsa. *I also said the crazy part didn't matter if all you were doing was having some fun. Now you've crossed her. Twice.*

It'll be fine.

I'm just glad I'm not you.

I have bad news for you...

Sam stood. The two troopers watched as he returned to the crime scene perimeter. "Gentlemen," Sam said by way of greeting.

Trooper Bailey—sympathy and understanding lingering in his eyes—had clearly witnessed the exchange. "Looks like the coffee helped."

"It always does. Marriage is about knowing what matters to your partner." Sam pretended not to notice the women eavesdropping like Cold War spies.

He dropped the act, meeting the troopers' eyes. "Thank you for your service. I'm sorry about your fallen officers. I lost friends on my tours too. There's nothing I can say that'll make it right—so I won't try. Just… I hope you catch the guy."

The troopers nodded. Said nothing.

Sam turned toward the park.

He'd woven a Kevlar vest from a fabric of lies, stitched with the thread of small-town gossip. It wouldn't protect him forever, but it should hold—for now. And with Polly's gun metaphorically holstered, he could turn his attention back to Ponytail.

And bring a little vengeance to the *Vengeance*.

Chapter Thirty-Two

S am entered the park, trailing after Ponytail, the damp
ground clinging to his shoes. To his right lay an open
field of grass sprinkled with a smattering of wildflowers. A
few people lounged on blankets, reading, sleeping, or just
talking. Some kids threw a frisbee. No *Vengeance* thug. Sam
turned down a forested trail.

Where do Mafiya slugs like him go to slither? Chet asked. *He's
not here for the surfing, the babes, or your stimulating company. They
took a risk sending him ashore. Why?*

*Well, our Russian friends have several problems. The first is that
I disabled their radar last night. That's going to make tooling around
the ocean very difficult. He could be here to get a new one or to get
that one fixed.*

*Don't forget you shot a flare into their bridge and blew a hole in the
bow. Things might be majorly effed and in need of repair. He could
be here for supplies.*

The sun's rays shone through the evergreen branches,
creating a patchwork quilt of light on the forest floor. The
gentle aroma of mulch and sap floated on a soft breeze as
he made his way through the pines.

Wow, I was way more productive than even I'd realized, Sam said. At the time, he'd only been interested in keeping the crew from filling his and Polly's collective asses full of lead.

Don't let your head swell up. You got lucky.

Lucky? Bro, I infiltrated a Mafiya ship in rough swells, committed a bit of strategic sabotage, stole secret documents, escaped while herds of guards with AK-47s hunted me, and survived my boat sinking, followed by a long swim in the middle of the freezing ocean. Not to toot my own horn or anything, but that's some serious skills right there. Instead of eliminating me, The Agency should give me the key to the city or something.

Chet tsked. *Are you done stroking your own ego, or do the two of you need to get a hotel room?*

Just pointing out that you seem to be having trouble reconciling the facts.

Sam paused, looking around, listening. Birds chirped, the wind blew, and in the distance, waves crashed. He didn't think that Ponytail had recognized him in the crowd, but if that assumption proved incorrect, then the security guard could be hiding among the trees and ferns hoping to get himself a piece of B&E retribution. Sam remained rooted in his spot, waiting. No snapping of twigs or crunching of cones indicated someone skulking through the underbrush. Confident he was still alone, Sam continued down the trail.

Chet said, *Another possibility is that Ponytail's here to help move Frank's body offshore.*

A fair point. *Even with the reduced patrols, the marinas are still heavily monitored. They can't just* Weekend at Bernie's *the corpse and pretend to take him for a ride through town in broad daylight.*

Polly said the patrols weren't cancelled until the state police arrived this morning. The clinic sits a full mile inland. Our KGB wannabes couldn't carry a corpse through town without someone noticing. I'm thinking they'll have to wait until dark.

Sam stopped by an especially thick tree whose canopy reached for the sky. He glanced around the trunk in both directions. When he didn't see anyone, he continued down the trail. *Why?*

Why what? Chet asked.

Why steal the body? I get the cell phone. Photographic evidence and all. But why steal back the corpse?

They fell silent as he exited the woods onto the shore of a small lake.

The bullet, they said in unison.

Has to be, Chet continued. *The gun was used in another crime they don't want tied back to this one.*

That means they don't need the whole body. They just need somewhere to stash it so they can do a little slice and dice. Sam glanced back at the woods. *That would be a pretty obvious place to hide a body.*

I didn't see anything, Chet said. *Maybe they haven't done it yet?*

Sam asked, *So are Ponytail and our murderer going to work together and perform some amateur medical examination? Or are they going to divide and conquer——one plays ME while the other fixes the radar?*

It doesn't take two to dig out a slug, Chet said.

We don't know where the body's at, but there are only a few places you can get boat hardware. Sam sat on a bench along the shore, the sun warm on his face. A gentle breeze blew through the grass and rippled the glossy surface of the lake. Good day to be alive and chasing bad guys.

He pulled out his phone and searched for local marine supply stores. The first two, Mario's and Pacific Marine, dealt in high-end and new electronics. The third, a junk yard named Waste Not Want Not, sounded like a place where professional thugs might like to hang out.

It wasn't the most solid lead ever, but Sam had done more with less. He was putting his chips on red. Time to see if the bet would pay off.

Chapter Thirty-Three

According to the locals, everything on Jellyfish Boulevard was owned by a man named Jebediah Dempsey. Derelict storefronts with weather-bleached siding and paper-thin roofs lined the potholed street.

A gray piece of plywood had been nailed over one of the twin windows of Waste Not Want Not. The other, cloudy as a dead man's eye, stared from the building's weathered skull. A cockeyed *Open* sign hung on the grime-coated glass door.

Sam instinctively put his hand on his gun as he pushed inside.

The scent of wet carpet, stale grease, and machine oil assaulted him like a junkie mugger desperate for a score. It took a moment for his eyes to adjust to the catacomb-like darkness. Beneath sickly yellow fluorescent lighting, steel shelves piled with ancient, leaking equipment ran from front to back.

Behind the counter, a man with a frumpy beard and wearing a stained t-shirt proclaiming he loved hot moms, reclined on a raggedy desk chair. He snored quietly while a baseball game droned from a nearby transistor radio.

Jebediah, I presume, Chet said. *Classy.*

"Excuse me," Sam said. When the man didn't move, Sam cleared his throat and repeated himself.

The proprietor cracked open an eye. "Help you?"

"Need to find a cable for an old radar."

When the grizzled man stretched and stood, both the ancient chair and his ancient bones squawked in protest.

Sam pulled out his phone and showed him the image of the radar.

Jebediah scratched his armpit and squinted at the screen. "Fella came in earlier asking about the same thing."

Sam nodded. "Red hair tied in a ponytail?"

He shook his head. "No. That wasn't him."

Sam thought back to the crew list. Of all the names and photos in Polly's notes, one stood out: Sergey Federov. Bald, tattooed from scalp to collarbone. He did a stint in the Norilsk penal colony for beating a man to death with the victim's own wooden leg, supposedly for cheating him at cards. His time behind bars didn't freeze the violence out of him, it distilled it. He slit the throats of three security guards during his escape into the sewer system, disappearing underground for several years, only to reemerged on the *Vengeance* as head of security.

"Happy-go-lucky fella with a spider tattoo on his head and webs on his neck?" Sam said. "Goes by Larry."

"Don't know his name, but ain't no one else in town with tats like that."

"Well, that explains it," Sam said. "He told me he was going for supplies—but he must've meant here. I'll call and get this straightened out. What did you say your name was?"

"Didn't." The *scritch* of him running a hand over his stubble-covered chin sounded like sandpaper. "Name's Jebediah. Jebediah Dempsey. Folks call me Jeb. There ain't nothing to straighten out neither." He reached into a box on the floor and began rummaging. "Told him I'd check my inventory. Thought it'd take a while, and fer him to come back tomorrow. Except, I got lucky."

He stood and slapped an old cable onto the counter.

Oh, shit. Sam had come in hoping for a lead to the next clue. Dempsey had just handed him the whole damn enchilada. Seemed his gamble had paid off in a big way. "When did Larry come by?"

Dempsey checked the cracked Timex strapped to his wrist. "About two hours ago. But I don't see no need for him to come back since you're here already."

"Right you are."

The old guy eyed Sam. "This is the only one of these in town."

And this is the part where he fleeces you, Chet said.

"One hundred and fifty dollars," Jebediah announced as though giving him the deal of a lifetime.

Sam would have paid triple. But he couldn't blow his cover by looking eager. "For an old cable?"

"Did I mention that this was the *only* one in town? Hell, it's probably the only one on the West Coast." He shrugged and reached for it. "But if you don't want it—"

"No. It's fine." Sam pulled out his wallet, counted out the bills, and made a show of being unhappy about Jeb taking him to the cleaners. "What time did Larry say he'd be coming by tomorrow?"

The proprietor shook his head. "Said he'd be here first thing after I opened."

"What time's that?"

"Nine, nine-thirty."

Sam pulled out five twenties and laid them on the counter. "You open at ten tomorrow, and there'll be five more of those for you."

Jeb snatched the cash. "I could use the extra sleep."

"Much appreciated." Sam took the cable and pushed through the door, squinting at the sunshine. He snapped a few pictures of the building, the nearby dilapidated structures, and the street. He turned and headed back to civilization.

Tomorrow, he'd come face-to-face with the man who broke into Polly's house and murdered Trooper Lane and Phil the Janitor.

If Sam went alone, he could hold a swift little trial—no judge, no jury, no loopholes. Just a verdict and a sentence. A *death* sentence. Maybe even squeeze a few answers out of Sergey about the murdered detective before turning the man's lights out.

Or he could loop in the California State Police. Let the system do what it was built to do—and let the staties have the satisfaction of getting justice for one of their own. But that meant evidence, red tape, lawyers… and praying the prosecutor could hold the case together.

It also meant risking everything if the Mafiya had their hooks in the chain of command.

Justice might be served—or vanish into a black hole of corruption and cover-ups.

Could he afford that gamble?

He didn't know.

As he reached the end of the block and turned toward town, the answer still didn't come.

But one thing he did know... Sergey was going to pay.

Chapter Thirty-Four

Back at his house, Sam slid the cable into the hidden floor compartment, the worn wood creaking beneath his knees. During the trip home, he'd dismissed the idea of bringing the staties with him tomorrow morning. Unless the police's photo unquestioningly implicated Sergey—which, based on the quality of most security systems, it may not—and they'd found the murder weapon with usable fingerprints on it, he could walk.

Sam wouldn't take that chance.

Skip all the court crap. He'd know the man's guilt or innocence the second he looked Sergey in the eyes.

In Sam's version of jurisprudence, trials had no need of a bailiff or a bench. His brand of justice didn't wait for permission or petitions. It was simple, swift, and uncompromising.

Similarly, he'd taken down a major drug operation in New York City, but his weapons hadn't been lawyers and legal proceedings. He'd answered bloody violence with bloody violence by turning his enemies against one another.

Criminals played by their own set of rules. Sam knew which to twist and which to break. He would go to that meet. Alone.

He could hardly wait.

Had he really considered giving up this job?

Having the murder investigation nearly complete, he set his tablet on the table and dug into the *Vengeance* documents. Time to find out what kind of Mafiya mayhem the Lion and her cubs had been up to. As he perused the first file, his stomach grumbled. Make that a working lunch.

A few minutes later, with his tablet tucked into his backpack, he wove between the packed slanted parking spaces in front of the diner. A pair of police cruisers sat shoulder to shoulder with VWs and Hondas. Inside, pseudo celebrity Sheriff Buford Austin and a pair of deputy wingmen sat at a center table. As Sam stepped across the threshold, he and the sheriff locked eyes.

The lawman's accusatory gaze implied he could tie Sam to the murders. He may have even entertained the notion that Sam had swung the tire iron used to kill Trooper Lane and Phil. Of course, he had no evidence and therefore no case.

Follow the clues and stop trying to shape reality to fit your bias, Sheriff.

In his peripheral vision, Sam noted the deputies following their boss' glower. The attack dogs had picked up the scent. They only awaited word from the alpha to attack. After several tense seconds, the sheriff gave Sam a sharp nod and refocused his attention on his meal. The wary mongrels also turned away.

Animated townsfolk filling the tables and deep red leather booths glanced between him and the fuzz. Their gazes were full of curiosity as they drew conclusions they'd embellish when they whispered their secrets to the gossip vines.

Accompanied by Jerry Lee Lewis' excited piano and zippy vocals pouring from a glimmering corner juke-box, Sam crossed the black-and-white checkered floor. The greasy aroma of fries, burgers, and bacon hung so heavy in the air, just inhaling bumped his cholesterol up several points. He took a silver sparkling barstool at the long counter.

A waitress, with a tight blouse and black hair pulled back, stopped at his elbow. She wielded a glass coffee pot like a samurai sword.

He flashed her his trademark smirk. "Hey, Trin!"

"Sam Bradford," she said, filling the large white mug in front of him without asking, "you scoundrel."

He looked into her dark eyes, feigning innocence, knowing exactly what she would say. "Scoundrel? Me?"

"Yes, you!" Triniti gave him a conspiratorial grin. "I hear congratulations are in order."

Interesting. Polly and I topped the headlines over the murders. He didn't know what that said about society—or people's priorities.

Sam mocked confusion. "What are you talking about?"

She smacked his arm. "Your *engagement*! I have it from a reliable source that you and Polly have been heating the sheets and are planning to tie the knot."

It wouldn't have surprised him if the townies had her knocked up by the end of the day. Cahill had no chance of distancing herself from him—none whatsoever. He added a flicker of genuine amusement to his smile. "It's an old fling that's become new again."

"I'll say! So, how did you ask her?"

Sam gave her a one-shouldered shrug and took a sip of the steaming brew. "I didn't."

Confusion crossed her face. "I don't understand."

He set his cup down and leaned in. "*She* asked *me*."

Triniti let out a surprised giggle. "You're kidding."

"Nope. Last night, she got down on one knee just like in the movies. It was over beer and pizza, not caviar and champagne, but that's more our speed anyhow."

Triniti's eyes grew huge. "What! Really?"

He nodded. "Said she wanted me to make an honest woman of her."

Polly is going to kill you, Chet predicted.

Wasn't that already inevitable?

Touché.

"She wants a simple wedding down on the beach," Sam said. "She's been dreaming about a flowy white dress her whole life. Saundy's going to be the flower girl."

Chet shook his head. *Your funeral to immediately follow the reception.*

Triniti looked completely aghast. "We cannot be talking about the same Polly. I'm talking about Polly *Cahill*. The Polly Cahill who works at the clinic. The same one who destroys a grappling dummy once a week with her kung fu or whatever. The same one who has more guns than the army and navy put together. The woman who didn't even flinch when she stuffed a guy's intestines back into his stomach after a boating accident last August."

Sam grinned and picked up his mug again. "One and the same. She's tough on the outside, I'll give you that. But she has a gentle, gooey nougat center. Tears up at Hallmark commercials, the whole nine yards."

Chet shook his head, for once at a loss for words.

Triniti blinked at the dissonance between the woman she knew and the one Sam had described. "Well. Okay. Just goes to show you life's full of surprises."

The cops at the nearby table laughed.

Her gaze flashed to them then back to Sam. "You working the case?"

"*Unofficially.*"

She chuckled. "That's your MO."

He took another sip from the warm mug, watching her over the rim.

As the cops' laughter died down, she commented, "Maybe instead of sitting around yukking it up at the diner on the taxpayers' dime, the sheriff and his good ol' boys should be out stopping those pirates from invading the Cove."

A sputtering laugh escaped Sam's lips before he could stop it, spraying coffee across the counter.

Oh, yeah, Chet said, chuckling. *You laid that pirate line on five and half feet of hot and crazy at the beach party yesterday. Guess she didn't keep it to herself after all.*

It wasn't a line. I told Savannah there were pirates on the Vengeance to keep her from insisting she come with me to check it out. I'd forgotten about it until just now.

Triniti cocked a manicured brow. "What's so funny?"

"It's nothing," he said, wiping splattered coffee off the counter with a napkin.

"It's clearly not nothing." She gave him a disapproving frown. "Surfing is a major part of this town's income. If people hear they might get pillaged, or plundered, or whatever, they might not come."

Sam swiped at his eyes, trying to rein in his amusement, as he set the used napkin aside. "The rumor mill has a way of turning a simple statement into a swashbuckling tale." He touched her hand. "I promise you have nothing to worry about."

She didn't look convinced, but before she could press him for details, he changed the subject. "Speaking of the rumor mill, what's the latest?"

Her look of suspicion vanished, replaced by a knowing gleam. It had been a banner day for the young rumor-monger, and she was excited to tell all. Triniti leaned in, the V of her blue blouse revealing acres of tanned cleavage. She'd been doing this trick to increase the size of her tips for so long that she probably didn't even think about it. "Besides you and Cahill and, of course, pirates? There're folks that claim it was Erebus who murdered those guys and the man that washed up on shore."

He shook his head in disbelief. "Wow."

"Right? Obviously, that's not true, since we were there when that bastard bit the farm."

He'd heard a lot of nonsense from the Cove's wagging tongues, but this was way out in left field. "What else? Anything that sounds legit?"

"Well, there're the usual conspiracy cranks claiming it was the FBI, CIA, and the KGB. It's amazing what some potheads with too much time and too much Panama Red in their system can dream up."

The KGB angle isn't as far off as she might think, Chet observed.

She thought for a moment, tapping her chin with a perfectly manicured nail. "There's also the brouhaha about that old ship parked offshore. Nothing really about it, except for the timing of it showing up and that it's just outside the Coast Guard's jurisdiction."

He didn't bother correcting her. If people found out *Vengeance* was Russian Mafiya, not pirates, they might panic. "What are people saying?" Sam asked, half expecting her to start in about flying the Jolly Roger or buried treasure.

"Not 'people.' Just one person. Josh Nordic. But he's been in the bottle for years. He's what the sheriff calls a 'non-credible witness.'"

Who he probably either didn't interview or didn't pay any attention to. "Humor me."

She dropped her voice, a little conspiratorial smile gracing her full lips. "He says the other day, a boat he ain't ever seen before pulls up at the marina. Two guys get off. One with red hair, the other, quote, 'burly with spiders,' end quote."

Sergey. Everything keeps coming back to him. Sam pretended like this was news. "Spiders?"

She shrugged. "He said the guy was covered in spiders. Also said they were speaking Russian or maybe Ukrainian."

Most people, the sheriff and his lot included, passed Triniti off as a boardhead simpleton. But she knew the town better than almost anyone. It would pay dividends for the lawman to trust her instincts. Sam took another sip of his coffee. "Sheriff talk to Josh?"

Triniti rolled her eyes in exasperation. "Yeah. They apparently took his statement, but when they came in here, they were all yammering about Josh being two sheets to the wind—which was probably true—and said he was just trying to get his fifteen minutes of fame."

"What about the state boys? Any of them talk to him?"

"As far as I know, no. Josh don't want nothin' to do with 'em."

Of course not. Sam suspected the sheriff, back in his prime, would have followed up with every lead—including a drunkard like Josh. Now, he just wanted to skate into retirement. Too lazy and content to do real police work anymore. "Thanks. Anything else in the mill I should know?"

Her face grew serious, and she leaned into Sam's ear. "Watch your back. The sheriff let it slip to the police about what happened here with that psychopath a few months ago."

Sam arched a brow as if this was a startling revelation. "What's the word?"

She glanced at the sheriff, who didn't seem to be paying them any attention. "Just that you are a 'person of interest.' They don't have your mug shot on the post office wall or nothing, but there're some of them poking around asking questions about you. Where you're from, where you live, that sort of stuff."

The sheriff hadn't exactly made it a secret that he disliked the coincidental timing of Erebus and Sam riding into town only a few days apart. Austin had never justified his suspicion with evidence to turn Sam from a person of interest to a legitimate suspect. But if the lawman thought he could rid himself of one Sam Bradford in the pursuit of justice through the state police, he might just do it.

Sam kissed her on the cheek. Her skin smelled of French fries—an occupational hazard. "Thanks for the heads up, Trin. I owe you one."

She straightened and blushed. "I'll keep my ears on and let you know if I hear anything else. You want to pay me back? Invite me to the wedding."

Sam chuckled. "Will do."

Switching gears, she asked, "Get you anything else besides coffee?"

"I'll have whatever the special is."

"You got it." She refilled his mug and flittered away.

From the corner of his eye, Sam watched as the sheriff and his men dropped a small pile of cash onto the table and made their way out the door. One deputy looked back, giving Sam the once over as if suspecting he might steal Triniti's tips. Then they were gone.

Sam pulled out his tablet. Still no reply from the translator app, and there never would be. He assumed Polly had sent the documents too. She may have had some luck, but if The Agency agenda truly had changed since Soren had assigned her the case, her request for information would also be ignored.

Whatever. He could do this the hard way. He pulled up the manifest documents on the tablet. Time to unlock the *Vengeance's* secrets.

Chapter Thirty-Five

Sam read through the manifest documents on his tablet, perusing the indecipherable Cyrillic. All around him, the din of energetic chatter back beat by scraping cutlery and clicking dishes provided the perfect white noise, helping him concentrate.

Triniti peeked at his screen as she set a plate down in front of him. Evidently, the special today was meatloaf, mashed potatoes, and some kind of vegetable medley. Sam didn't bother to cover his tablet. She wouldn't know what it meant any more than he did. "Looks like fun," she commented.

"You have no idea."

She wandered off to attend to her tables.

He grouped the files into types—supplies, fuel receipts, and manifests—based on their English headings and titles.

He opened a translation website and selected the first document. Even if he'd spoken the language, the sloppy half-English, half-Russian handwriting was almost illegible. Zooming in on the individual letters, he laboriously typed in the Cyrillic characters.

Based on the fuel and supply receipts, it appeared the *Vengeance* had been cruising around the Pacific for the last few months. Samoa, Fiji, Solomon Islands, Puerto Vallarta. Ports where the inspectors and guards would turn a blind eye for a few bucks and not ask questions.

As he worked, the meatloaf and gravy congealed into a cold, lacquer-like substance. Sam ate it anyway. The rations from his military days made the diner food look like a Thanksgiving feast at grandma's house.

Triniti breezed by every so often. As she refilled his coffee and made idle chitchat, she fleetingly surveyed his work.

Had she been hoping he was planning a wedding? *Sorry, Trin, no gossip to be had.*

A low-level throb had formed behind his eyes as he finished the first batch of documents. Though he had revealed some clear patterns—repeats of destinations, receivers, and so on—the deciphered text proved less than informative.

Besides a list of ports, the manifest headings contained nonsense like salty fish, Neptune, lunar sea, and aqua blue. Maybe he'd translated the text wrong, or the words were code. Frustration nibbled at his nerves. He wished for the thousandth time he could tap into The Agency's resources for help.

Sighing, he stretched his aching neck. The diner had grown quiet, the lunch crowd having long ago vacated. A busboy wiped down the booths and tables. According to Sam's watch, he'd been in the trenches with the shipping documents for over three hours.

"Hopefully, what you're working on doesn't disrupt your wedding plans," Triniti said on one of her passes.

"Don't worry about that. Polly——"

Sam's tablet pinged, interrupting his train of thought. He glanced at the screen. The background check he'd ordered from his deep-dive investigator had arrived. Odd, he didn't think it would come for at least a few more days. *You were a lot faster than I expected, but The Agency's report came first.*

"Polly, what?" Triniti prompted.

He pulled his attention off his inbox. "Nothing on this Earth would stop her from achieving her vision."

"I don't doubt that." She looked like she was about to turn away but cocked her head, studying his face. "You alright?"

Sam patted her arm reassuringly. He gave a small nod toward his tablet. "Of course. Just my mind still working on things even when I'm talking to the prettiest waitress in town." He gave her a little wink.

"Hmmm." She didn't appear as though she quite believed him, but she took the hint and headed off.

Sam looked at the email again. Why was it so much earlier than normal? Did that matter? Maybe. Something niggled at the back of his mind, but he didn't understand the significance.

Letting the oddity go for now, he almost filed the email away. Did he really need to know more about Polly? Yes and no. He still had some unanswered questions, but after all they'd been through, he didn't know if they were relevant anymore.

Instead of closing the message, he read through the attachments. Nothing new stood out in Polly's family history. The timeline of her days on the Boston PD aligned with Zach Ghinhart's recollection, not The Agency's report—no surprise there. No mention, of course, about her employment with The Agency. The report read *Unemployed, but receiving an income. Source unknown.*

He paused at a large document labeled *Termination for Cause.* Sam opened it.

The Agency's intel regarding Polly's 86 from the force had been a couple of pages of redacted court proceedings. His investigator must have known someone because it looked like he'd gotten the entire case unsealed.

Maybe you should close that, Sputnik, Chet said.

Why?

Sometimes it's best to leave the past in the past.

Aren't you the one who's always telling me I should think and do my homework before acting? Now you're telling me to remain ignorant?

Chet hesitated. *In this one case, I think ignorance will bring you more bliss than...* He waved a hand at the tablet. *...whatever's in there.*

You didn't say shit when I was looking at everything else. Now you're talking in riddles.

Sometimes it's better to ignore logic and listen to your gut.

On occasion—like now—Chet went all Nostradamus on him, advising an action without justification. Those same instincts had saved his life a dozen times over. But in this situation, no one had him lined up in their crosshairs. No IEDs awaited him under the diner's checkered floor.

This is information, Sam said. *Nothing else. The more I know and all of that.*

You sure about that?

He had been, but now that certainty fled like a startled deer. He almost closed the file.

Almost.

Under the disapproving stink eye of his inner conscience, Sam scrolled. He found the snippet from the direct examination he'd seen in The Agency's background check—but this time, he had the full transcript.

He began where the redacted version had left off. Tattersall, the narcissistic prosecutor, twisting the narrative and bending the law to fit his agenda. Not for justice, but to persecute a decorated detective. A political move, nothing more, to nurture his career and further his campaign of "policing the police."

Tattersall: And you had no other motivation for the deaths of the victims besides protecting the public?

Cahill: They weren't victims, they were cartel members who sold drugs to anyone with cash, including children. It wasn't murder. It was justifiable homicide. And no—I had no other motivation than to end a very dangerous situation.

Tattersall: You were working solely for the Boston PD at the time?

Cahill: Yes. Same as now. Same as every day I wear the shield.

Sam continued to read. Tattersall kept working Polly over, implying—though not substantiating—ulterior motives for killing the drug cartel members in her final case with the Boston PD. At some point, the defense counsel objected.

Judge: Sustained. What's your point, Counselor?

Tattersall: Your Honor, there is evidence—albeit inconclusive—that Polly Cahill has ties to Roman "The Undertaker" Dubrovnik, and that work she performed for the Boston PD may have indirectly benefited him and his organization. I'm simply trying to uncover the truth.

Judge: Then present your evidence.

Tattersall: There's no physical evidence at this time.

Judge: You're speculating, Counselor. Move on.

Tattersall didn't mention Dubrovnik again until his closing arguments, where he hinted at a connection with Polly, but had to leave it at that.

Who the hell is Roman Dubrovnik and why bring him up during Polly's trial?

Sam opened a browser and found a Wikipedia page.

Roman Dubrovnik earned the moniker "The Undertaker" not only for his funeral business but for his ruthless efficiency in eliminating rivals. He buries "problems," literally and figuratively.

Sam scanned the rest of the laughable article—half rumors, half fluff. That was it. No charges. No mugshots. No real record. Just vapor.

Time to go dark.

Sam accessed a hidden menu hardwired into the tablet for just these situations. Tails OS, Tor browser, VPN tunnel.

The dark web. A world of ghosts.

He skipped past the usual garbage of hitman scams, fake passports, stolen credit cards. What he needed was intel on Dubrovnik, a.k.a. The Undertaker. He moved from page to page. The posts were fragmented—screen names and scrambled grammar, but a pattern emerged.

Dubrovnik had been a kingpin in Massachusetts, specializing in pharmaceuticals, human trafficking, and mid-level gun trades. He'd built the US Mafiya branch of the Black Volga with smuggled ex-Spetsnaz and American turncoats. A few months before Polly's trial, an FBI task force had burned half his network.

Why had Prosecutor Tattersall suspected Polly had ties to Dubrovnik, a Mafiya *vor*? Clearly, Tattersall had no real evidence, or Polly would be in prison, but someone had said something that had pricked the lawyer's intuition. Sam rescanned the trial transcript. Upon a second read, Sam realized the prosecutor seemed to be hoping she'd incriminate herself.

Except, whatever theory, whatever source he had, was flawed and misleading. Had to be. Polly was a patriot. Polly was dedicated to her country and justice.

But Polly the operative was... a liar.

Zach Ghinhart—the cop she'd saved by running into a hailstorm of bullets and pulling him to safety—had called her "dedicated." Was it possible she had just been dedicated to pretending?

Or perhaps she'd been involved in the FBI's sting operation that had taken Dubrovnik's East Cost bratva down. If she'd been working undercover, she wouldn't have been allowed to talk about it. There could have been evidence of her involvement with the bratva, but for her own security and those she'd worked with, the details of the case would have been sealed.

Again, completely possible.

Sam dug deeper, making notes as the posts shifted in tone.

Dubrovnik's fled the East Coast, but he's not gone.

A newer post showed a blurry image of a customs manifest tied to a shell company. The container was scanned entering the Port of Los Angeles. The contents—weapons and drugs—disappeared without a trace. Dubrovnik's bratva, Black Volga, the suspected receiver.

The Gabisonia Enterprise is bleeding. Black Volga is carving up Koreatown. Dubrovnik is running the show.

New fronts popping up in South LA. Imports. Strip clubs. Security contracts. That's Dubrovnik's money.

Someone's been spotted making deals and meeting contacts in Long Beach and Alabaster Cove—same tattoos, same MO.

Sam sat back staring at the screen. This last entry had been made just a few months ago.

Dubrovnik had been in Boston when Polly worked for the BPD. As per the prosecutor's not-so-subtle accusations, she'd been removing cartel members who just happened to be the bratva's competitors. Eliminating the competition would put more money in Dubrovnik's pocket. It would also put cold cash into the pockets of anyone working for him.

Now, here in the Cove, Polly again, just as Dubrovnik is setting up shop.

No way that's a coincidence.

Sam's heart raced as he rebooted the tablet back to the real world. Black Volga in Los Angeles, run by Dubrovnik, was a fierce rival of the Gabisonia Enterprise.

The pieces fell into place like a Plinko game from hell.

Levka Belikov—captain of the *Vengeance* and daughter of a high ranking Mafiya officer with ties to the KGB—ran one of the most successful bratvas for Gabisonia. She'd parked her ship not ten miles off the coast where Polly lives.

Polly had taken the Frank Boreman case as a personal project, which just so happened to have them investigating the *Vengeance*. Sam had boarded the ship and stolen documents telling them what Levka had been up to and who she'd been doing business with. Exactly the sort of information Dubrovnik would need to undermine her operation.

At the time, he'd thought it had been his idea. Now he understood Polly had somehow manipulated him.

This entire situation sounded like something from a Joseph Finder novel. It seemed impossible, yet the facts were equally impossible to ignore.

Sam was the prey. Polly the predator.

"Son of a bitch," he said, just a little too loudly. Several people at nearby tables glanced his way.

He didn't pay them any attention.

Sam's shell-shocked mind whirred. A corrupt cop with the skills and—as Tattersall had alluded to but couldn't prove—ties to the Mafiya. She was later recruited by

The Agency for her connections, survival skills, and ability to manipulate—after she was fired from her detective position.

She had ties to Dubrovnik's bratva, Black Volga. Dubrovnik had been spotted doing business in Alabaster Cove—where recently reactivated Operative Polly Cahill worked and lived.

It seemed unlikely The Agency would have hired someone with Mafiya connections... unless her employer had a Mafiya connection as well.

As Dubrovnik edged in on Gabisonia's territory, Soren—Polly's Agency handler—had tapped the one person who'd been in the right place to help him.

Polly Cahill, and Soren, and the Mafiya. The chain linking them together was undeniable.

The only question that remained was: Were Polly and Soren working alone, or were others in Agency command also helping Dubrovnik undermine Gabisonia?

Sam couldn't know that. Not yet anyway. What he did know was that the entire time he'd been helping Polly dig into the murder of a fallen Marine, he'd really been helping her investigate a competing bratva.

He could barely wrap his head around it, but it seemed the impossible was possible.

Polly. The Mafiya.

Jesus Christ.

His phone buzzed, tearing him back to the present. He glanced at the screen.

Polly: *Meet me at my house.*

Raw rage struck him like a sledgehammer.

He'd been played a fool. The Agency had put a hit on him. Polly had been using him, not to stop the Mafiya but to help it and to serve her own self interests.

Lies. Deceit. Manipulation.

Sam squeezed the phone so hard, it was a wonder he didn't crack its plastic case. His vision turned red. The room around him—booths, counter, floor, walls—was drenched in the blood of his anger.

"You bet, Polly," he whispered, in a voice he barely recognized. "I'll be right there." He shoved the tablet into his bag and dropped a couple of twenties on the counter. He pushed through the door and stormed his way across town.

Time to end this.

Chapter Thirty-Six

The closer Sam got to Polly's house, the faster he ran. His mind brewed and bubbled like a witch's cauldron, steaming with an angry stew of deception, revenge, and subterfuge. Nothing escaped The Agency without Josha's knowledge, meaning his handler had left him to die at the hands of a fellow operative. No warning, no thanks for ten years of faithful service, nothing.

Sam didn't have a mark on his back because he'd gone rogue. That was just the party line. He'd gotten too close to the truth. A truth that started with the Monica case and ended with Polly, Frank Boreman's death, and the Mafiya together in one nice, neat package.

He was done with The Agency. He knew that now. They'd cast him aside. But, despite repaying ten years of dedication with a knife to the back, somehow Polly's deception cut deeper. She had fooled him good. Made him believe they were partners. Made him believe she wanted justice and to make the world a better place. That she cared.

Worst of all, she'd manipulated him into caring back.

And all along, she'd been in the Mafiya's pocket.

Sam blazed down the pathway leading from the street to her front stoop. He hopped over the porch steps, flinging his bag to the floor. Drawing his Smith & Wesson .45, he raised his foot and kicked. Splinters of wood erupted from the frame as the door smashed into the wall with a thunderous crack.

Sam stormed the fort.

Wait! Chet yelled.

Too late.

As he transitioned from bright sunshine to the shadowed hallway, a pair of strong hands shot out of the blackness, seized Sam's gun arm, and yanked him down. His S&W hit the floor with a muted clang, bouncing out of his grip as a head slammed into the side of his face—the sharp sting of impact reverberating through his skull.

Even as stars burst across his vision, two things registered at once: the faint scent of cherry blossoms and his assailant's petite frame.

Polly.

Something deep inside him growled with satisfaction. *Let's roll.*

He had her on mass and strength. She had agility, limberness, and speed. Everything else—their hand-to-hand training, marksmanship, aggression—more or less balanced each other out.

Given his opponent's attack vector and adjusting for her physical size, Sam's body moved on autopilot. He shifted his weight and raised a knee, blocking the kick intended for his groin.

Polly's leg glanced off his and looped around behind his knee.

As she yanked his leg out from under him, he wrapped an arm around her waist. Falling, he used his greater weight and sudden momentum to bring her with him. They collapsed to the floor, the hardwood groaning as it absorbed their combined weight.

As she landed on top of him, her hand darted to her belt. Metal glinted in the weak light.

A fraction of a second before the dagger could plunge into his chest, he blocked with a sweep of his arm. The wicked blade sliced across his skin, spraying his face in a fan of blood.

Growling, she raised the dagger and drove it toward his throat.

He grabbed her wrist. Twisted. Her fingers spasmed. The knife clattered to the hardwood.

She yanked free of his grip. A barrage of cobra-quick punches struck his eyes, neck, and nose. Left. Right. Left. Right.

Instead of tensing, he relaxed, allowing the avalanche of blows to bounce off.

Her aggression had left an opening in her defenses. Driving his arms up through her pummeling fists and into her abdomen, he shoved.

Polly flew.

His head still clanging like a church bell, Sam snatched his Smith & Wesson from the floor and rocketed to his feet.

In a single motion, Polly landed, rolled, and grabbed a gun off a magnetic plate glued to the bottom of the entryway table. Rebounding as if immune to the laws of gravity, she sprang off the wall.

Raising his weapon, Sam launched himself.

Their outstretched arms slipped by one another. Their bodies slammed together. Newton's second law prevailed—his velocity and greater mass overcame her momentum, driving her back into the wall.

Keeping her pinned to the sheetrock so she couldn't knee or knife him, he pressed the barrel of his Smith & Wesson against her temple.

She jammed the barrel of her revolver into the side of his head.

Faces inches apart, they froze, chests heaving.

Time crawled. His senses hyperaware, Sam absorbed every detail, every nuance of the moment. Coffee and chocolate on her hot breath. Fine silver hairs interspersed in her black brows. Her eyes red from a lack of sleep. Tiny beads of sweat dotting her cheeks and forehead. Polly's hard, muscular legs gripping his thighs.

But what really drew his focus was her heart. With their chests mashed together, he could feel it drumming against his own. As though the two organs battled it out from within their respective rib bone cages.

Polly cocked the hammer of the revolver, the reverberating *click* as ominous as the pull of a grenade pin.

"You're an operative of The Agency," he snarled.

"I don't know what—"

"Your handler *ordered* you to murder me."

A jolt vibrated through Polly's body. She gave him a look so heavy it could have tipped the Scales of Justice.

Sam held her gaze. Didn't flinch. Didn't blink.

She snorted and went with an operative's last resort: the truth. "That's right. He did." Her icy glower sharpened to pinpricks.

"The first honest thing you've said to me since we met."

"*You* betrayed The Agency."

"The Agency betrayed *me*," Sam snapped. "It betrayed us all."

"You're a *rogue* agent," she bit back.

That old line is getting tired. I caught you red-handed. You may not know it yet. But you will. "I'm not rogue. I'm fighting for justice. I'm working for America." Sam had gotten a little lost for a while, but he'd found his place in the universe again. Found his purpose. He might leave The Agency, but he would *never* give up on what he believed in.

Polly scoffed. "You're working for someone, but it sure as shit isn't America."

"I'm not. And even if it were true, it's better than being in the Mafiya's pocket."

A slew of emotions flashed through Polly's green eyes. Anger. Apprehension. And, of course, denial. "You don't know what you're talking about."

"Yes, I do, and so do you."

A flicker of bewilderment crossed her face then vanished, replaced by animosity. "I don't have any damned idea. Maybe we should talk about *you* in the pocket of terrorists."

What?

Before he could ask her what she meant, she continued. "I should have dropped you the second you wandered into town. Your traitorous incompetence led to a dozen people getting killed."

He didn't know what she meant by terrorists, but he suddenly understood what about the Erebus case had so thoroughly pissed her off. It wasn't that Sam had succeeded in eliminating the psycho at the expense of the town. It was that her Erebus—whoever that equivalent was from either her operative or detective days—had gotten away. Others had paid with their lives, and Polly had failed to stop him.

Time to grind that wound and knock her off her game. "Well, at least I caught my guy. Unlike you."

Rage filled her face. "Shut up."

"Who was it, Polly? Serial killer? Rapist? Pedophile? It's no wonder they kicked you off the force, and The Agency parked you in this backwater corner of the world. If you're so incompetent you can't even get a killer off the streets, and since your Mafiya buddy is either dead or in a cell somewhere, you're worthless. I may be on The Agency's hit list today, but you'll be there tomorrow."

Polly pushed the gun into the side of his head so hard, a bead of blood rolled down his cheek. "I said, shut up."

"Do it, Polly," he growled, leaning into the barrel. "You got the confirm on my identity. You've got your orders and a verification. Do the drop. Finish your fucking mission, but you'd better know who you're killing me for and why."

"When I pull this trigger, there'll be one less sellout terrorizing America."

She seemed to be trying to rattle him with senseless, baseless accusations. He wouldn't bite. "You sure about that?"

Her heart beat so hard against his, it was a wonder it didn't crack a rib.

No. You're not. You and I both know you're full of shit. You're projecting your own corruption onto me.

If he was going to get the upper hand, he needed to keep her guessing. Time to change the subject again. "After you kill me, are you burning your identity?" he asked.

"What?"

"Polly Cahill, paramedic practitioner and RU team lead, can't go down for murdering her fiancé. So are you doing a fade or do you have a story?"

Her chest rose and fell with each breath. The hard muscles in her abdomen and shoulders tight as bow strings. "You broke in. Gun drawn. I had to protect myself."

"That's what you're going with?" Sam released a scathing, mocking chuckle. "You need to do better, Cahill. The powder burns on my temple make this an execution, not a defensive wound. Any ME fresh from the turnip truck will tell you that. And when the cops run ballistics on the bullets from the intruder's gun from last night—and trust me, now that we're *engaged,* the sheriff has his eye on you so he *will*—you'll need a story that covers the broken light, the busted furniture, all of it."

"Fine. *You* broke in last night. We fought. And—"

He had her on the ropes. Keep the pressure hard and hot. "I broke in twice? The first time, I stole the evidence *illegally* in your possession. Then we went to the marina together and we spent the night together?" Condescension dripped from his words. "Our Agency instructors would be so disappointed. Try again."

Her jaw worked. "I—"

"Also, there's no excuse for not calling in last night's B&E. That story won't fly, *Polly*."

"You broke in with your gun drawn. Crazy with jealousy. I'll patch the house up and tell them I was just protecting—"

Sam's rage exploded like a neutron star. He'd had enough of the lies, the secrets, the manipulation. Now that he'd gotten a peek past the blinders, he saw the ludicrousness of the entire thing. If he had to listen to one more line of bullshit, he would combust. When the police arrived, they'd find two ashen corpses. "They died in the heat of passion," the cops would say. "Case closed."

"No!" he yelled. "Shit or get off the pot, Cahill."

"I could have killed you a dozen times over in the last two days," she informed him.

"Then why didn't you?"

"I told you last night. I owed you for saving my life."

Polly had been out of the game too long. The lie smelled as rank as Frank Boreman's corpse. "That's not true. You and I both know it. What's the *truth*, Polly?"

She pinched her lips together, forming a dagger-sharp line.

Continuing to keep her off balance, Sam shifted gears again. "I know about your history with Dubrovnik—the bribes, the payouts. The Agency knew it too, yet they hired you anyway. Maybe you'd gone straight once you joined them. Or maybe they've been using you because of your past."

She knit her brows together. "You have no idea what you're talking about."

Not a denial. But not a confirmation either. She didn't need to say anything—he saw it in the way her jaw clenched tight enough to crack teeth. Her world had detonated, and she was scrambling to hold the pieces together.

But there was something else, something off—something behind the fury and the confusion he couldn't quite name. "What happened?" he asked, voice low. "Something went sideways. What was it?"

A flicker of heat flashed in her emerald-green eyes. Fear? Regret? Rage? Despite their precarious position, despite her accusations and her attacking him, her anger—though burning hot—wasn't entirely for him. Their fight was a proxy for the civil war burning inside her.

Her body tensed, her knuckles whitening on the grip of her gun. Was she going to pull the trigger?

Then his mind clicked. "Your handler's dead," he whispered.

She flinched as if he'd shivved her ribs.

"You called in. Soren didn't answer. Someone else did." He leaned in even closer. "And no one at the handler level leaves unless it's in a body bag."

Her reply came in a fractured whisper. "I don't know that. I——"

"Yes, you do."

Sam felt her chest expand and her pulse steady as she took in a deep breath. She exhaled slowly, bathing his face with sweet chocolate, burnt coffee, and hot anxiety. "I don't know how," she said. "But I think I know *why*."

An accusation? A confession? Was she implicating him in her handler's death? "I didn't murder your boss. The

Agency's corruption did. But you already knew that. Hell, you were part of it."

She didn't argue. She didn't even blink.

They stared at one another—guns raised, hearts beating in unison, pasts colliding.

She'd worked for the Mafiya. That was a fact. Whether it was out of desperation or greed, he didn't know. But now... now he saw something else. A crack in her armor. A hint that maybe, just maybe, she'd been used. Just like he had.

As Sam stared into her eyes, he saw the pain buried deep beneath her mask—pain held in check by sheer force of will. Her foundation was crumbling, and everything she thought she knew and stood for was collapsing with it.

He knew that feeling all too well.

Or was he just seeing what he wanted to see? Was he projecting his own shattered loyalties onto her because, in some selfish, battered corner of his heart, he wanted the partnership they almost had to be real?

He searched himself for the answer. Came up empty.

The only thing he knew for certain was she couldn't be trusted.

And right now, neither could he.

Focus on what you can control. Trust is irrelevant if you're both dead.

"Here's the bitch of your situation," he said. "You pull the trigger, my reflexes will pull mine. It's not a threat. It's simple physiology."

She held his gaze. "You pull yours and you're dead too. Same reason."

"Mutually assured destruction," he said, nodding.

"Are you bargaining for your life? You should know, I don't negotiate with terrorists."

"Wow. You really have been brainwashed. I'm not rogue, and I sure as shit am not a terrorist. I'm a Marine. I eat terrorists for breakfast."

She let out a dry, ironic chuckle. "Me? You're the one brainwashed if you think I've got anything to do with the Mafiya—besides a burning desire to stop them. I don't know who the fuck this Dubrovnik is, but I haven't been doing business—or whatever—with him."

He searched her face, trying to read the sincerity behind her words. She looked honest. Convincing.

Of course she did. She was a trained liar.

Same as him.

I warned you about reading that document, Chet said.

Except now I know the truth.

Do you?

Yes. Remember, the prosecutor thought she was involved with the Mafiya.

Chet huffed. *Since when did you start siding with lawyers?*

I'm not siding with lawyers. I saw—

You saw what, exactly? How hard do you think it would be to fake that transcript and toss a few breadcrumbs on the dark web?

This gave Sam pause. *I don't know. Probably not very.* He thought it over for a moment. *You think she's innocent?*

Not by a million miles. But she may be innocent of what you're accusing her of.

Sam tried once more to read her face and parse what was real from what was a false front. But he couldn't. He just didn't know.

You may as well give it up, Chet said. *What's truth, what's fiction—it's irrelevant.*

What are you talking about?

I mean, you! You're rusty.

I'm not. I'm just—

Chet barreled over his objection. *You've been surfing and hanging with your friends instead of keeping your wits and skills sharp. Because you're so dull and out of practice, the lady assassin has been running circles around you without breaking a sweat.*

Chet paused for a beat. *Sam of old,* he said, *would never have been played such a fool.*

Sam let that sink in for a second as a new flame of determination burned in his heart. *Well, I'm back.*

"I've been where you are," he said to Polly, his voice low. "Had the mark in my sights. Finger on the trigger. I held off just long enough to find out the truth. Didn't like it, not one bit, but it kept me from putting an innocent into the ground."

She swallowed. "Say that's true."

"It is."

"Whatever." Polly stared at him for several seconds, her eyes a locked vault. "What are you proposing?"

"The chance to walk away before either of us makes a mistake we can't come back from."

"You're just trying to save your own ass."

"You know that's not true."

She hesitated. "How?"

"We release on three," Sam said.

"How do I know you won't kill me?"

"You don't." Their noses nearly touched as he held her gaze. "But if you plan to see another sunrise, you're just going to have to trust me."

"I don't trust anyone."

"Well then, you'd better learn fast."

She didn't blink, nor did her expression falter. But Sam felt Polly's heart pounding against his chest—fast and hard, like an MMA fighter scrapping for the title. "Fine."

"One," he said.

Would she kill him?

Should he kill her?

"Two."

Eternity, as black as gunpowder and as cold as a full metal jacket, held its breath.

His finger tightened on the trigger. It would be so easy to squeeze. So much easier—and so much safer—to give in to instinct.

Either him or her.

He looked into her eyes, searching, desperate, determined.

"Three."

To be continued in *122 Rules – Vengeance*...

Stars and Vengeance

Thank you for purchasing this copy of *122 Rules - Mafiya*, Book Three in the 122 Rules Series. If you enjoyed this book by Deek, please let him know by posting a short review. If you purchased this book through Amazon, it is eligible for a free Kindle Match.

When you're done, come back and continue reading the acknowledgements and, so forth._

But first, go ahead and leave your stars. I'll wait.

Thanks for handling that bit of business.

Ready for the next book in the series? *Vengeance* can be yours.

122 Rules - Vengeance
He came for justice. He found *Vengeance*.

Sam Bradford and his partner, Polly Cahill—a fellow operative ordered to assassinate him—are pursuing the killer of an undercover detective. But every clue pulls them deeper into the Russian Mafiya—and toward the *Vengeance*, a ghost ship fueling the syndicate's smuggling empire along the West Coast.

Officially, the ship doesn't exist. Unofficially, anyone who gets too close never makes it back to shore alive.

To uncover its secrets, Sam infiltrates the crew, stepping into a brutal underworld of drugs, weapons, and human trafficking. The deeper he digs, the clearer it becomes: loyalty is a lie, betrayal is currency, and death comes for everyone.

Out on the open sea, there are no rules. No mercy.

Only *Vengeance*.

With a pulse-pounding cadence, feverish anticipation, and deft comedic satire, Deek Rhew's latest thriller, *122 Rules-Vengeance*, will keep fans of Nelson DeMille and Joseph Finder riveted to their last death-defying breath.

Author Notes

In this story, Sam Bradford is a Marine turned federal assassin, who, even after ten years non-active duty, continues to identify as a Marine. Erin and I come from a long line of proud soldiers, including my own father who spent his career serving our country. There is simply no way to repay the sacrifices made by our brave warriors and their families.

To help honor them and give back, 10% of all the 122 Rules Series' proceeds are donated to benefit soldiers through charities like the Wounded Warrior Project and Special Operations Warrior Foundation.

By purchasing or reading the KU version of this book, you are helping empower and honor Wounded Warriors and their families. To find out how you can help more, please visit WoundedWarriorProject.org (www.facebook.com/wwp) or https://specialops.org (https://www.facebook.com/WarriorFoundation).

~Deek

Acknowledgements

First and foremost, I want to thank my readers. I love sharing adventures with you. Through stories we get to experience a thousand different lives. We put ourselves in the hearts and minds of others, allowing us to empathize in a way not possible through any other medium. Experiences bond us together and together, we journey.

Becky Hartsfield, a.k.a. Guido. I've said it a hundred times before, but it warrants repeating: Sister friend, you rock. I'm incredibly grateful to you for your diligence and your typo-finding hawk eyes. I'm proud *122 Rules - Mafiya* bears the Guido gold seal of approval.

To my father for whom this book is dedicated. Thank you for your service to our country, for being my role model, and your valuable insights into my books. My life is a tribute to your strong, proud, and kind example.

My beta team: Kathy, Lorraine, Anastasia, and Nicole. Thank you for your feedback and for wrangling so many of the little things that somehow still got through. It amazes me how many there still were. I am eternally grateful to your hard work in helping me catch those slippery little devils.

And, while I am truly appreciative of your help improving the story, I most look forward to hearing about you and your lives. While this is only a dip in the proverbial well, I thought I'd share a story shared with me.

One of my beta team members used to be a paramedic and talked about her experience performing CPR—comparing it to Polly's technique. I'm really pleased to have gotten that right, but even happier to have made that connection—to learn about her real experiences. We all have stories to tell, and I'm grateful to get to know some of yours.

To my editor, Erin Rhew. Thank you for lending your amazing editorial skills. Your talents and efforts have not only made this book a thousand times better, but you've made me a much better writer. You are the best in the business, and I'm incredibly lucky to have you as my editor.

To my bride, Erin Rhew. Thank you for being my partner, best friend, and fellow world adventurer. Your love, support, and unending patience are everything. I adore you more than there are words in the English language to describe.

About the Author

Deek Rhew writes thrillers where psychology is the weapon and human nature decides who survives. A lifelong traveler with an insatiable curiosity about what makes people tick, Deek draws inspiration from years spent exploring the world with his bride, Erin Rhew. Different cultures, unfamiliar terrain, and quiet moments of observation become the seeds for stories rooted in motive, fear, and the choices people make under pressure.

Fueled by dark coffee and a fascination with the human psyche, Deek's work asks: when pressure, circumstance, and perception strip away reason and logic, does anyone truly have limits? This obsession drives the 122 Rules series, where psychological principles predict behavior and operatives like Sam Bradford and Polly Cahill survive by manipulating others into choices that betray their own morals, even when the consequences are fatal.

His career in software development sharpened his understanding of technology and the unintended consequences of its misuse, themes that echo through his speculative fiction. The Fall of Civilization series feels less like imagination and more like an early warning.

Deek's father, a proud Air Force veteran, taught him commitment, discipline, and sacrifice. These threads are woven throughout Deek's life's work. When he's not writing, Deek is adventuring with Erin, scouting the next horizon, or debating human behavior and motives over cups of strong coffee.

Find Deek online at www.DeekRhewBooks.com or on Facebook at Deek Rhew – Author.